I0816594

Editorial project:
© 2022 **booq** publishing, S.L.
c/ Domènech, 7-9, 2º 1ª
08012 Barcelona, Spain
T: +34 93 268 80 88
www.booqpublishing.com

ISBN 978-84-9936-661-6 [EN]
ISBN 978-84-9936-651-7 [DE]

monsa
publications
© 2022 Instituto Monsa de ediciones, S.L.
c/ Gravina, 43
08930 Sant Adrià de Besós, Barcelona, Spain
T: +34 93 381 00 93
www.monsa.com
monsa@monsa.com

ISBN: 978-84-17557-61-4

Editorial coordinator:
Claudia Martínez Alonso

Art director:
Mireia Casanovas Soley

Editor:
Sergio Asensio

Layout:
Cristina Simó Perales

Translation:
© **booq** publishing, S.L.

Printing in Spain

Pastel Park

Bricks have been in constant use for a long time. Brick is inexpensive and flexible in its use and, today, the appreciation for its versatile application, constructive qualities and eco-efficiency remains intact.
This book presents selected designs through detailed descriptions accompanied by beautiful images, site and floor plans, elevations and sections.
Focusing on residential and interior architecture, this impressive volume is a celebration of contemporary Brick Architecture, a great exploration of the most surprising, fascinating and inspiring recent projects.

Ziegel sind seit langem in ständiger Verwendung. Ziegel ist preiswert und flexibel einsetzbar, und auch heute noch ist die Wertschätzung für seine vielseitige Verwendung, seine konstruktiven Qualitäten und seine Ökoeffizienz ungebrochen.
In diesem Buch werden ausgewählte Entwürfe anhand detaillierter Beschreibungen vorgestellt, die von schönen Bildern, Lage- und Grundrissen, Ansichten und Schnitten begleitet werden.
Mit dem Schwerpunkt auf Wohn- und Innenarchitektur ist dieser beeindruckende Band ein Fest der zeitgenössischen Backsteinarchitektur, eine großartige Erkundung der überraschendsten, faszinierendsten und inspirierendsten Projekte der letzten Zeit.

Les briques sont utilisées en permanence depuis longtemps. La brique est peu coûteuse et flexible dans son utilisation et, aujourd'hui, l'appréciation de son application polyvalente, de ses qualités constructives et de son éco-efficacité reste intacte.
Ce livre présente une sélection de conceptions à travers des descriptions détaillées accompagnées de belles images, de plans de site et d'étage, d'élévations et de sections.
Axé sur l'architecture résidentielle et intérieure, cet impressionnant volume est une célébration de l'architecture contemporaine en briques, une grande exploration des projets récents les plus surprenants, fascinants et inspirants.

Los ladrillos se utilizan desde hace mucho tiempo. El ladrillo es barato y flexible en su uso y, hoy en día, el aprecio por su aplicación versátil, sus cualidades constructivas y su ecoeficiencia sigue intacto.
Este libro presenta diseños seleccionados mediante descripciones detalladas acompañadas de bellas imágenes, planos de obra y de planta, alzados y secciones.
Centrado en la arquitectura residencial y de interiores, este impresionante volumen es una celebración de la arquitectura de ladrillo contemporánea, una gran exploración de los proyectos recientes más sorprendentes, fascinantes e inspiradores.

AST 77 is a strongly locally committed architectural and engineering firm where architects, engineers and interior architects work together on high-quality projects.
The team has built up great expertise in design, research and technical analysis over the past 15 years. Contemporary and innovative solutions were developed for present-day assignments - varying in scale and nature - for both new construction and renovation and with different functions. The architecture developed is characterized by three key words: Context, Structure and Integral quality. Specific project-related aspects such as function, location, typology, social context, materialization, energy, environment and circularity are linked to these keywords. With this forward-looking view, AST 77 aroused the interest of national and international awards such as the Belgian Building Awards and Terra Fibra Award.

AST 77 est un cabinet d'architecture et d'ingénierie fortement engagé localement, où architectes, ingénieurs et architectes d'intérieur travaillent ensemble sur des projets de haute qualité.
L'équipe a acquis une grande expertise en matière de conception, de recherche et d'analyse technique au cours des 15 dernières années. Des solutions contemporaines et innovantes ont été développées pour des missions actuelles - d'échelle et de nature différentes - tant pour des constructions neuves que pour des rénovations et avec des fonctions différentes. L'architecture développée se caractérise par trois mots clés : Contexte, Structure et Qualité intégrale. Des aspects spécifiques liés au projet tels que la fonction, l'emplacement, la typologie, le contexte social, la matérialisation, l'énergie, l'environnement et la circularité sont liés à ces mots clés. Avec cette vision prospective, AST 77 a suscité l'intérêt de prix nationaux et internationaux tels que les Belgian Building Awards et Terra Fibra Award.

AST 77 ist ein stark lokal engagiertes Architektur- und Ingenieurbüro, in dem Architekten, Ingenieure und Innenarchitekten gemeinsam an hochwertigen Projekten arbeiten.
Das Team hat in den letzten 15 Jahren ein großes Fachwissen in den Bereichen Design, Forschung und technische Analyse aufgebaut. Es wurden zeitgemäße und innovative Lösungen für aktuelle Aufgabenstellungen - unterschiedlicher Größe und Art - sowohl für Neubau als auch für Renovierung und mit verschiedenen Funktionen entwickelt. Die entwickelte Architektur zeichnet sich durch drei Schlüsselbegriffe aus: Kontext, Struktur und ganzheitliche Qualität. Mit diesen Schlüsselwörtern sind spezifische projektbezogene Aspekte wie Funktion, Standort, Typologie, sozialer Kontext, Materialisierung, Energie, Umwelt und Kreislaufwirtschaft verbunden. Mit dieser zukunftsweisenden Sichtweise hat AST 77 das Interesse nationaler und internationaler Auszeichnungen wie der Belgian Building Awards und Terra Fibra Award geweckt.

AST 77 es una empresa de arquitectura e ingeniería con un fuerte compromiso local en la que arquitectos, ingenieros y arquitectos de interiores trabajan juntos en proyectos de alta calidad.
El equipo ha acumulado una gran experiencia en diseño, investigación y análisis técnico durante los últimos 15 años. Se han desarrollado soluciones contemporáneas e innovadoras para los encargos actuales -de diferente escala y naturaleza- tanto para nuevas construcciones como para renovaciones y con diferentes funciones. La arquitectura desarrollada se caracteriza por tres palabras clave: Contexto, Estructura y Calidad integral. A estas palabras clave se vinculan aspectos específicos del proyecto como la función, la ubicación, la tipología, el contexto social, la materialización, la energía, el medio ambiente y la circularidad. Con esta visión de futuro, AST 77 despertó el interés de premios nacionales e internacionales como los Belgian Building Awards y Terra Fibra Award.

AST77 ARCHITECTEN EN INGENIEURS

PETER VAN IMPE

www.ast77.be

BRUTALIST BRICK HOUSE

Landen, Belgium

Program: Private home | *Project director:* Arch.-ing. Peter Van Impe
Design team: Arch. Philippe Dirix, Arch. Stijn Creten, Arch. Joris Brouns
Contractor: Berben Martin, Makke Dakwerken, ALU2+ | *Engineer:* V2S, 2B-Safe
Built surface: 105 m² | *Photos:* © Steven Massart

The design of the house starts from the characteristics of the place, combined with the needs and wishes of the client. Despite the generous available space, which is arranged as the garden of the parental home, vigilant use has been made of this plot. The house has been realized in a setting of front gardens and municipal parks, where it can complement the two houses behind, but can also function perfectly on its own in the steep slope of limestone and marl layers.
The home is built with atypical industrial materials. The highly reflective stained glass windows and the (prefab) concrete retaining wall elements give the house a brutalistic look to the public domain. On the north and garden side, the closed cores are rather soft and tactile. One of the most striking features of this home is perhaps the use of different recovery bricks. The two cores are covered with this and form a knitted thick warm sweater.

Der Entwurf des Hauses geht von den Eigenschaften des Ortes aus, kombiniert mit den Bedürfnissen und Wünschen des Bauherrn. Trotz des großzügigen Platzangebots, das als Garten des Elternhauses angelegt ist, wurde das Grundstück mit Bedacht genutzt. Das Haus wurde in einem Umfeld von Vorgärten und städtischen Parks realisiert, wo es die beiden dahinter liegenden Häuser ergänzen kann, aber auch perfekt für sich allein in dem steilen Hang aus Kalkstein- und Mergelschichten funktioniert.
Das Haus wurde mit atypischen Industriematerialien gebaut. Die stark reflektierenden Glasfenster und die (vorgefertigten) Stützmauerelemente aus Beton verleihen dem Haus ein brutalistisches Aussehen im öffentlichen Raum. Auf der Nord- und Gartenseite sind die geschlossenen Kerne eher weich und taktil. Eines der auffälligsten Merkmale dieses Hauses ist vielleicht die Verwendung unterschiedlicher Verwertungsziegel. Die beiden Kerne sind damit verkleidet und bilden einen dicken, warmen Winterpulli.

La conception de la maison part des caractéristiques du lieu, combinées aux besoins et aux souhaits du client. Malgré l'espace généreux disponible, aménagé comme le jardin de la maison parentale, une utilisation vigilante a été faite de cette parcelle. La maison a été réalisée dans un cadre de jardins de devant et de parcs municipaux, où elle peut compléter les deux maisons situées derrière, mais aussi fonctionner parfaitement seule dans la pente raide des couches de calcaire et de marne.
La maison est construite avec des matériaux industriels atypiques. Les vitraux très réfléchissants et les éléments du mur de soutènement en béton (préfabriqué) donnent à la maison un aspect brutal sur le domaine public. Du côté nord et du jardin, les noyaux fermés sont plutôt doux et tactiles. L'une des caractéristiques les plus frappantes de cette maison est peut-être l'utilisation de briques de récupération différentes. Les deux noyaux en sont recouverts et forment un épais pull d'hiver chaud.

El diseño de la casa parte de las características del lugar, combinadas con las necesidades y deseos del cliente. A pesar del generoso espacio disponible, dispuesto como jardín de la casa paterna, se ha hecho un uso inteligente de esta parcela. La casa se ha realizado en un entorno de jardines y parques municipales, donde puede complementar las dos casas de detrás, pero también puede funcionar perfectamente por sí sola en la empinada pendiente de capas de caliza y marga.
La casa está construida con materiales industriales atípicos. Las vidrieras muy reflectantes y los elementos del muro de contención de hormigón (prefabricado) dan a la casa un aspecto brutalista. En el lado norte y el jardín, los núcleos cerrados son más bien suaves. Una de las características más llamativas de esta casa es quizá el uso de diferentes ladrillos de recuperación. Los dos núcleos están recubiertos formando un grueso y cálido jersey de invierno.

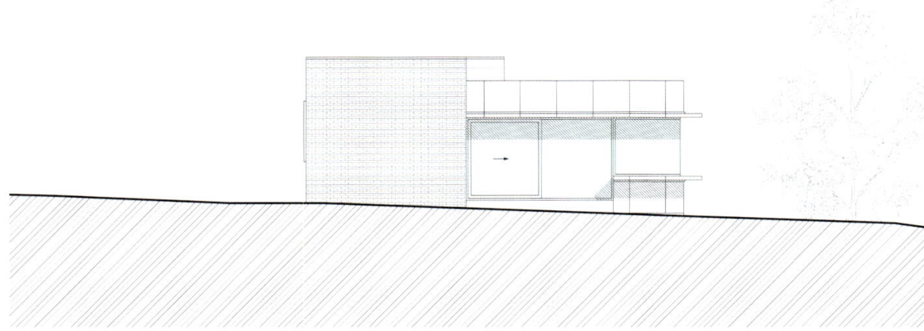

Northwest elevation

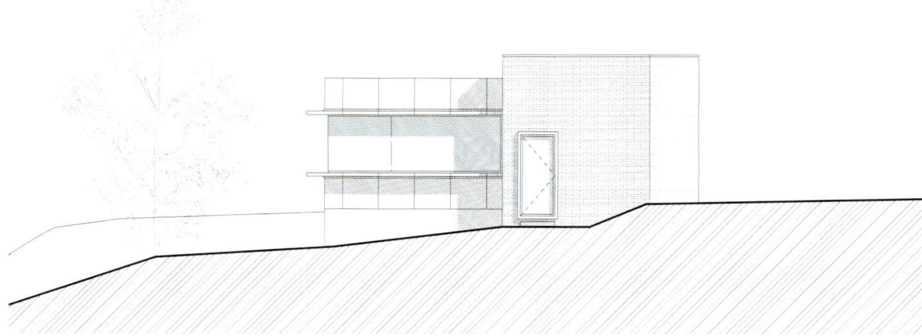

Souteast elevation

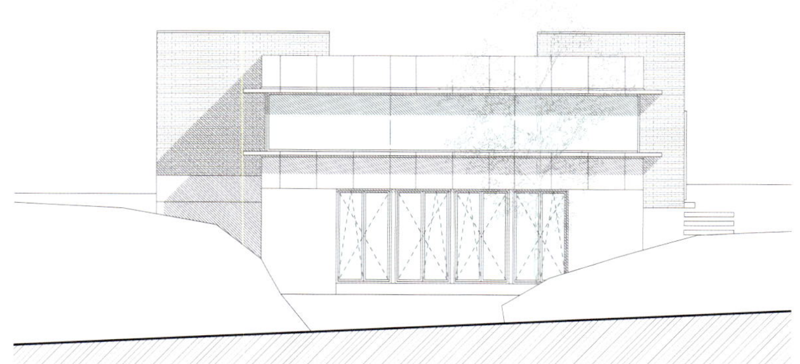

Southwest elevation

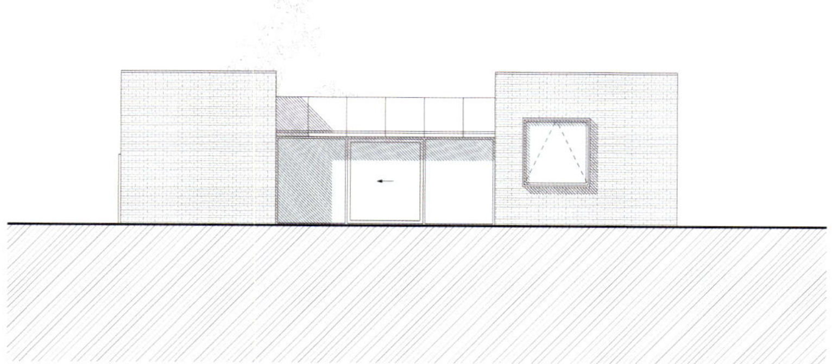

Northeast elevation

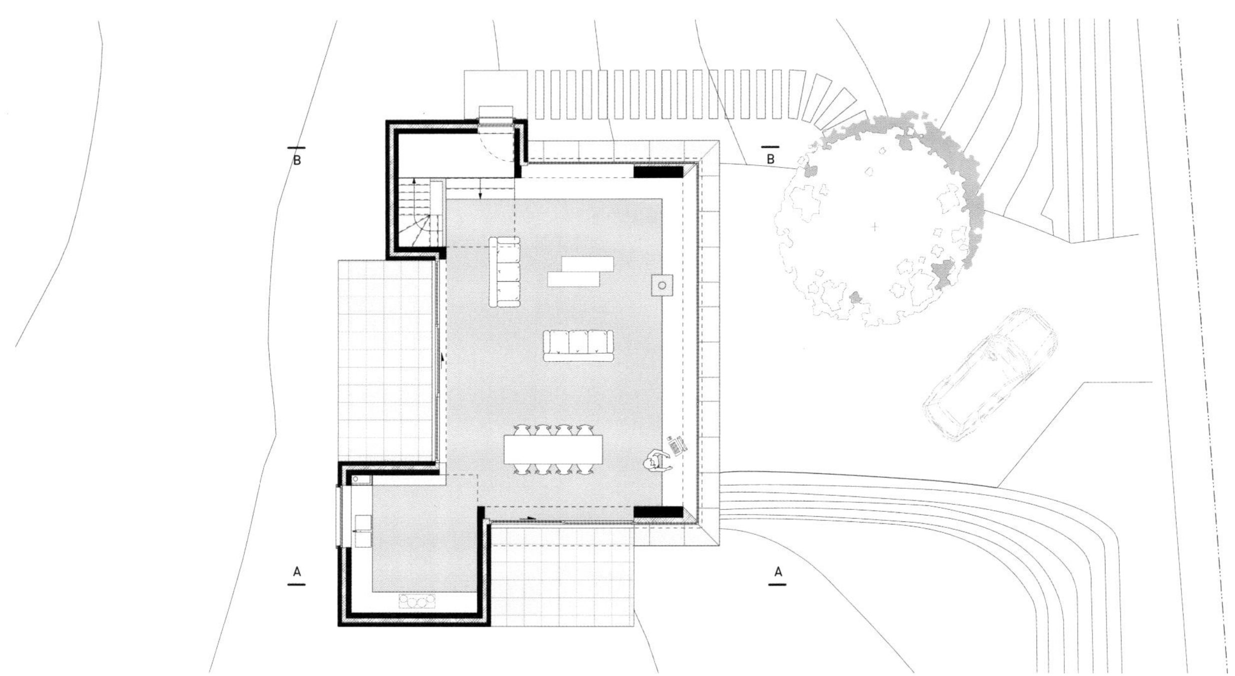

First floor plan

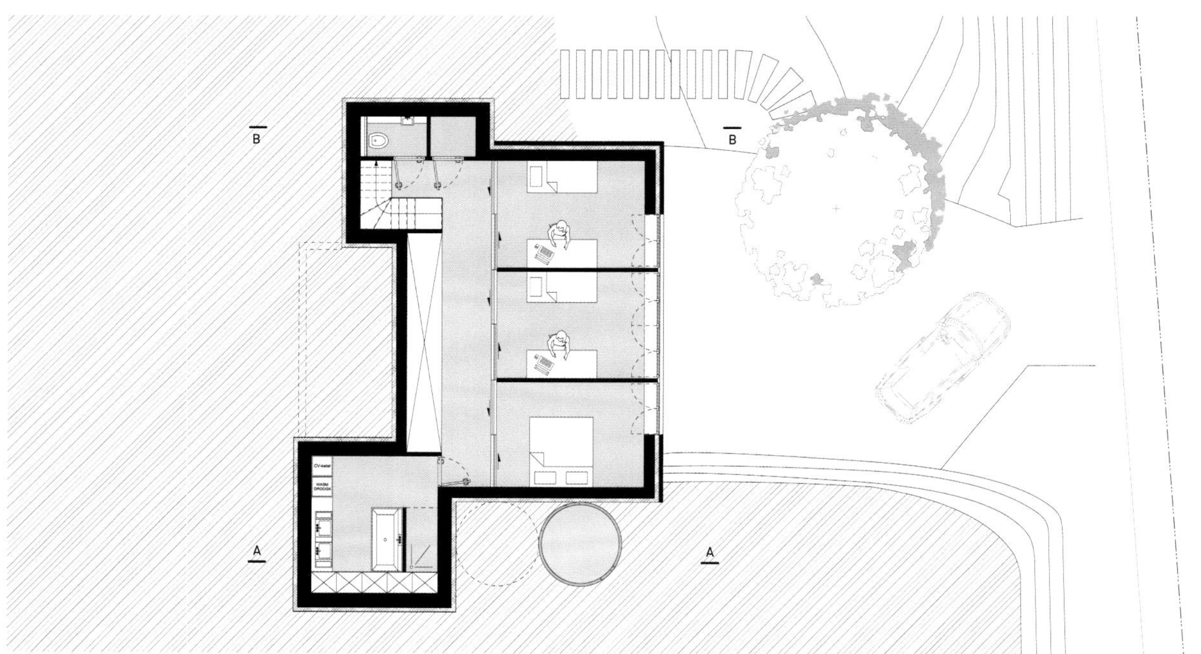

Ground floor plan

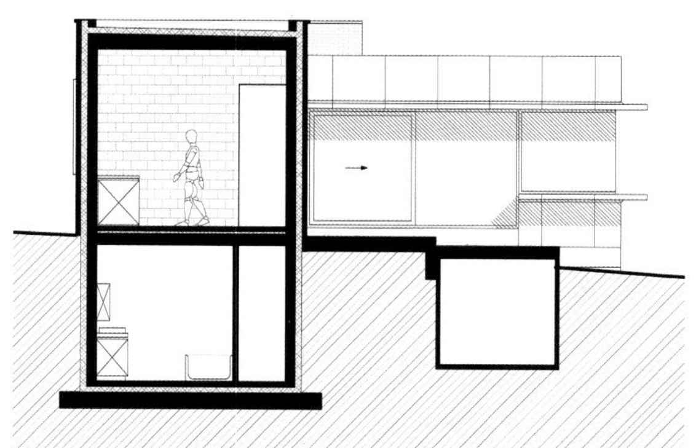

A-A section

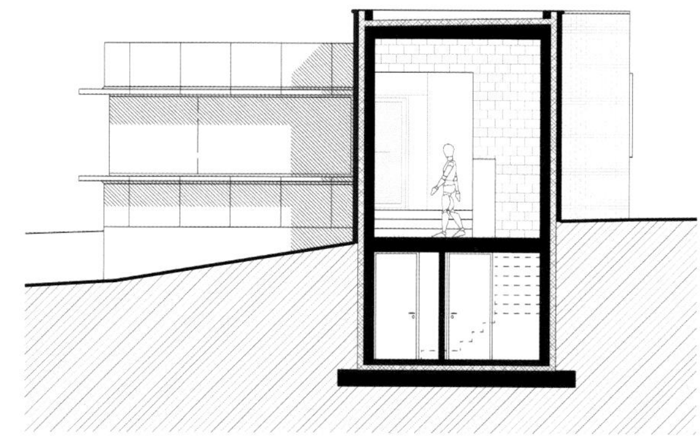

B-B section

CIRCULAR BRICK HOUSE

Tienen, Belgium

Project team: **Peter Van Impe, Jordi Gijzen, Marijke Peeters, Evelien Broeckx** | *Total built area:* **250 m²** | *General contractor:* **Inter ID, Kestens Montage, Elektriciteitswerken Degens, Sollec, Ronan Marteau, Dakwerken Makkedak, Gert Smets, Air Service Center, Alu2+, Het Leemniscaat** *Engineers:* **BC Studies, Util, Yuvico, 2B-Safe** | *Photos:* **© Steven Massart, Maarten De Bouw, Philippe Van den Panhuyzen**

On the premise that good architecture often begins with accepting that one's own knowledge is incomplete, AST 77 director Peter Van Impe involved a large number of external experts in the construction of his private home and explored the innovative possibilities of team building. The project involves the construction of a sustainable dwelling at the end of a row of 12 houses, which becomes a transitional element between the residential complex and the adjacent park. Its west façade, made entirely of reflective glass, allows nature to penetrate the interior while providing privacy. The basic structural material of the house is earth in combination with steel, wood and concrete. A 15 m high wall of rammed earth from the site excavation stands at the central core of the house and is the result of an innovative process that involved all the project collaborators. The three outer walls of the house, 50 cm thick and made of terracotta bricks, are joined to the earth wall by steel plate floors. The house is designed as a "sustainable tailor-made suit". The exterior envelope has been determined, but the floor plan and its interpretation are free and fully adaptable to the different needs of current and future residents.

Unter der Prämisse, dass gute Architektur oft damit beginnt, zu akzeptieren, dass das eigene Wissen unvollständig ist, bezog AST 77-Direktor Peter Van Impe eine Vielzahl von externen Experten in die Realisierung seines Privathauses ein und erforschte die innovativen Möglichkeiten der Teambildung. Das Projekt umfasst den Bau eines nachhaltigen Wohnhauses am Ende einer Reihe von zwölf Häusern, das zu einem Übergangselement zwischen der Wohnanlage und dem angrenzenden Park wird. Seine Westfassade, die komplett aus reflektierendem Glas besteht, lässt die Natur in den Innenraum eindringen und bietet gleichzeitig Privatsphäre. Das Grundbaumaterial des Hauses ist Erde in Kombination mit Stahl, Holz und Beton. Eine 15 m hohe Stampflehmwand aus der Baugrube bildet den zentralen Kern des Hauses und ist das Ergebnis eines innovativen Prozesses, an dem alle Projektbeteiligten beteiligt waren. Die drei Außenwände des Hauses, 50 cm dick und aus Terrakotta-Ziegeln, sind durch Stahlplattenböden mit dem Erdwall verbunden.Das Haus ist wie ein „nachhaltiger Maßanzug" konzipiert. Die äußere Hülle ist festgelegt, aber der Grundriss und seine Interpretation sind frei und vollständig an die unterschiedlichen Bedürfnisse der aktuellen und zukünftigen Bewohner anpassbar.

Partant du principe qu'une bonne architecture commence souvent par l'acceptation du fait que ses propres connaissances sont incomplètes. Le directeur d'AST 77, Peter Van Impe, a impliqué un grand nombre d'experts externes dans la réalisation de sa maison privée et a exploré les possibilités innovantes de la formation d'équipes. Le projet prévoit la construction d'un logement durable à la fin d'une rangée de douze maisons, qui devient un élément de transition entre le complexe résidentiel et le parc adjacent. Sa façade ouest, entièrement constituée de verre réfléchissant, permet à la nature de pénétrer à l'intérieur tout en assurant l'intimité. Le matériau structurel de base de la maison est la terre, combinée à l'acier, au bois et au béton. Un mur de terre battue de 15 mètres de haut, provenant de l'excavation du site, se dresse au centre de la maison, est le résultat d'un processus innovant qui a impliqué tous les collaborateurs du projet. Les trois murs extérieurs de la maison, d'une épaisseur de 50 cm et réalisés en briques de terre cuite, sont reliés au mur de terre par des planchers en tôle d'acier. La maison est conçue comme un « costume sur mesure durable ». L'enveloppe extérieure a été déterminée, mais le plan d'étage et son interprétation sont libres et entièrement adaptables aux différents besoins des résidents actuels et futurs.

Con la premisa de que la buena arquitectura suele empezar por aceptar que los conocimientos propios son incompletos, el director de AST 77, Peter Van Impe, implicó a un gran número de expertos externos en la realización de su vivienda privada y exploró las posibilidades innovadoras de la construcción en equipo. El proyecto aborda la construcción de una vivienda sostenible situada en el extremo de una hilera de doce casas, que se convierte en un elemento de transición entre el conjunto residencial y el parque adyacente. Su fachada oeste, totalmente de cristal reflectante, permite que la naturaleza penetre en el interior y a la vez proporciona privacidad. El material estructural básico de la casa es la tierra en combinación con el acero, la madera y el hormigón. Un muro de 15 m de altura de tierra apisonada procedente de la excavación de la obra se erige en el núcleo central de la casa y constituye el resultado de un proceso innovador que involucró a todos los colaboradores del proyecto. Los tres muros exteriores de la casa, de 50 cm de grosor y construidos con de ladrillos de barro cocido, se unen al muro de tierra mediante suelos de plancha de acero. La casa está diseñada como un «traje a medida sostenible». La envolvente exterior se ha determinado, pero la planta y su interpretación son libres y totalmente adaptables a las diferentes necesidades de los residentes actuales y futuros.

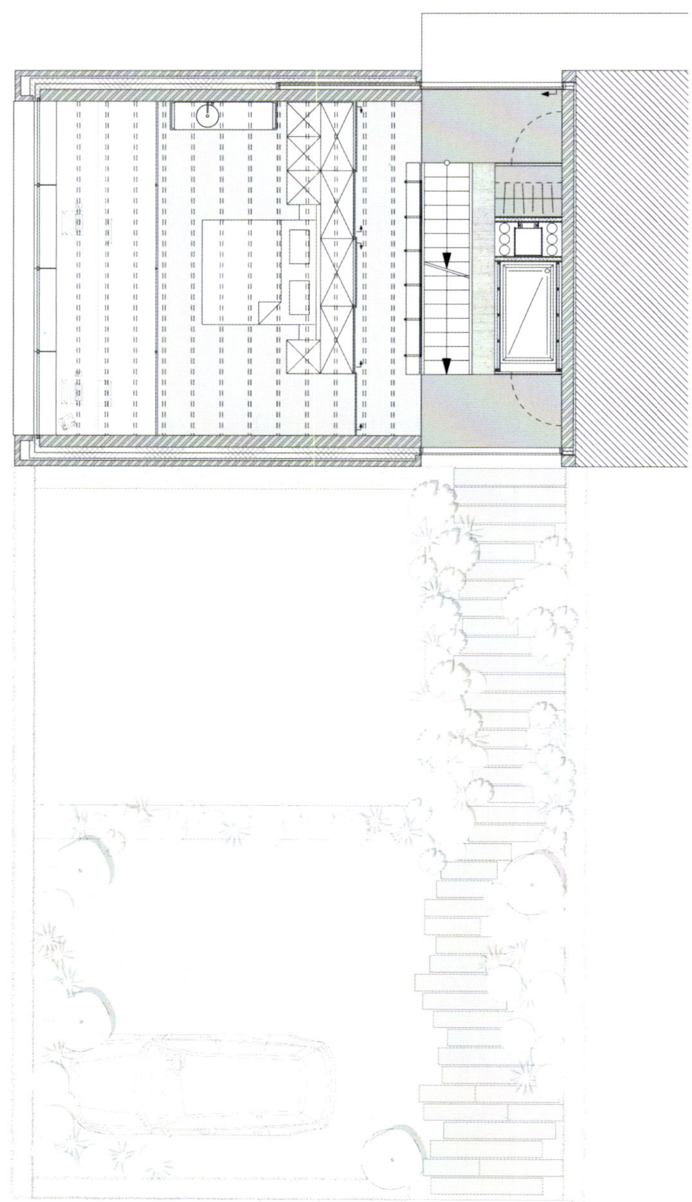

First level plan

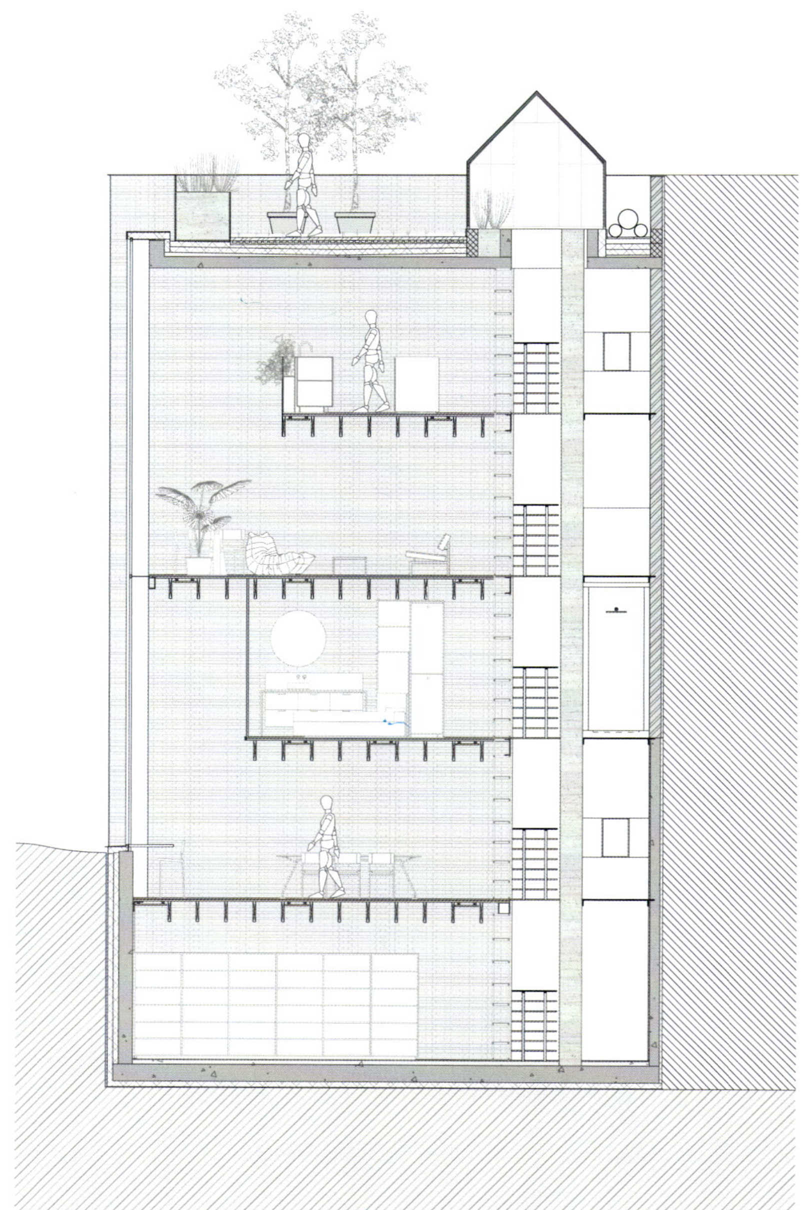

Section

Established by Principals Susan Bowen and Revital Kaufman Meron in 2009, Bekom Design, Inc. is a boutique design firm, specializing in Custom single-family homes. The design process is driven by the core belief, that the site should be designed as a whole with the form , Interior and Hardscape planned simultaneously and in close relation with one another. Each home is its own unique expression of the owner's vision, expressed through carefully crafted spaces, integration of indoor-outdoor living, natural lighting and custom details.

Fondé par les directrices Susan Bowen et Revital Kaufman Meron en 2009, Bekom Design, Inc. est un cabinet de design spécialisé dans les maisons individuelles sur mesure. Le processus de conception est guidé par la conviction fondamentale que le projet doit être conçu comme un tout, la forme, l'intérieur et l'extérieur étant planifiés simultanément et en étroite relation les uns avec les autres. Chaque maison est l'expression unique de la vision du propriétaire, exprimée par des espaces soigneusement conçus, l'intégration de la vie intérieure et extérieure, l'éclairage naturel et les détails personnalisés.

Bekom Design, Inc. wurde 2009 von den Geschäftsführern Susan Bowen und Revital Kaufman Meron gegründet und ist ein Boutique-Designbüro, das sich auf individuelle Einfamilienhäuser spezialisiert hat. Der Entwurfsprozess wird von der grundlegenden Überzeugung geleitet, dass das Projekt als Ganzes entworfen werden sollte, wobei Form, Innen- und Außenbereich gleichzeitig und in enger Beziehung zueinander geplant werden. Jedes Haus ist ein einzigartiger Ausdruck der Vision des Eigentümers, die sich in durchdacht gestalteten Räumen, der Integration von Innen- und Außenbereichen, natürlicher Beleuchtung und individuellen Details ausdrückt.

Fundada por los directores Susan Bowen y Revital Kaufman Meron en 2009, Bekom Design, Inc. es una empresa de diseño boutique, especializada en casas unifamiliares personalizadas. El proceso de diseño es impulsado por la creencia fundamental de que el proyecto debe ser diseñado como un todo con la forma, el interior y el exterior planeados simultáneamente y en estrecha relación unos con otros. Cada casa es una expresión única de la visión del propietario, expresada a través de espacios cuidadosamente diseñados, integración de la vida interior y exterior, iluminación natural y detalles personalizados.

BEKOM DESIGN, INC.

SUSAN BOWEN, REVITAL KAUFMAN MERON

www.bekomdesign.com

LOS ALTOS HILLS RESIDENCE

Los Altos Hills, California, United States

Total property size: **7,120 sq. ft.** | *Main house size:* **4,680 sq. ft.** | *Structural engineering:* **Sung Engineering, Inc.** | *Geotech engineering:* **Murray Engineers, Inc.** | *Civil engineering:* **GREEN Civil Engineering, Inc.** | *Landscape architecture:* **John Merten, RLA / Studio Green Landscape Architecture and Site planning** | *Photos:* **© Rich Anderson LucidPic Photography**

Nestled in the mountains of Los Altos Hills and with dramatic views to San Francisco Bay area, this property features three structures and generous outdoor grounds. The design process was inspired by a combination of the unique site, a specific set of functions reflecting the lifestyle of the owners and creating an aesthetic that is both contemporary and timeless. Construction was done in two phases. The first phase was a complete transformation of the existing guest unit. The second included the construction of the new home, remodel of an existing cabana and installation of hardscape features, including pool, outdoor kitchen, fire pit and patios along with carefully placed landscape to create a uniform singular estate.

Eingebettet in die Berge von Los Altos Hills und mit spektakulärem Blick auf die Bucht von San Francisco, verfügt dieses Anwesen über drei Gebäude und ein großzügiges Außengelände. Der Entwurfsprozess wurde durch eine Kombination aus einem einzigartigen Standort, einer Reihe von spezifischen Funktionen, die den Lebensstil der Eigentümer widerspiegeln, und der Schaffung einer zeitgemäßen und zeitlosen Ästhetik inspiriert. Der Bau wurde in zwei Phasen durchgeführt. Die erste bestand in der vollständigen Umgestaltung der bestehenden Gästeeinheit. Das zweite Projekt umfasste den Bau des neuen Hauses, die Umgestaltung einer Cabana und die Installation von Außenelementen wie Pool, Außenküche, Feuerstelle und Terrassen sowie die sorgfältige Bepflanzung des Geländes, um ein einheitliches und einzigartiges Ensemble zu schaffen.

Nichée dans les montagnes de Los Altos Hills et offrant une vue spectaculaire sur la baie de San Francisco, cette propriété comprend trois structures et de généreux terrains extérieurs. Le processus de conception a été inspiré par la combinaison d'un site unique, d'un ensemble spécifique de fonctions qui reflètent le style de vie des propriétaires, et de la création d'une esthétique à la fois contemporaine et intemporelle. La construction a été réalisée en deux phases. La première consistait en la transformation complète de l'unité d'accueil existante. La seconde comprenait la construction de la nouvelle maison, le réaménagement d'une cabane et l'installation d'éléments extérieurs tels que la piscine, la cuisine extérieure, la cheminée et les patios, ainsi qu'un aménagement paysager soigneusement planté pour créer un ensemble uniforme et singulier.

Enclavada en las montañas de Los Altos Hills y con espectaculares vistas a la bahía de San Francisco, esta propiedad cuenta con tres estructuras y generosos terrenos exteriores. El proceso de diseño se inspiró en una combinación de un emplazamiento único, un conjunto específico de funciones que reflejan el estilo de vida de los propietarios y la creación de una estética que es a la vez contemporánea y atemporal. La construcción se llevó a cabo en dos fases. La primera consistió en la transformación completa de la unidad de invitados ya existente. La segunda incluyó la construcción de la nueva casa, la remodelación de una cabaña y la instalación de elementos exteriores, como la piscina, la cocina al aire libre, chimenea y los patios, junto con un paisajismo cuidadosamente plantado para crear un conjunto uniforme y singular.

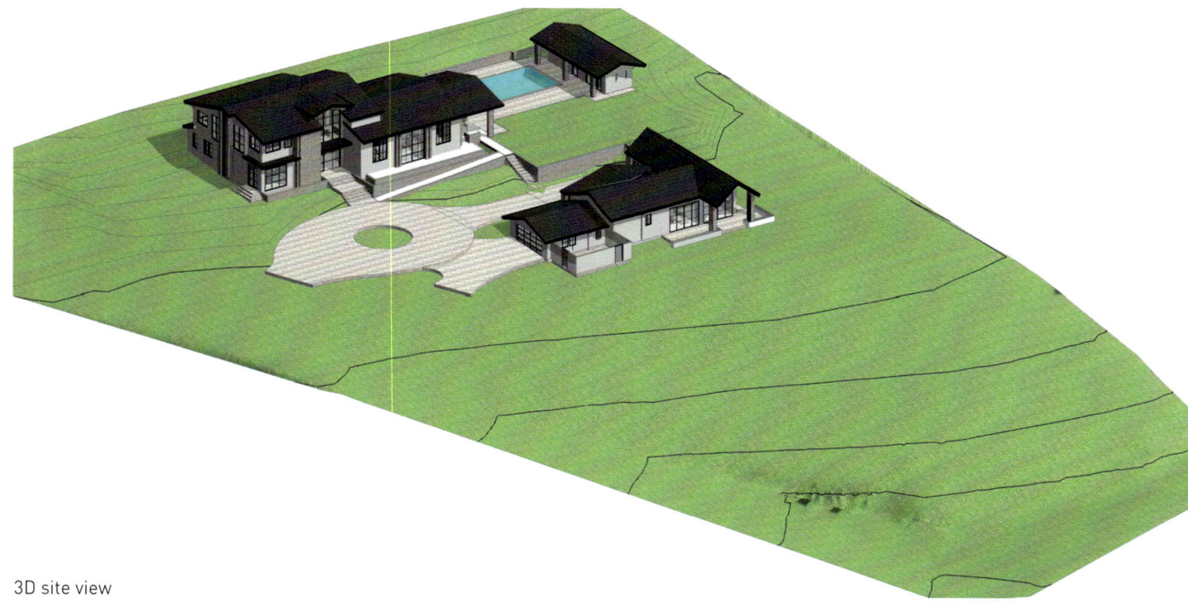

3D site view

1. Seating area/bar
2. Master bedroom
3. Master bathroom 1
4. Office 1
5. Fireplace
6. Office 2
7. Master bathroom 1
8. Walk-in closet
9. Elevator
10. Mechanical room

Main house: second floor plan

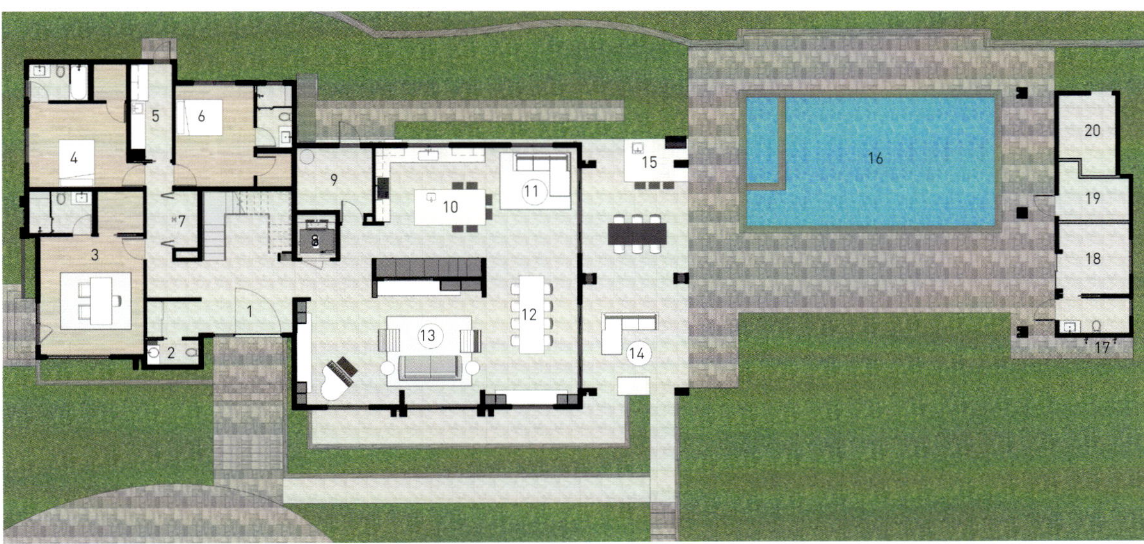

Main house
1. Entry
2. Powder room
3. Office/bedroom suite 1
4. Bedroom suite 2
5. Laundry
6. Bedroom suite 3
7. Storage
8. Elevator
9. Pantry
10. Kitchen
11. Family room
12. Dining
13. Living room
14. Outdoor fireplace
15. Outdood kitchen and dining
16. Pool/spa
17. Outdoor shower

Cabana
18. Gym
19. Sauna
20. Mechanical room

Main house and cabana: first floor plan

1. Kitchen/living area
2. Office
3. Bedroom suite
4. Powder room
5. Laundry
6. Garage

Guest unit floor plan

Leonardo Neve, Founding Partner and Principal of Cafeina Design, a provocative international firm with offices in Mexico City and New York that promotes human, innovative, and positive architecture. Their work has been recognized internationally for its innovative approach, such as The Build Magazine as the Best Innovative and Creative Architecture (2022), America's Property Awards (Toronto, 2017), The Architecture Biennale of Puebla (2018 & 2016), and the Top 100 Projects of Archdaily (2016).
Additionally he is certified by NYU in Real Estate Development, a member of the National Academy of Architecture in Mexico, as well as an International Member of the American Institute of Architects (IAIA).

Leonardo Neve, partenaire fondateur et directeur de Cafeina Design, un cabinet international provocateur avec des bureaux à Mexico et à New York qui promeut une architecture humaine, innovante et positive. Son travail a été reconnu internationalement pour son approche innovante, notamment par le magazine The Build comme la meilleure architecture innovante et créative (2022), les America's Property Awards (Toronto, 2017), la Biennale d'architecture de Puebla (2018 et 2016) et le Top 100 des projets d'Archdaily (2016).
Il est également certifié par l'Université de New York en développement immobilier, membre de l'Académie nationale d'architecture du Mexique et membre international de l'American Institute of Architects (IAIA).

Leonardo Neve, Gründungspartner und Leiter von Cafeina Design, einem provokativen internationalen Büro mit Niederlassungen in Mexiko-Stadt und New York, das sich für menschliche, innovative und positive Architektur einsetzt. Die Arbeit von Cafeina Design wurde international für ihren innovativen Ansatz anerkannt, z. B. vom Build Magazine als beste innovative und kreative Architektur (2022), bei den America's Property Awards (Toronto, 2017), bei der Architekturbiennale von Puebla (2018 & 2016) und bei den Top 100 Projekten von Archdaily (2016).
Darüber hinaus ist er von der NYU in Real Estate Development zertifiziert, Mitglied der Nationalen Akademie für Architektur in Mexiko sowie internationales Mitglied des American Institute of Architects (IAIA).

Leonardo Neve es Socio Fundador y Director de Cafeina Design, una provocadora firma internacional con oficinas en la Ciudad de México y Nueva York que promueve una arquitectura humana, innovadora y positiva. Su trabajo ha sido reconocido internacionalmente por su enfoque innovador, como The Build Magazine como Mejor Arquitectura Innovadora y Creativa (2022), America's Property Awards (Toronto, 2017), La Bienal de Arquitectura de Puebla (2018 y 2016), y los 100 mejores proyectos de Archdaily (2016).
Adicionalmente está certificado por la NYU en Desarrollo Inmobiliario, es miembro de la Academia Nacional de Arquitectura en México, así como Miembro Internacional del Instituto Americano de Arquitectos (IAIA).

CAFEINA DESIGN

LEONARDO NEVE

www.cafeina.design

DESIGN TEAM

SOCIAL LOUNGE

Santa Cruz de la Sierra, Bolivia

Program: **Residential** | *Project director:* **Leonardo Neve** | *Leading architect:* **Jesus Amezcua**
Design team: **Otli Campos, Max Pasquel, Rita Bustos, Itzhel Zambrano** | *Built surface:* **148 m^2**
Photos: **© Paul Renaud**

Social Lounge is a pleasure centered extension of an existing residence in Santa Cruz de La Sierra Bolivia, where the idea of a contemporary paradise is evoked as an unusual discovery. The architecture is not only peculiar, but also it nourishes the imagination, and provides a space suitable for relaxation and socialization. Located at the backyard of an existing family residence, the project provides a ludic and social program that includes a swimming pool, BBQ area for guests, a sauna, a studio, and a guest room. The design premises were to first respect the existing trees, second the position of the pool aims to create an intimate social spot at the back of the building, third a raised platform gives the appearance of a floating structure while the sculptural columns mimic and frame the existing trees, and finally, the upper level serves as an observation deck, providing views to the surrounding trees of the adjacent natural reserve. The predominant use of raw clay bricks and their different arrangements, originates from an intention to reappropriate and reinterpret one of the most traditional construction materials in the Santa Cruz area.

Social Lounge ist eine auf das Vergnügen ausgerichtete Erweiterung eines bestehenden Wohnhauses in Santa Cruz de La Sierra, Bolivien, wo die Idee eines zeitgenössischen Paradieses als ungewöhnliche Entdeckung hervorgerufen wird. Die Architektur ist nicht nur ungewöhnlich, sondern regt auch die Fantasie an und bietet einen Raum, der zur Entspannung und Geselligkeit einlädt. Das Projekt befindet sich im Hinterhof eines bestehenden Familienhauses und bietet ein Freizeit- und Sozialprogramm, das einen Swimmingpool, einen Grillbereich für Gäste, eine Sauna, ein Studio und ein Gästezimmer umfasst. Die Entwurfsprämissen waren erstens, die vorhandenen Bäume zu respektieren, zweitens zielt die Position des Pools darauf ab, einen intimen sozialen Ort im hinteren Teil des Gebäudes zu schaffen, drittens gibt eine erhöhte Plattform den Anschein einer schwimmenden Struktur, während die skulpturalen Säulen die vorhandenen Bäume nachahmen und einrahmen, und schließlich dient die obere Ebene als Aussichtsplattform, die den Blick auf die umliegenden Bäume des angrenzenden Naturschutzgebietes freigibt. Die überwiegende Verwendung von rohen Lehmziegeln und deren unterschiedliche Anordnung entspringt der Absicht, sich eines der traditionellsten Baumaterialien in der Region Santa Cruz wieder anzueignen und neu zu interpretieren.

Social Lounge est une extension centrée sur le plaisir d'une résidence existante à Santa Cruz de La Sierra en Bolivie, où l'idée d'un paradis contemporain est évoquée comme une découverte insolite. L'architecture n'est pas seulement singulière, elle nourrit aussi l'imagination et offre un espace propice à la relaxation et à la socialisation. Situé à l'arrière d'une résidence familiale existante, le projet offre un programme ludique et social comprenant une piscine, un espace barbecue pour les invités, un sauna, un studio et une chambre d'amis. Les prémisses de la conception étaient les suivantes : premièrement, respecter les arbres existants ; deuxièmement, la position de la piscine vise à créer un lieu social intime à l'arrière du bâtiment ; troisièmement, une plateforme surélevée donne l'apparence d'une structure flottante tandis que les colonnes sculpturales imitent et encadrent les arbres existants ; enfin, le niveau supérieur sert de terrasse d'observation, offrant des vues sur les arbres environnants de la réserve naturelle voisine. L'utilisation prédominante de briques d'argile brutes et leurs différentes dispositions, provient d'une intention de se réapproprier et de réinterpréter l'un des matériaux de construction les plus traditionnels de la région de Santa Cruz.

Social Lounge es una extensión centrada en el placer de una residencia existente en Santa Cruz de La Sierra Bolivia. La propuesta surge de una concepción de paraíso contemporáneo evocada desde un descubrimiento inusual donde la arquitectura es peculiar, a la vez que alimenta la imaginación y brinda un espacio adecuado para la relajación y la socialización. Ubicado en el patio trasero de una residencia familiar existente, el proyecto ofrece un programa lúdico y social que incluye una piscina, un área de barbacoa, una sauna, un estudio y una habitación para invitados. El punto de partida del diseño surge del respeto de los árboles existentes; seguido por la posición de la piscina, que tiene como objetivo crear un lugar social íntimo en la parte posterior del edificio; posteriormente, una plataforma elevada que da la apariencia de tener una estructura flotante, mientras que las columnas escultóricas imitan y enmarcan el trazo de los árboles existentes y, finalmente, el nivel superior funciona como plataforma de observación, proporcionando vistas a los árboles circundantes de la reserva natural adyacente. El uso predominante de ladrillos de arcilla cruda y sus diferentes arreglos, se origina en la intención de reapropiarse y reinterpretar uno de los materiales de construcción más tradicionales de la zona de Santa Cruz.

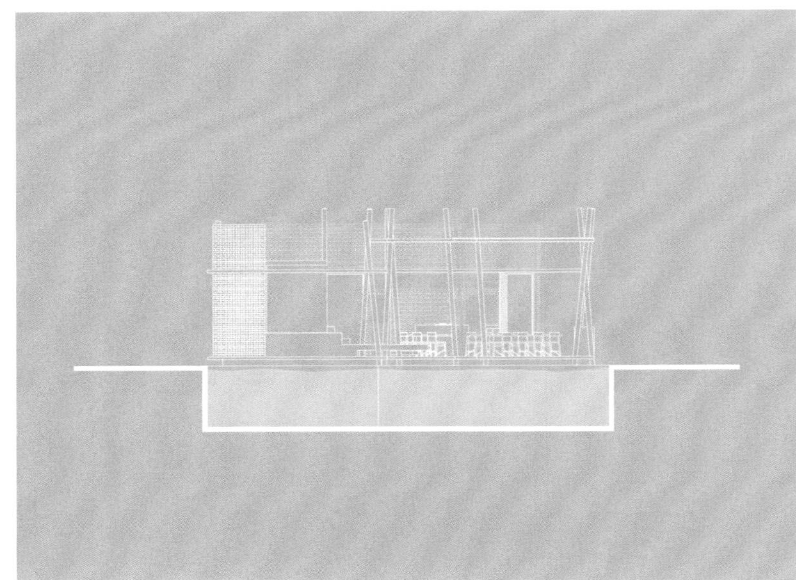

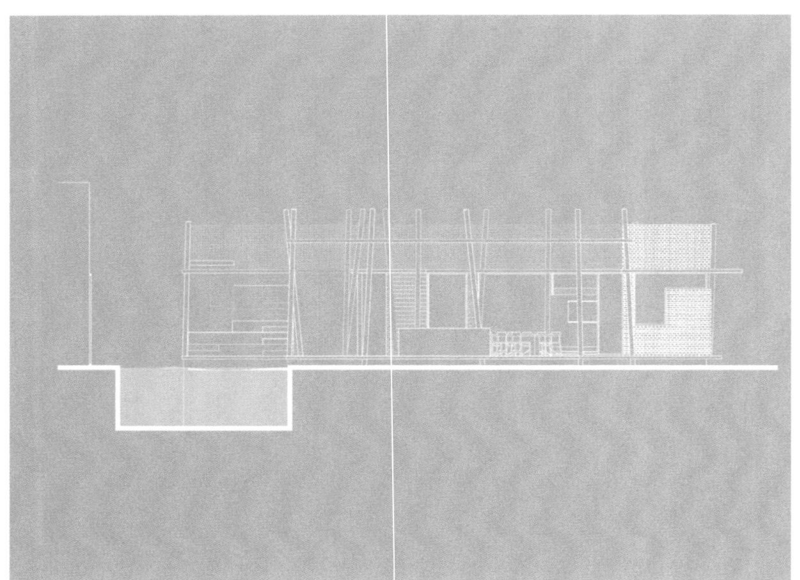

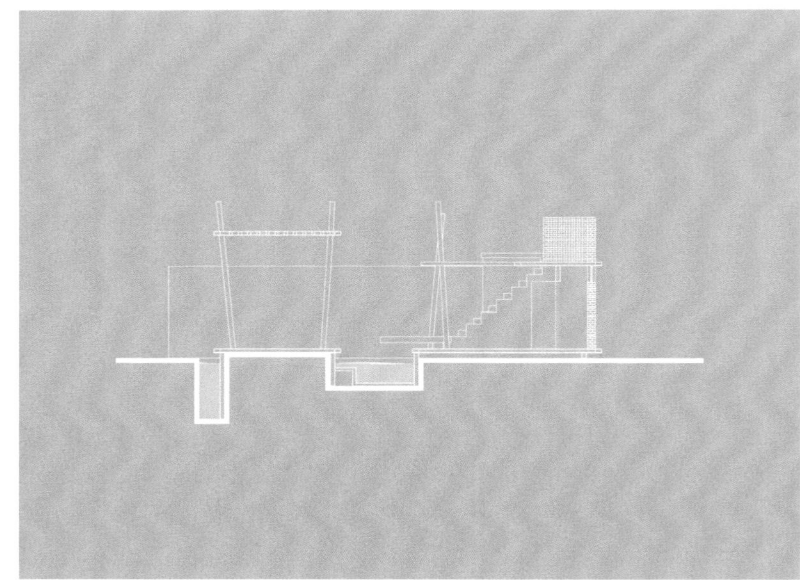

Elevations

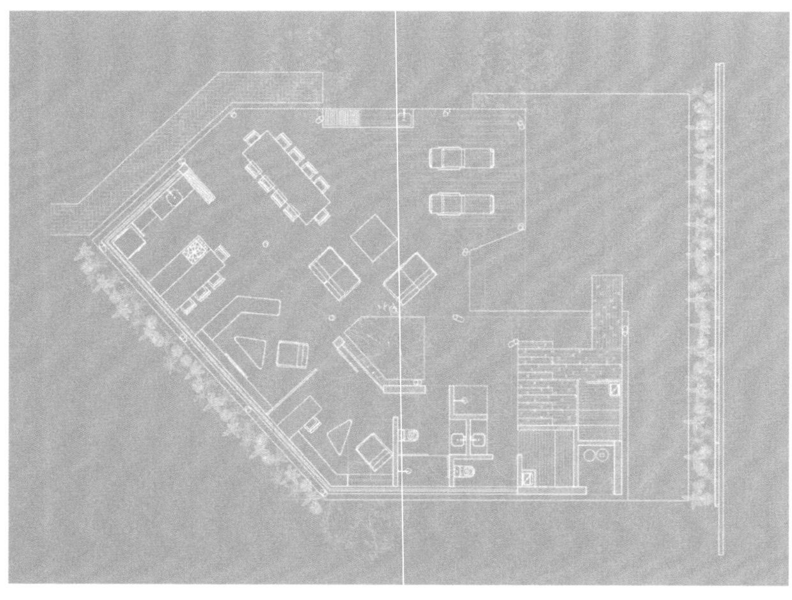

Ground floor plan

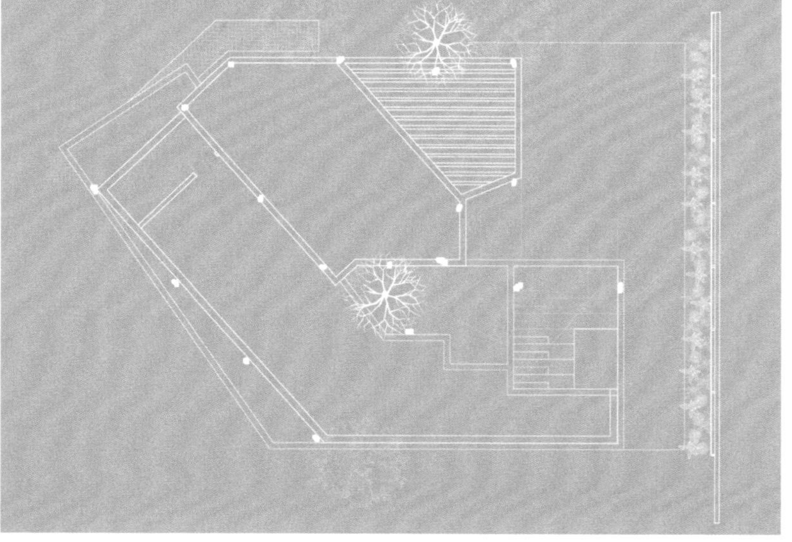

Roof plan

David is an Architect Designer, Master in Project Planning and Urbanism from the Faculty of Architecture and Design of the PUJ (Pontificia Universidad Javeriana) in Bogota and associate member of the SCA (Colombian Society of Architects). His speciality and professional practice has focused on architectural and urban design for more than 15 years.
He divides his profession between the direction of his architecture studio DMAU (DAVID MACIAS ARQUITECTURA Y URBANISMO) and the practice of teaching, directing degree projects and design workshops in different universities.
The studio promotes project management from concept stage to the built work. The implementation of Bioclimatic architecture and Eco-Urbanism in their designs has determined and differentiated their projects, which has led to their work being distinguished as an avant-garde architectural production associated with a sustainable conscience.

David est architecte-concepteur, titulaire d'un master en planification de projets et urbanisme de la faculté d'architecture et de design de la PUJ (Pontificia Universidad Javeriana) de Bogota et membre associé de la SCA (Société colombienne des architectes). Sa spécialité et sa pratique professionnelle sont axées sur la conception architecturale et urbaine depuis plus de 15 ans.
Il partage sa profession entre la direction de son studio d'architecture DMAU (DAVID MACIAS ARQUITECTURA Y URBANISMO) et la pratique de l'enseignement, en dirigeant des projets de diplôme et des ateliers de conception dans différentes universités.
Le studio promeut la gestion de projet depuis le stade de la conceptualisation jusqu'à l'œuvre construite. La mise en œuvre de l'architecture bioclimatique et de l'éco-urbanisme dans leurs conceptions a caractérisé et différencié leurs projets, ce qui a permis de distinguer leur travail comme une production architecturale d'avant-garde associée à une conscience durable.

David ist Architekt, Designer, Master in Projektplanung und Städtebau an der Fakultät für Architektur und Design der PUJ (Pontificia Universidad Javeriana) in Bogota und assoziiertes Mitglied der SCA (Colombian Society of Architects). Sein Spezialgebiet und seine berufliche Praxis konzentrieren sich seit mehr als 15 Jahren auf Architektur und Stadtplanung.
Er teilt seinen Beruf zwischen der Leitung seines Architekturbüros DMAU (DAVID MACIAS ARQUITECTURA Y URBANISMO) und der Lehrtätigkeit auf, indem er Studienprojekte und Designworkshops an verschiedenen Universitäten leitet.
Das Studio fördert das Projektmanagement von der Konzeptionsphase bis zum fertigen Werk. Die Umsetzung der bioklimatischen Architektur und des Öko-Urbanismus in ihren Entwürfen hat ihre Projekte charakterisiert und differenziert, was dazu geführt hat, dass ihre Arbeit als eine avantgardistische architektonische Produktion in Verbindung mit einem nachhaltigen Bewusstsein wahrgenommen wird.

David es Arquitecto Diseñador, Magister en planificación de proyectos y Urbanismo de la Facultad de Arquitectura y Diseño de la PUJ (Pontificia Universidad Javeriana) de Bogotá y miembro asociado de la SCA (Sociedad Colombiana de Arquitectos). Su especialidad y ejercicio profesional se ha centrado en el diseño arquitectónico y urbano por más de 15 años.
Su profesión la divide entre la dirección de su estudio de arquitectura DMAU (DAVID MACIAS ARQUITECTURA Y URBANISMO) y la práctica de la docencia, la dirección de trabajos de grado y talleres de diseño en diferentes universidades.
El estudio promueve la gestión de proyectos desde la etapa de conceptualización hasta la obra construida. La implementación de la arquitectura Bioclimática y el Eco-Urbanismo en sus diseños ha caracterizado y diferenciado sus proyectos, lo que ha llevado a que su trabajo se distinga como una producción arquitectónica de vanguardia asociado a una conciencia sostenible.

DAVID MACIAS ARQUITECTURA & URBANISMO

DAVID MACIAS

www.davidmacias.com.co

CASA DE LA ACACIA

Villavicencio Meta, Colombia

Program: **Residential – Private Housing** | *Project director and leading architect:* **David Macias** *Design team:* **Julian Macias, Victor Macias B., Consuelo Rubio, John Saavedra** | *Built surface:* **280 m^2 interior, 315 m^2 exterior** | *Photos:* **© Santiago Robayo**

The project, located on a vast plain lacking in vegetation of great coverage as a shading strategy, set out a clear design determinant, recovering the splendour of an old native tree, making it itself the great actor of the project. The construction, carried out by local labour, is built using 3 types of bricks. The first are clay blocks with a double chamber, masoned and plastered with lime and crushed white granite, a strategy that minimises solar absorption and allows the house to be thermally regulated. The second are bricks in the form of lattice construction and handmade manufacture that offer solar control and cross ventilation screening on one of the longest facades where the bedrooms are located. Lastly, the bricks in natural stone of the spacato type, typical of the place, allow the stone to be used as a finishing element on the façade that contrasts with the white colour of the bricks, generating a chromatic symbiosis between the house and the exuberant green of the surroundings.

Das Projekt, das sich in einer weiten Ebene befindet, in der es keine großflächige Vegetation als Beschattungsstrategie gibt, war ein klarer gestalterischer Faktor, der die Pracht eines alten einheimischen Baumes wiederherstellte und ihn selbst zum Hauptdarsteller des Projekts machte. Der Bau, der von einheimischen Arbeitskräften ausgeführt wird, besteht aus 3 Arten von Ziegeln. Die ersten sind Lehmziegel mit einer Doppelkammer, gemauert und verputzt mit Kalk und gebrochenem weißem Granit, eine Strategie, die die Sonnenabsorption minimiert und die Wärmeregulierung des Hauses ermöglicht. Das zweite sind Ziegel in Form einer Gitterkonstruktion und handgefertigter Herstellung, die an einer der längsten Fassaden, an der sich die Schlafzimmer befinden, Sonnenschutz und Querlüftung bieten. Die Natursteinziegel vom Typ Spacato, die für den Ort typisch sind, ermöglichen es schließlich, den Stein als Abschlusselement an der Fassade zu verwenden, das mit der weißen Farbe der Ziegel kontrastiert und eine farbliche Symbiose zwischen dem Haus und dem üppigen Grün der Umgebung schafft.

Le projet, situé sur une vaste plaine dépourvue de végétation de grande couverture comme stratégie d'ombrage, a établi un déterminant de conception clair, récupérant la splendeur d'un vieil arbre indigène, faisant de lui le grand acteur du projet. La construction, réalisée par la main d'œuvre locale, utilise 3 types de briques. Les premiers sont des blocs d'argile à double chambre, maçonnés et enduits de chaux et de granit blanc concassé, une stratégie qui minimise l'absorption solaire et permet de réguler thermiquement la maison. Les secondes sont des briques en forme de treillis et de fabrication artisanale qui offrent un contrôle solaire et un écran de ventilation transversale sur l'une des façades les plus longues où se trouvent les chambres. Enfin, les briques en pierre naturelle de type *spacato*, typiques du lieu, permettent d'utiliser la pierre comme élément de finition sur la façade qui contraste avec la couleur blanche des briques, générant une symbiose chromatique entre la maison et le vert exubérant des environs.

El proyecto, localizado sobre una vasta llanura resiliente y carente de vegetación de gran cobertura como estrategia de sombreamiento, dispuso una clara determinante de diseño, recuperar el esplendor de un viejo árbol nativo convirtiéndolo por sí mismo en el gran actor del proyecto. La construcción, llevada a cabo por mano de obra local, se edifica mediante 3 tipos de ladrillos. Los primeros son bloques de arcilla con cámara doble, mampuestos y pañetados con cal y triturado de granito blanco, estrategia que minimiza la absorción solar y permite regular térmicamente la vivienda. Los segundos son ladrillos en forma de celosías de construcción y manufactura artesanal que ofrecen control solar y tamizaje de ventilación cruzada sobre una de las fachadas más largas donde se localizan las alcobas. Por último, los ladrillos en piedra natural tipo espacato, propios del lugar, permiten aprovechar la piedra como elemento de acabado en fachada que contrasta con el color blanco de las mismas, generando una simbiosis cromática de la casa con el verde exuberante del entorno.

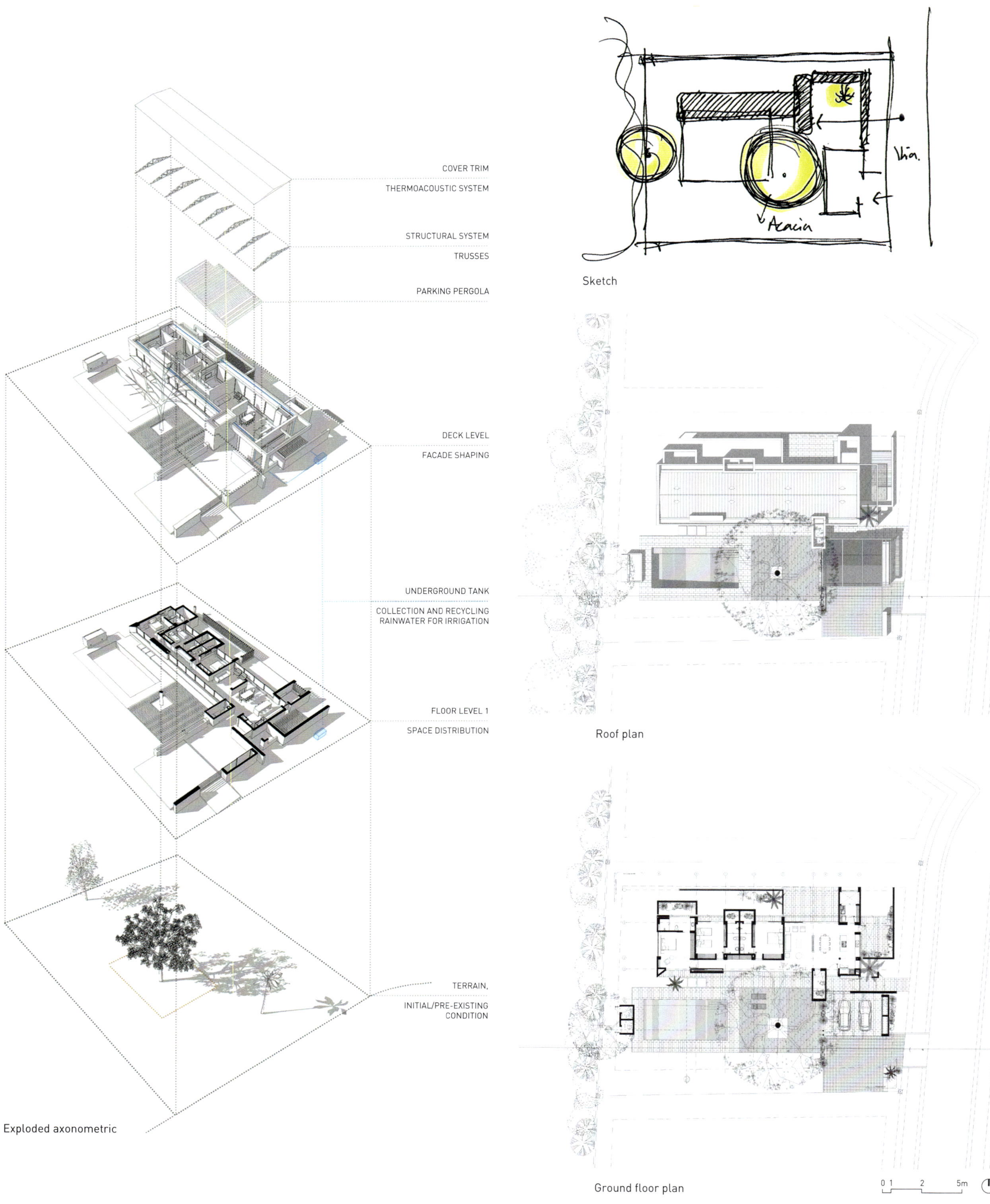

Exploded axonometric

Sketch

Roof plan

Ground floor plan

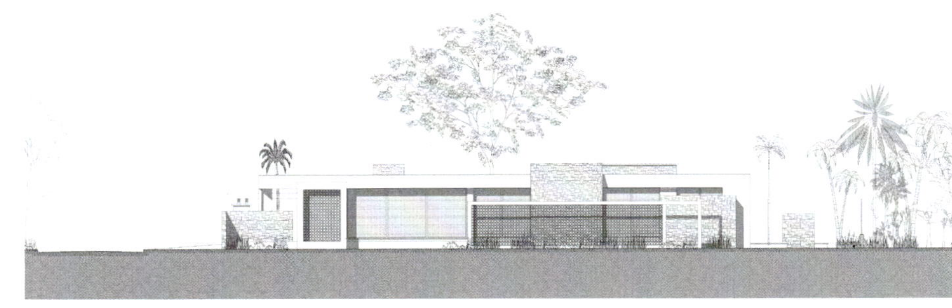
North elevation

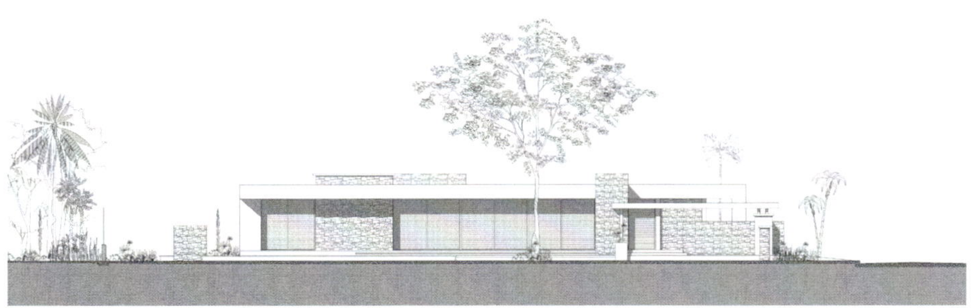
South elevation

East elevation

Sketch

1-1 section

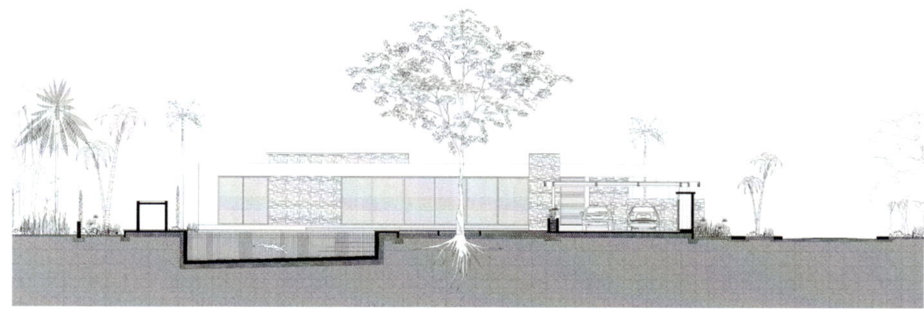
2-2 section

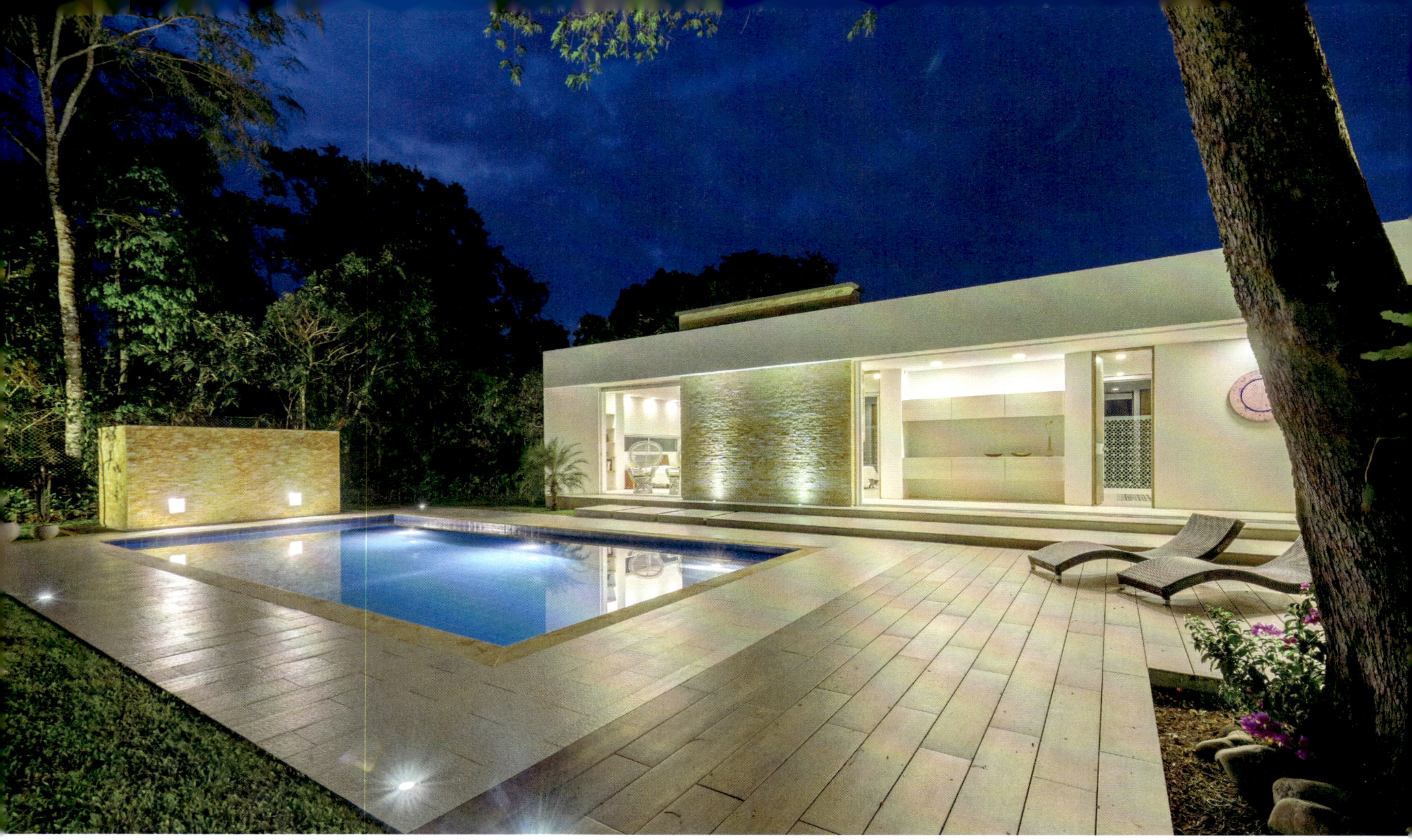

Stephanie Davidson and Georg Rafailidis have collaborated as Davidson Rafailidis since 2013. Davidson (1977) grew up in rural Ontario. She earned a degree in fine art from Mount Allison University in Sackville, then studied architecture at London's Architectural Association and Dalhousie University in Halifax, where she earned her M.Arch.
Rafailidis (1972, Furstenfeldbruck, Germany) holds degrees from the University of Applied Sciences in Munich and the Architectural Association in London. Their work has been recognized by multiple awards. They are also authors of the book "Processes of Creating Space: An Architectural Design Workbook" (Routledge, 2017) with endorsements by Herman Hertzberger, Jacques Rousseau and Rachel Whiteread.
For the past years, both Davidson and Rafailidis have taught at various architecture schools. Currently, Davidson is an assistant professor at the Ryerson University in Toronto, while Rafailidis is associate professor at the State University of New York at Buffalo.

Stephanie Davidson et Georg Rafailidis collaborent sous le nom de Davidson Rafailidis depuis 2013. Stephanie Davidson (1977) a grandi dans la campagne ontarienne. Elle a obtenu un diplôme en beaux-arts de l'Université Mount Allison à Sackville, puis a étudié l'architecture à l'Architectural Association de Londres et à l'Université Dalhousie à Halifax, où elle a obtenu sa maîtrise en architecture.
Rafailidis (1972, Furstenfeldbruck, Allemagne) est diplômé de l'Université des sciences appliquées de Munich et de l'Architectural Association de Londres. Leur travail a été récompensé par de nombreux prix. Ils sont également les auteurs du livre « Processes of Creating Space : An Architectural Design Workbook » (Routledge, 2017), auquel ont souscrit Herman Hertzberger, Jacques Rousseau et Rachel Whiteread.
Ces dernières années, Davidson et Rafailidis ont tous deux enseigné dans diverses écoles d'architecture. Actuellement, Davidson est professeur adjoint à l'université Ryerson de Toronto, tandis que Rafailidis est professeur associé à l'université d'État de New York à Buffalo.

Stephanie Davidson und Georg Rafailidis arbeiten seit 2013 unter dem Namen Davidson Rafailidis zusammen. Davidson (1977) wuchs im ländlichen Ontario auf. Sie erwarb einen Abschluss in Bildender Kunst an der Mount Allison University in Sackville und studierte anschließend Architektur an der Architectural Association in London und an der Dalhousie University in Halifax, wo sie ihren M.Arch. erwarb.
Rafailidis (1972, Fürstenfeldbruck, Deutschland) hat Abschlüsse von der Hochschule für angewandte Wissenschaften in München und der Architectural Association in London. Ihre Arbeit wurde mit mehreren Preisen ausgezeichnet. Sie sind auch Autoren des Buches „Processes of Creating Space: An Architectural Design Workbook" (Routledge, 2017) mit Beiträgen von Herman Hertzberger, Jacques Rousseau und Rachel Whiteread.
In den vergangenen Jahren haben sowohl Davidson als auch Rafailidis an verschiedenen Architekturschulen unterrichtet. Derzeit ist Davidson Assistenzprofessor an der Ryerson University in Toronto, während Rafailidis außerordentlicher Professor an der State University of New York in Buffalo ist.

Stephanie Davidson y Georg Rafailidis colaboran como Davidson Rafailidis desde 2013. Davidson (1977) creció en la zona rural de Ontario. Se licenció en Bellas Artes en la Universidad Mount Allison de Sackville, y después estudió arquitectura en la Architectural Association de Londres y en la Universidad Dalhousie de Halifax, donde obtuvo su máster en Arquitectura.
Rafailidis (1972, Furstenfeldbruck, Alemania) es licenciado por la Universidad de Ciencias Aplicadas de Múnich y la Architectural Association de Londres. Su trabajo ha sido reconocido con múltiples premios. También son autores del libro «Processes of Creating Space: An Architectural Design Workbook» (Routledge, 2017) con avales de Herman Hertzberger, Jacques Rousseau y Rachel Whiteread.
Durante los últimos años, tanto Davidson como Rafailidis han impartido clases en varias escuelas de arquitectura. En la actualidad, Davidson es profesor asistente en la Universidad Ryerson de Toronto, mientras que Rafailidis es profesor asociado en la Universidad Estatal de Nueva York en Buffalo.

DAVIDSON RAFAILIDIS

STEPHANIE DAVIDSON, GEORG RAFAILIDIS

www.davidsonrafailidis.net

CONTINUAL CONSTRUCTION / TOGETHER APART

Buffalo, New York, United States

Design team: **Stephanie Davidson, Georg Rafailidis** | *Engineer of record:* **John Banaszak**
General contractor: **CFR Construction & Restoration** | *Custom fabrication:* **Spielman Fabrication**
Photos: **© Florian Holzherr**

Design studio Davidson Rafailidis has completed the renovation and addition of a century-old, two-story brick building in Buffalo, NY. Built in 1900 with a 1940s extension, the historic structure has operated as a grocery store, strip club, attorney's office, and hair salon, among other businesses. Davidson Rafailidis received a brief to transform the space into a cat café for a local entrepreneur, Buckminster's Cat Café. Cat cafés offer a unique typology, given health regulations that demand air-tight separation between animals and food preparation—in this case, cats and coffee. This requirement allowed Davidson Rafailidis to expand on the studio's interest in designing partitioned spaces that support flexibility but still imply and encourage togetherness and community. The project, called Together Apart, is the first phase of a continual construction on the lot, which responds to new city zoning that encourages high density construction and furthers Davidson Rafailidis' efforts to design heterogenous, mixed-use spaces for a wide range of users.

Das Designbüro Davidson Rafailidis hat die Renovierung und Erweiterung eines jahrhundertealten, zweistöckigen Backsteingebäudes in Buffalo, NY, abgeschlossen. Das 1900 erbaute und in den 1940er Jahren erweiterte historische Gebäude wurde unter anderem als Lebensmittelgeschäft, Stripclub, Anwaltskanzlei und Friseursalon genutzt.
Davidson Rafailidis erhielt den Auftrag, die Räumlichkeiten in ein Katzencafé für einen örtlichen Unternehmer, Buckminster's Cat Café, umzuwandeln. Katzencafés sind aufgrund der Gesundheitsvorschriften, die eine luftdichte Trennung zwischen Tieren und Lebensmittelzubereitung - in diesem Fall zwischen Katzen und Kaffee - vorschreiben, eine einzigartige Typologie. Diese Vorschrift ermöglichte es Davidson Rafailidis, das Interesse des Studios an der Gestaltung von abgetrennten Räumen zu erweitern, die Flexibilität unterstützen, aber dennoch Zusammengehörigkeit und Gemeinschaft implizieren und fördern. Das Projekt mit dem Namen Together Apart ist die erste Phase eines fortlaufenden Bauprojekts auf dem Grundstück, das auf die neue städtische Flächennutzungsplanung reagiert, die eine Bebauung mit hoher Dichte fördert, und das die Bemühungen von Davidson Rafailidis um die Gestaltung heterogener, gemischt genutzter Räume für ein breites Spektrum von Nutzern unterstützt.

Le studio de design Davidson Rafailidis a terminé la rénovation et l'agrandissement d'un bâtiment centenaire en briques de deux étages à Buffalo, dans l'État de New York. Construite en 1900 et agrandie dans les années 1940, cette structure historique a servi, entre autres, d'épicerie, de club de strip-tease, de bureau d'avocat et de salon de coiffure.
Davidson Rafailidis a reçu un mandat pour transformer l'espace en un café pour chats pour un entrepreneur local, Buckminster's Cat Café. Les cafés pour chats offrent une typologie unique, étant donné les réglementations sanitaires qui exigent une séparation hermétique entre les animaux et la préparation des aliments ; dans ce cas, les chats et le café. Cette exigence a permis à Davidson Rafailidis de développer l'intérêt du studio pour la conception d'espaces cloisonnés qui favorisent la flexibilité tout en impliquant et en encourageant la convivialité et la communauté. Le projet, appelé Together Apart, est la première phase d'une construction continue sur le terrain, qui répond à un nouveau zonage de la ville qui encourage la construction à haute densité et poursuit les efforts de Davidson Rafailidis pour concevoir des espaces hétérogènes et à usage mixte pour un large éventail d'utilisateurs.

El estudio de diseño Davidson Rafailidis ha completado la renovación y ampliación de un edificio centenario de dos plantas de ladrillo en Buffalo, Nueva York. Construido en 1900 con una ampliación en la década de 1940, la estructura histórica ha funcionado como tienda de comestibles, club de striptease, despacho de abogados y peluquería, entre otros negocios.
Davidson Rafailidis recibió el encargo de transformar el espacio en una cafetería para gatos para un empresario local, Buckminster's Cat Café. Los cafés para gatos ofrecen una tipología única, dada la normativa sanitaria que exige una separación hermética entre los animales y la preparación de alimentos; en este caso, los gatos y el café. Este requisito permitió a Davidson Rafailidis profundizar en el interés del estudio por el diseño de espacios divididos que permitan la flexibilidad, pero que impliquen y fomenten la unión y la comunidad. El proyecto, denominado Together Apart, es la primera fase de una construcción continua en el solar, que responde a la nueva zonificación de la ciudad que fomenta la construcción de alta densidad y fomenta los esfuerzos de Davidson Rafailidis por diseñar espacios heterogéneos de uso mixto para una amplia gama de usuarios.

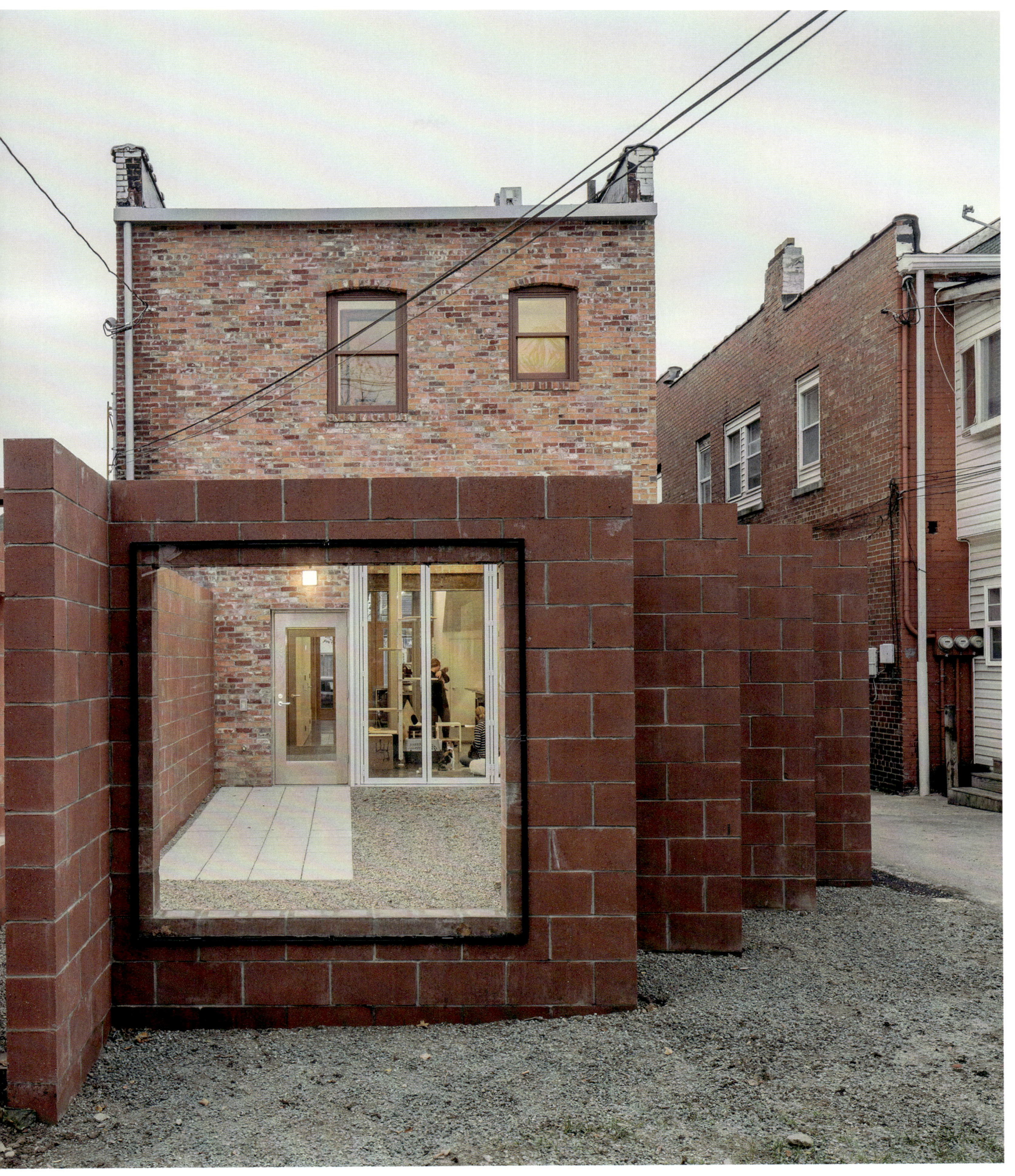

Old Building front facade

Old Building rear facade

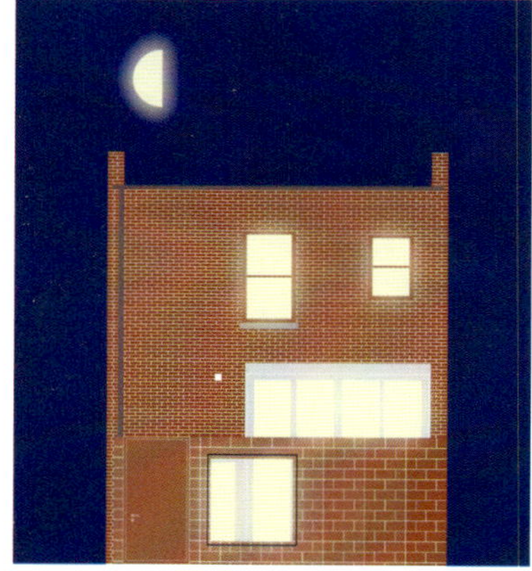

Front elevation

Rear elevation

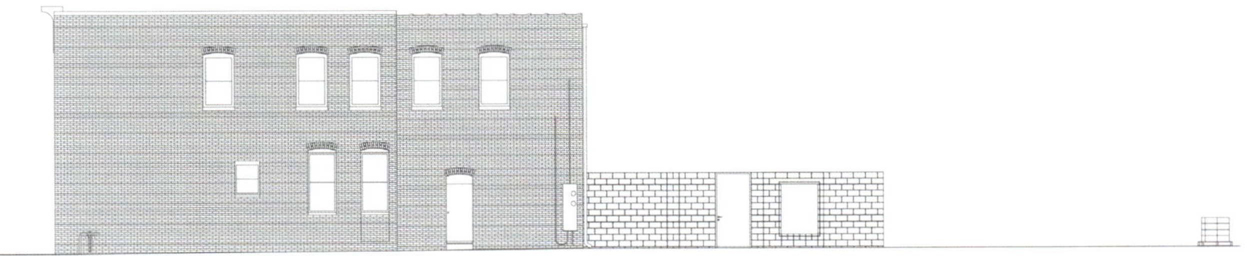

Lateral elevation

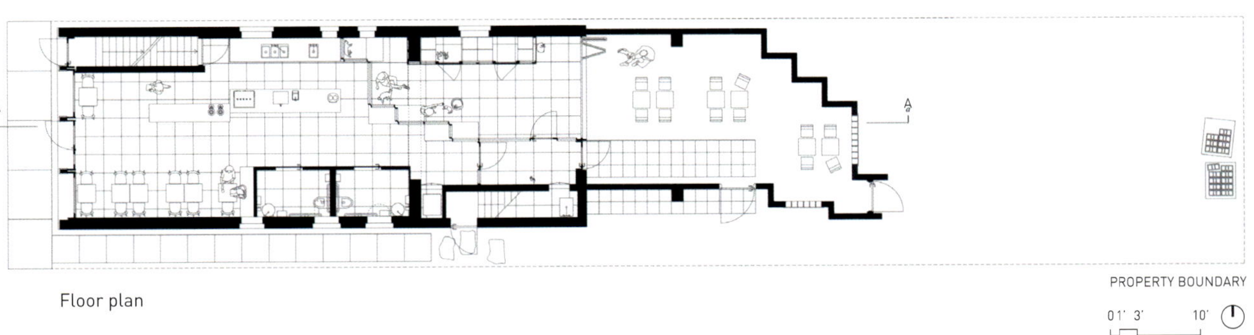

Floor plan

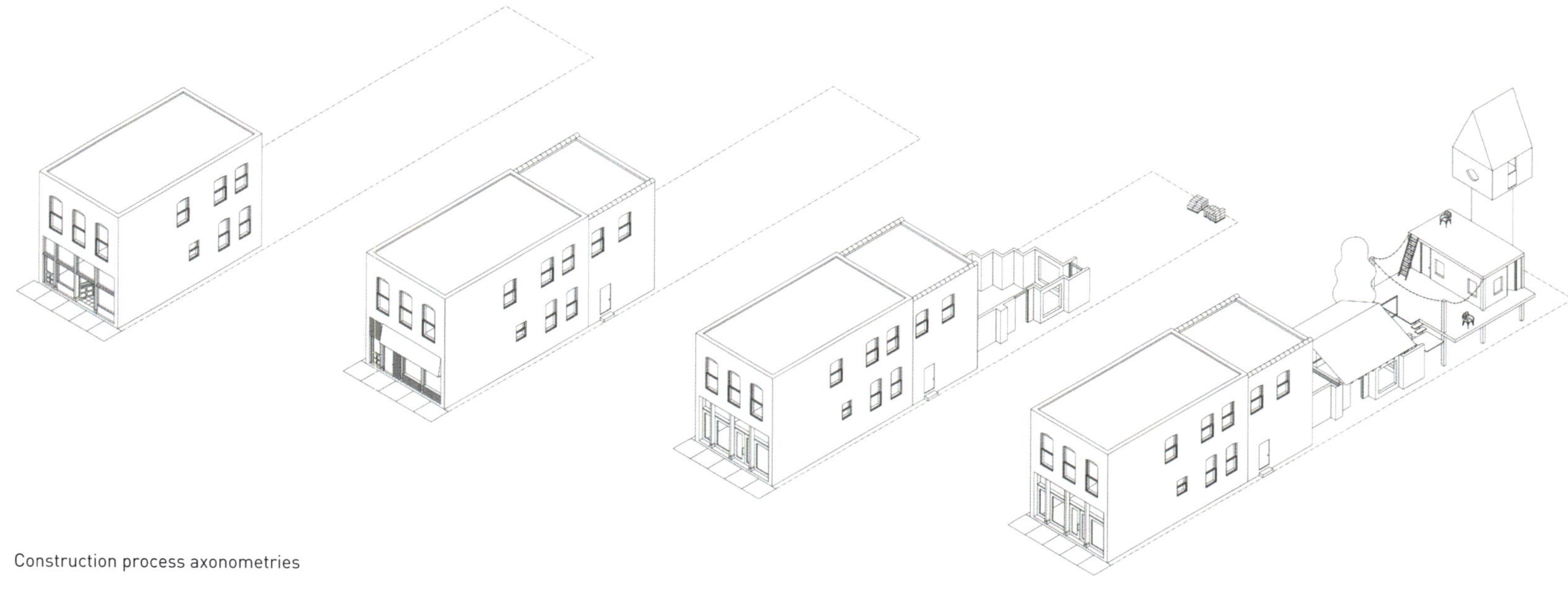

Construction process axonometries

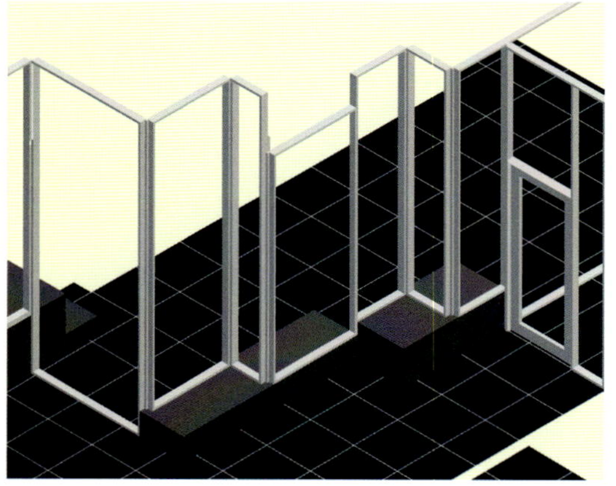

Zig zag glass wall

Zig zag glass wall

Cat meet kitchen

Opening in catio wall

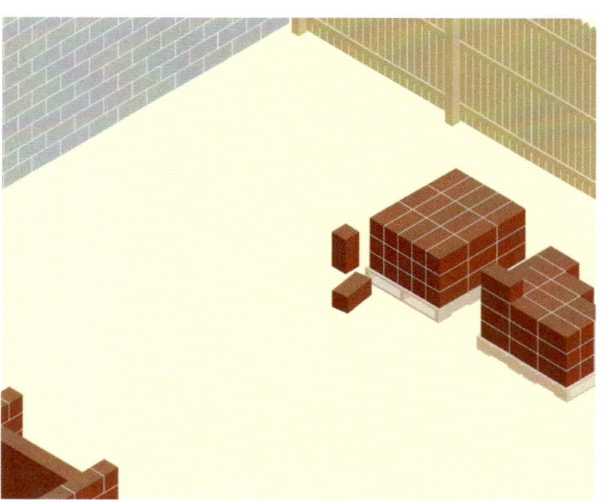

Iso catio wall blocks for future construction

Iso front facade

David Driesen and Tom Verschueren passion for architecture led to dmvA, 'door middel van Architectuur' ('by means of Architecture'). A noble goal to provide a critical answer using architecture to respond to social, economic and collective matters. The creative process doesn't follow a manifesto, but it is expressed through experimenting in architecture: A research on form, material and sustainability... Architecture that always starts with a question, a context and a budget. The work of dmvA can be described as expressive and meticulous, achieving maximalism through minimalism. It also entails dedication to refined details and materiality. By claiming to have no defined style, the entire range of styles is in fact appropriated. This attitude eliminates all conformity restrictions and at the same time makes a statement that timeless architecture doesn't exist.

La passion de David Driesen et Tom Verschueren pour l'architecture a donné naissance à la dmvA, « door middel van Architectuur » (« par l'architecture »). Un noble objectif qui consiste à donner une réponse critique en utilisant l'architecture pour répondre à des questions sociales, économiques et collectives. Le processus créatif s'exprime à travers l'expérimentation en architecture : une recherche sur la forme, le matériau et la durabilité. Une architecture qui commence toujours par une question, un contexte et un budget. Le travail de la dmvA peut être décrit comme expressif et méticuleux, atteignant le maximalisme par le minimalisme. Elle implique également un dévouement aux détails raffinés et à la matérialité. En affirmant qu'elle n'a pas de style défini, la gamme complète des styles est en fait appropriée. Cette attitude supprime toutes les restrictions de conformité et affirme en même temps que l'architecture intemporelle n'existe pas.

Aus der Leidenschaft von David Driesen und Tom Verschueren für Architektur entstand dmvA, „door middel van Architectuur" („durch Architektur"). Sie haben sich als Ziel gesetzt, eine kritische Antwort zu geben, indem die Architektur genutzt wird, um auf soziale, wirtschaftliche und kollektive Probleme zu reagieren. Der kreative Prozess drückt sich durch das Experimentieren in der Architektur aus: Es werden Untersuchung von Form, Material und Nachhaltigkeit durchgeführt – eine Architektur, die immer mit einer Frage, einem Kontext und einem Budget beginnt. Die Arbeit von dmvA kann als ausdrucksstark und akribisch beschrieben werden, wobei Maximalismus durch Minimalismus erreicht wird. Dazu gehört auch die Hingabe zu raffinierten Details und Materialität. Durch die Vorgabe, dass sie keinen klaren Stil haben, ist in der Tat die gesamte Bandbreite an Stilen vorhanden. Diese Haltung hebt alle Beschränkungen der Konformität auf und trifft gleichzeitig die Aussage, dass es keine zeitlose Architektur gibt.

La pasión de David Driesen y Tom Verschueren por la arquitectura dio lugar a dmvA, «door middel van Architectuur» («por medio de la arquitectura»). Un noble objetivo de dar una respuesta crítica usando la arquitectura para responder a los asuntos sociales, económicos y colectivos. El proceso creativo se expresa a través de la experimentación en la arquitectura: una investigación sobre la forma, el material y la sostenibilidad... Una arquitectura que siempre empieza con una pregunta, un contexto y un presupuesto. El trabajo del dmvA puede describirse como expresivo y meticuloso, logrando el maximalismo a través del minimalismo. También implica la dedicación a los detalles refinados y la materialidad. Al afirmar que no tiene un estilo definido, toda la gama de estilos es, de hecho, apropiada. Esta actitud elimina todas las restricciones de conformidad y al mismo tiempo hace una declaración de que la arquitectura atemporal no existe.

dmvA ARCHITECTEN

DAVID DRIESEN, TOM VERSCHUEREN

www.dmva-architecten.be

ARTS CENTER NONA

Mechelen, Belgium

Program: **Renovation & extension of arts center nOna** | *Client:* **vzw Theater Teater** | *Design team:* **David Driesen, Tom Verschueren, Kobe Van Praet, Valerie Lonnoy, Michael De Roeck, Gert-Jan Schulte, Lukas Versteele** | *Structural engineer:* **UTIL struktuurstudies** | *Surface:* **687 m² (arts center) + 275 m² (front building with apartments)** | *Photos:* **© Sergio Pirrone**

Twenty years ago the arts center nOna suffered from lack of space. In 1999 they built a second hall on the adjacent printing business site. In the meantime, the printing plant was transformed into three temporary rehearsal rooms for artists called nOva. In 2016 the actual renovation and extension started. The project fits in the urban planning of Mechelen to boost the cultural axis between the Grand Place and the congress center Lamot.
The site is situated in the middle of a block with a medieval alley that separates the new and old sites. The new extension got embedded in the urban fabric by the succession of interior and exterior rooms with their own atmosphere, capitalizing on the capricious form of the plot.Three patios as urban 'rooms' were created around the new theatre hall and the forum, a multifunctional space with a covered market hall. The first patio connects the Begijnenstraat with the inner area. The large patio is an extension of the forum and the long courtyard gives access to the artists' foyer at the back. The exterior patios were created in collaboration with artist Nick Ervinck with the concept 'brick in motion'.

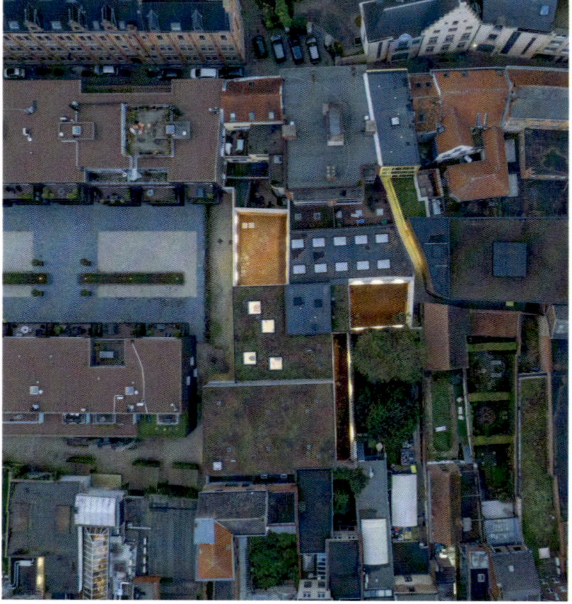

Vor zwanzig Jahren litt das Kunstzentrum nOna unter Platzmangel. Im Jahr 1999 wurde auf dem benachbarten Druckereigelände ein zweiter Saal gebaut. In der Zwischenzeit wurde die Druckerei in drei temporäre Proberäume für Künstler namens nOva umgewandelt. Im Jahr 2016 wurde mit der eigentlichen Renovierung und Erweiterung begonnen. Das Projekt fügt sich in die Stadtplanung von Mechelen ein, um die kulturelle Achse zwischen dem Grand Place und dem Kongresszentrum Lamot zu stärken.
Der Standort befindet sich in der Mitte eines Blocks mit einer mittelalterlichen Gasse, die den neuen und den alten Standort trennt. Der neue Erweiterungsbau wurde durch die Abfolge von Innen- und Außenräumen mit eigener Atmosphäre in das Stadtgefüge eingebettet, wobei die kapriziöse Form des Grundstücks ausgenutzt wurde: Um den neuen Theatersaal und das Forum, einen multifunktionalen Raum mit einer überdachten Markthalle, wurden drei Innenhöfe als städtische „Räume" geschaffen. Der erste Innenhof verbindet die Begijnenstraat mit dem Innenbereich. Der große Innenhof ist eine Erweiterung des Forums und der lange Innenhof ermöglicht den Zugang zum Künstlerfoyer im hinteren Teil. Die Außenhöfe wurden in Zusammenarbeit mit dem Künstler Nick Ervinck nach dem Konzept „brick in motion" gestaltet.

Il y a vingt ans, le centre artistique nOna souffrait d'un manque d'espace. En 1999, on a construit une deuxième salle sur le site adjacent de l'imprimerie. Entre-temps, l'imprimerie a été transformée en trois salles de répétition temporaires pour les artistes, appelées nOva. En 2016, la rénovation et l'extension proprement dites ont commencé. Le projet s'inscrit dans la planification urbaine de Malines pour dynamiser l'axe culturel entre la Grand Place et le centre de congrès Lamot.
Le site est situé au milieu d'un bloc avec une allée médiévale qui sépare le nouveau et l'ancien site. La nouvelle extension s'est inscrite dans le tissu urbain par la succession de pièces intérieures et extérieures avec leur propre atmosphère, capitalisant sur la forme capricieuse de la parcelle.Trois patios comme des « pièces » urbaines ont été créés autour de la nouvelle salle de théâtre et du forum, un espace multifonctionnel avec une halle couverte. Le premier patio relie la Begijnenstraat à la zone intérieure. Le grand patio est une extension du forum et la longue cour donne accès au foyer des artistes à l'arrière. Les patios extérieurs ont été créés en collaboration avec l'artiste Nick Ervinck selon le concept « brick in motion ».

Hace veinte años, el Centro de Artes nOna sufría de falta de espacio. En 1999 se construyó una segunda sala en el terreno adyacente de la imprenta. Mientras tanto, la imprenta se transformó en tres salas de ensayo temporales para artistas llamadas nOva. En 2016 comenzó la renovación y ampliación propiamente dicha. El proyecto encaja en la planificación urbana de Malinas para impulsar el eje cultural entre la Grand Place y el centro de congresos Lamot.
El solar está situado en el centro de una manzana con un callejón medieval que separa el nuevo y el antiguo emplazamiento. La nueva ampliación se incrustó en el tejido urbano mediante la sucesión de salas interiores y exteriores con ambiente propio, aprovechando la forma caprichosa del solar. Se crearon tres patios como «salas» urbanas en torno a la nueva sala de teatro y el foro, un espacio multifuncional con un mercado cubierto. El primer patio conecta la Begijnenstraat con la zona interior. El gran patio es una extensión del foro y el largo patio da acceso al vestíbulo de los artistas en la parte trasera. Los patios exteriores fueron creados en colaboración con el artista Nick Ervinck con el concepto «ladrillo en movimiento».

Second floor plan

Roof plan

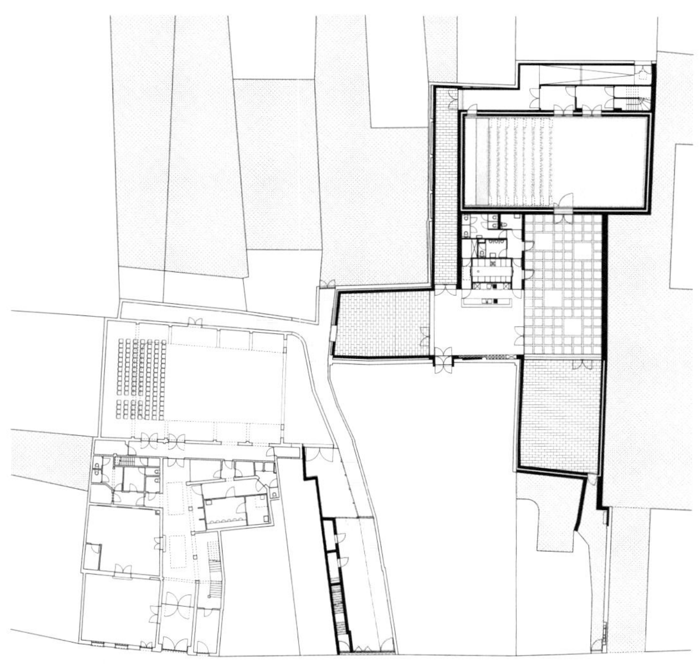
Ground floor plan

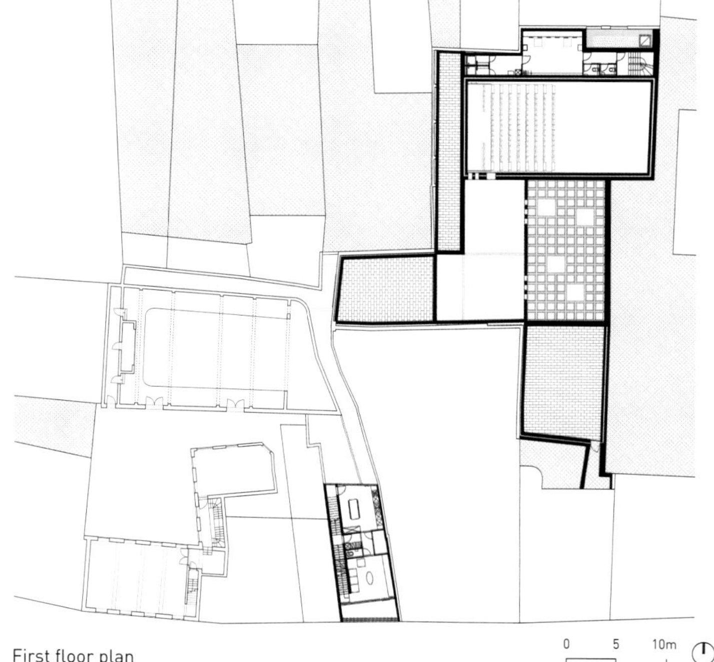

First floor plan

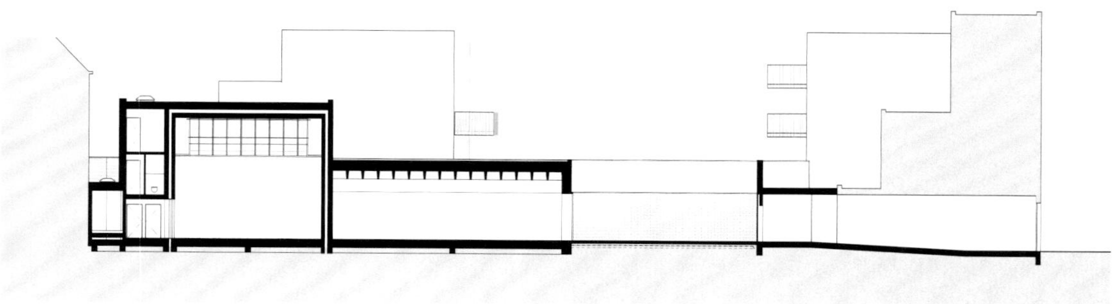
Section

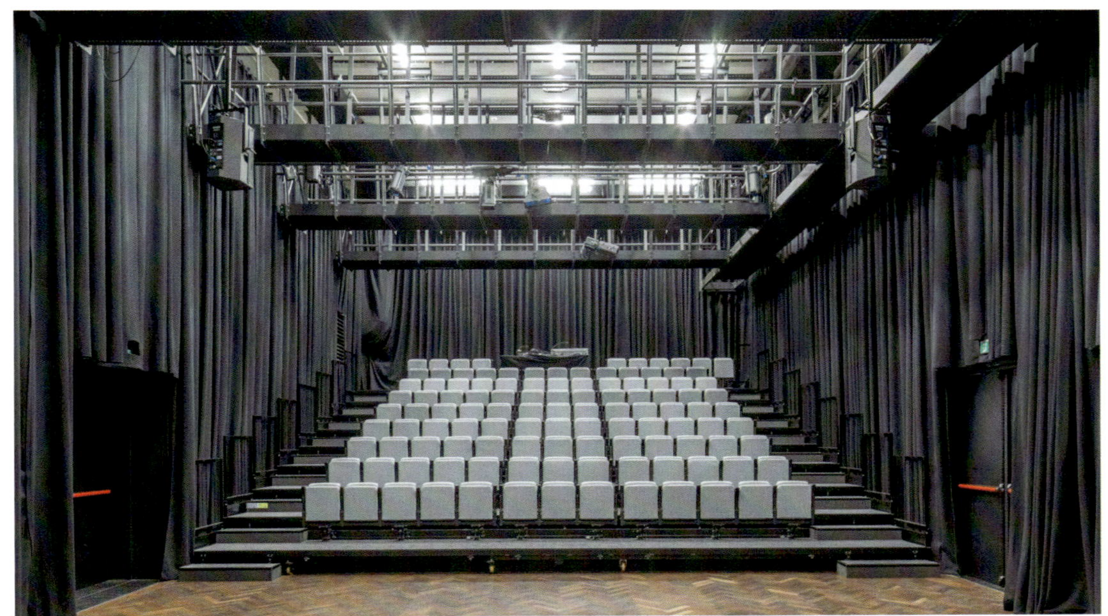

SITE APOSTOLINNEN

Mechelen, Belgium

Concept: **Conversion of an old convent site to inner city living** | *Design team:* **Tom Verschueren, David Driesen, Valerie Lonnoy, Veerle Delaunay, Gert-Jan Schulte** | *Client:* **Phase 1: Visbende / Phase 2: AB nv / B-apart** | *Contractor:* **Phase 1: Harry Hendrickx / Phase 2: FDT Construct + AB nv** | *Gross area:* **Phase 1: 350 m² / Phase 2: 1050 m²** | *Photos:* **© Bart Gosselin**

Site Apostolinnen is a project combination of new building, renovation and restoration. The client asked dmvA initially about the possibilities of the site where his bed factory was located. Based on an archaeological research, a non-binding master plan was made that divided the site in different housing units. In the middle of the site was the "Somerhuys" ("Summer house"), of which dmvA did the restoration as a first assignment. Later the entire master plan was taken into option by the client and dmvA became the engine behind the project "Site Apostolinnen".
The site is located between the Onze-Lieve-Vrouwestraat, the Lange Nieuwstraat and the narrow Tessestraat. According to the historical research, many streets have disappeared since the Middle Ages. dmvA decided to bring back the alleys by cleaning out the inner area of the site. Giving space to the historical volumes. New outdoor spaces are created, making the inner area liveable.

Site Apostolinnen ist ein Projekt, das Neubau, Renovierung und Restaurierung kombiniert. Der Auftraggeber fragte dmvA zunächst nach den Möglichkeiten des Geländes, auf dem sich seine Bettenfabrik befand. Auf der Grundlage einer archäologischen Untersuchung wurde ein unverbindlicher Masterplan erstellt, der das Gelände in verschiedene Wohneinheiten unterteilte. In der Mitte des Geländes befand sich das „Somerhuys" („Sommerhaus"), dessen Restaurierung dmvA als erste Aufgabe übernahm. Später wurde der gesamte Masterplan vom Auftraggeber in Betracht gezogen, und dmvA wurde zum Motor des Projekts „Site Apostolinnen".
Das Gelände befindet sich zwischen der Onze-Lieve-Vrouwestraat, der Lange Nieuwstraat und der schmalen Tessestraat. Der historischen Forschung zufolge sind viele Straßen seit dem Mittelalter verschwunden. dmvA beschloss, die Gassen wieder aufleben zu lassen, indem der Innenbereich des Geländes gereinigt wurde. Den historischen Volumen wird Raum gegeben. Es werden neue Außenräume geschaffen, die das Innere des Geländes bewohnbar machen.

Site Apostolinnen est un projet combinant une nouvelle construction, une rénovation et une restauration. Le client a d'abord demandé à dmvA quelles étaient les possibilités du site où se trouvait sa fabrique de lits. Sur la base d'une recherche archéologique, un plan directeur non contraignant a été établi, divisant le site en différentes unités de logement. Au milieu du site se trouvait la « Somerhuys » (« Maison d'été »), dont dmvA a assuré la restauration dans un premier temps. Plus tard, le maître d'ouvrage a pris en considération l'ensemble du plan directeur et dmvA est devenu le moteur du projet « Site Apostolinnen ».
Le site est situé entre la Onze-Lieve-Vrouwestraat, la Lange Nieuwstraat et l'étroite Tessestraat. D'après les recherches historiques, de nombreuses rues ont disparu depuis le Moyen Âge. dmvA a décidé de faire revivre les ruelles en nettoyant la zone intérieure du site. Donner de l'espace aux volumes historiques. De nouveaux espaces extérieurs sont créés, rendant la zone intérieure vivable.

Site Apostolinnen es un proyecto que combina construcción nueva, renovación y restauración. El cliente preguntó inicialmente a dmvA sobre las posibilidades del emplazamiento donde se encontraba su fábrica de camas. Basándose en una investigación arqueológica, se elaboró un plan maestro no vinculante que dividía el solar en diferentes unidades de vivienda. En el centro del solar estaba la «Somerhuys» («Casa de verano»), de la que dmvA hizo la restauración como primer encargo. Más tarde, el plan maestro completo fue tomado en opción por el cliente y dmvA se convirtió en el motor del proyecto «Site Apostolinnen».
El sitio está situado entre la Onze-Lieve-Vrouwestraat, la Lange Nieuwstraat y la estrecha Tessestraat. Según la investigación histórica, muchas calles han desaparecido desde la Edad Media. dmvA decidió recuperar las callejuelas limpiando la zona interior del solar. Dando espacio a los volúmenes históricos. Se crean nuevos espacios exteriores, haciendo habitable la zona interior.

Site plan

Axonometry

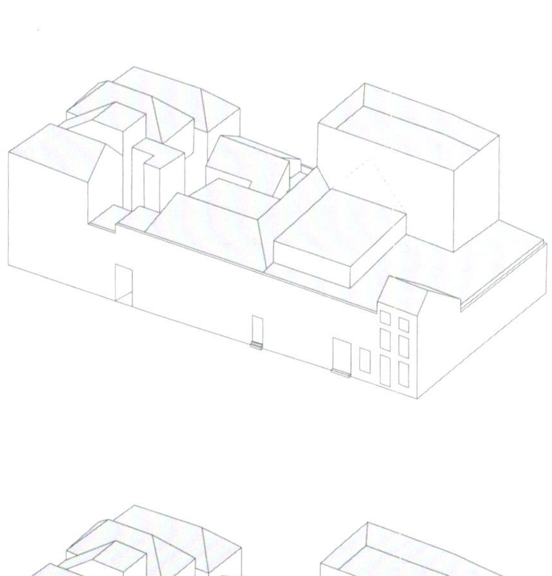

Before and after diagrams

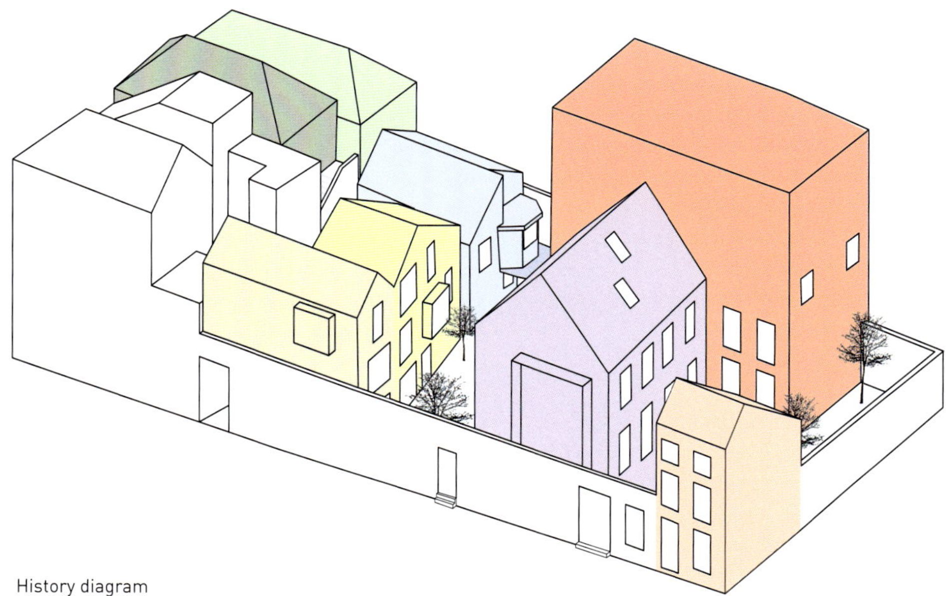

History diagram

Guest house
Worker's house, 20th century, neoclassicism

Private house
Somerhuys, 17th century

8 student studios
Warehouse, was part of the convent of the Apostolins, 18th century

Triplex house
New building

Triplex house
New building

Triplex house
Restored bay window house, 18th century

Duplex (+2 and +3)
Ground floor: commercial retail spaces, 19th century building
Building with modernist facade 1950's

Duplex (+2 and +3)
Ground floor: commercial spaces, 19th century building

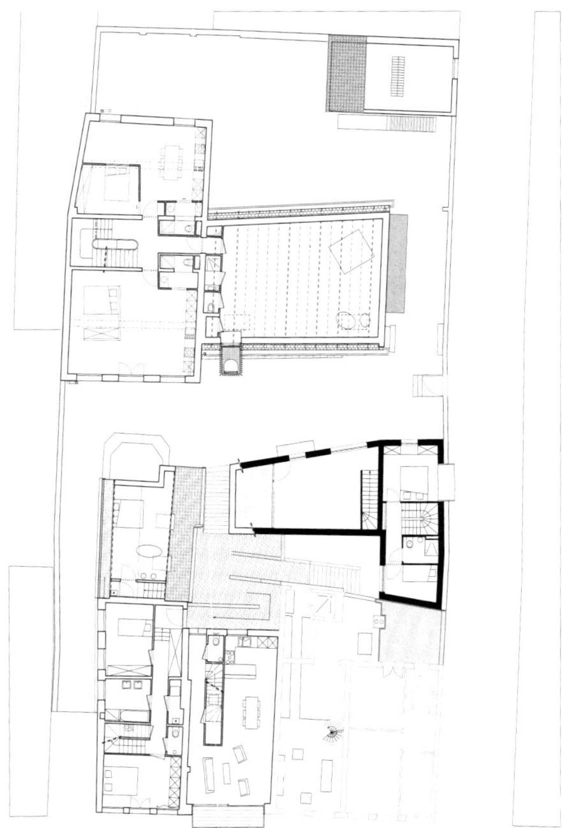

Second floor plan

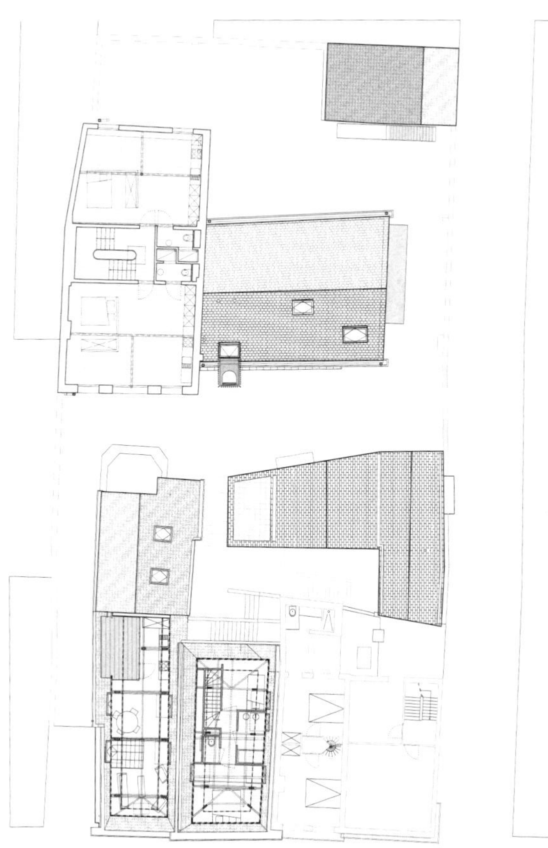

Third floor plan

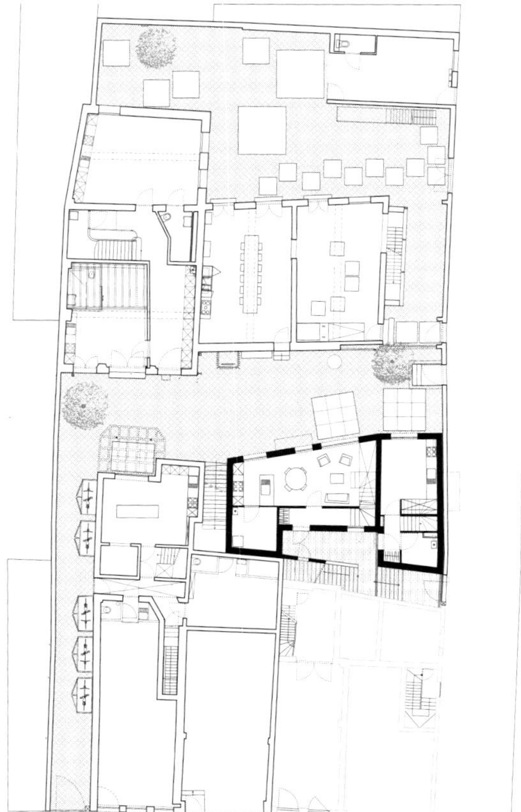

Ground floor plan

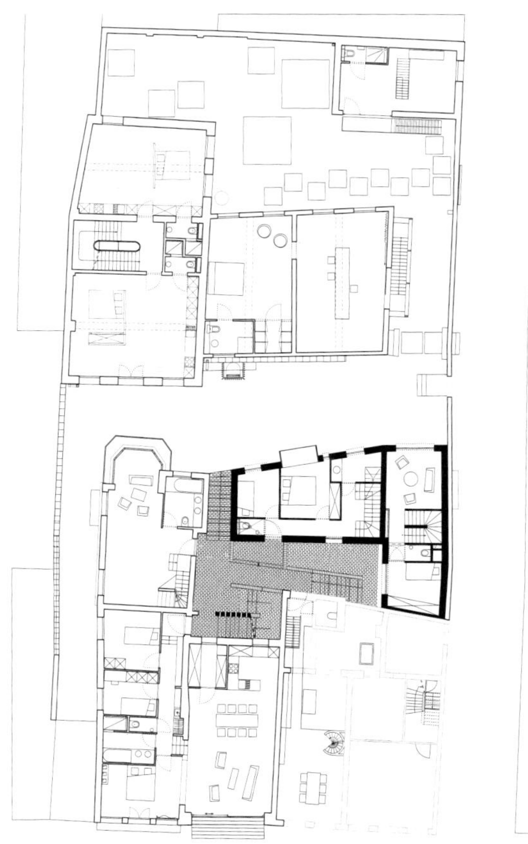

First floor plan

Hooman Balazadeh established HOOBA Design in 2007 with the aim of developing projects in harmony with the cultural and geographical characteristics of the site so that each project forms a new platform for research and investigation. This office has focused on various topics such as light, color, the relation between architecture and the city, building materials, the development of spatial diagrams in Persian Architecture, etc. Using the latest design methods and construction technologies, HOOBA Design tries to create projects which are sustainable and cost-efficient.
In HOOBA Design, one of the main design criteria is to create consistency between the whole and the pieces. Therefore, in the majority of the projects designed by this Group, details are formed and organized following the overall design concept. Projects by Hooba Design have been praised and awarded by various national and international organizations.

Hooman Balazadeh a créé HOOBA Design en 2007 dans le but de développer des projets en harmonie avec les caractéristiques culturelles et géographiques du site afin que chaque projet constitue une nouvelle plateforme de recherche et d'investigation. Ce bureau s'est concentré sur divers sujets tels que la lumière, la couleur, la relation entre l'architecture et la ville, les matériaux de construction, le développement de diagrammes spatiaux dans l'architecture persane, etc. En utilisant les dernières méthodes de conception et technologies de construction, HOOBA Design tente de créer des projets durables et rentables.
Chez HOOBA Design, l'un des principaux critères de conception est de créer une cohérence entre l'ensemble et les pièces. Par conséquent, dans la majorité des projets conçus par ce groupe, les détails sont formés et organisés en fonction du concept de design global. Les projets de Hooba Design ont été salués et récompensés par diverses organisations nationales et internationales.

Hooman Balazadeh gründete HOOBA Design im Jahr 2007 mit dem Ziel, Projekte im Einklang mit den kulturellen und geografischen Besonderheiten des Ortes zu entwickeln, so dass jedes Projekt eine neue Plattform für Forschung und Untersuchung bildet. Das Büro hat sich auf verschiedene Themen wie Licht, Farbe, die Beziehung zwischen Architektur und Stadt, Baumaterialien, die Entwicklung von Raumdiagrammen in der persischen Architektur usw. konzentriert. Unter Verwendung der neuesten Entwurfsmethoden und Bautechnologien versucht HOOBA Design, Projekte zu schaffen, die nachhaltig und kosteneffizient sind.
Eines der wichtigsten Designkriterien von HOOBA Design ist es, die Kohärenz zwischen dem Ganzen und den Teilen herzustellen. Daher werden bei den meisten von dieser Gruppe entworfenen Projekten die Details nach dem Gesamtkonzept gestaltet und organisiert. Die Projekte von Hooba Design wurden von verschiedenen nationalen und internationalen Organisationen gelobt und ausgezeichnet.

Hooman Balazadeh fundó HOOBA Design en 2007 con el objetivo de desarrollar proyectos en armonía con las características culturales y geográficas del lugar, de modo que cada proyecto constituya una nueva plataforma de investigación. Esta oficina se ha centrado en diversos temas como la luz, el color, la relación entre la arquitectura y la ciudad, los materiales de construcción, el desarrollo de diagramas espaciales en la arquitectura persa, etc. Utilizando los últimos métodos de diseño y tecnologías de construcción, HOOBA Design intenta crear proyectos que sean sostenibles y rentables.
En HOOBA Design, uno de los principales criterios de diseño es crear coherencia entre el conjunto y las piezas. Por ello, en la mayoría de los proyectos diseñados por este Grupo, los detalles se forman y organizan siguiendo el concepto de diseño general. Los proyectos de Hooba Design han sido elogiados y premiados por diversas organizaciones nacionales e internacionales.

HOOBA DESIGN

HOOMAN BALAZADEH

www.hoobadesign.com

HITRA OFFICE & COMMERCIAL BUILDING

Tehran, Iran

Architect: **Hooman Balazadeh** | *Project architect:* **Elham Seyfiazad**
Design Team: **Elham Seyfiazad, Parima Jahangard, Mona Razavi, Saeed Farshbaf**
Total building area: **5960 m²** | *Photos:* **© Parham Taghioff, Deed Studio, Sadegh Miri, Khatereh Eshghi**

In Kohan Ceram project, our mission was to have minimum formal disturbance to the city. Hitra Commercial-Office Building is located at the intersection of two main streets in Tehran. Above ground floors are dedicated to office units. The commercial zone and the entrances were arranged to create outdoor green patios for people to relax. These platforms are aligned with street levels on both sides to create an urban plaza for the public, a win-win opportunity for both the commercial spaces and the city by creating a new public space. The main criteria was to reevaluate the morphology of a typical office building by improving the quality of natural lighting and views without altering the built area.
Two of the main considerations were to create an integrated volume and to reevaluate the 40 % glass use on the façade. A double skin façade was created with the outer porous skin formed by brick and metal frames. The combination of brick and metal form modules which enable bigger openings on the façade.

Bei dem Projekt Kohan Ceram war es unser Ziel, die Stadt so wenig wie möglich zu stören. Das Hitra Commercial-Office Building befindet sich an der Kreuzung von zwei Hauptstraßen in Teheran. Die oberirdischen Stockwerke sind für Büroeinheiten vorgesehen. Der gewerbliche Bereich und die Eingänge wurden so angeordnet, dass grüne Außenbereiche entstehen, in denen sich die Menschen entspannen können. Diese Plattformen sind auf beiden Seiten auf das Straßenniveau ausgerichtet, um einen städtischen Platz für die Öffentlichkeit zu schaffen, von dem sowohl die Gewerbeflächen als auch die Stadt durch die Schaffung eines neuen öffentlichen Raums profitieren können. Das Hauptkriterium bestand darin, die Morphologie eines typischen Bürogebäudes neu zu bewerten, indem die Qualität der natürlichen Beleuchtung und der Ausblicke verbessert wird, ohne die bebaute Fläche zu verändern.
Zwei der Hauptüberlegungen waren die Schaffung eines integrierten Volumens und die Neubewertung des 40 %igen Glasanteils an der Fassade. Es wurde eine zweischalige Fassade geschaffen, deren äußere poröse Haut aus Ziegeln und Metallrahmen besteht. Die Kombination von Ziegeln und Metall bildet Module, die größere Öffnungen in der Fassade ermöglichen.

Dans le projet Kohan Ceram, notre mission était de minimiser la perturbation formelle de la ville. Le bâtiment commercial et de bureaux Hitra est situé à l'intersection de deux rues principales de Téhéran. Les étages supérieurs sont consacrés à des bureaux. La zone commerciale et les entrées ont été aménagées de manière à créer des patios verts extérieurs où les gens peuvent se détendre. Ces plateformes sont alignées avec les niveaux des rues des deux côtés afin de créer une place urbaine pour le public, une opportunité gagnant-gagnant à la fois pour les espaces commerciaux et pour la ville en créant un nouvel espace public. Le critère principal était de réévaluer la morphologie d'un immeuble de bureaux typique en améliorant la qualité de l'éclairage naturel et des vues sans altérer la zone construite.
Deux des principales considérations étaient de créer un volume intégré et de réévaluer l'utilisation de 40 % de verre sur la façade. Une façade à double peau a été créée, la peau extérieure poreuse étant formée de briques et de cadres métalliques. La combinaison de la brique et du métal forme des modules qui permettent des ouvertures plus grandes sur la façade.

En el proyecto de Kohan Ceram, nuestra misión era tener la mínima perturbación formal de la ciudad. El edificio comercial y de oficinas Hitra está situado en la intersección de dos calles principales de Teherán. Las plantas superiores están dedicadas a oficinas. La zona comercial y las entradas se dispusieron para crear patios verdes exteriores para disfrute de la gente. Estas plataformas están alineadas con los niveles de la calle en ambos lados para crear una plaza urbana para el público, una oportunidad en la que ganan tanto los espacios comerciales como la ciudad al crear un nuevo espacio público. El criterio principal era revalorizar la morfología de un típico edificio de oficinas mejorando la calidad de la iluminación natural y las vistas sin alterar la superficie construida.
Dos de las principales consideraciones fueron crear un volumen integrado y re evaluar el uso del 40 % de vidrio en la fachada. Se creó una fachada de doble piel con la parte exterior porosa formada por ladrillos y marcos metálicos. La combinación de ladrillo y metal forma módulos que permiten mayores aberturas en la fachada.

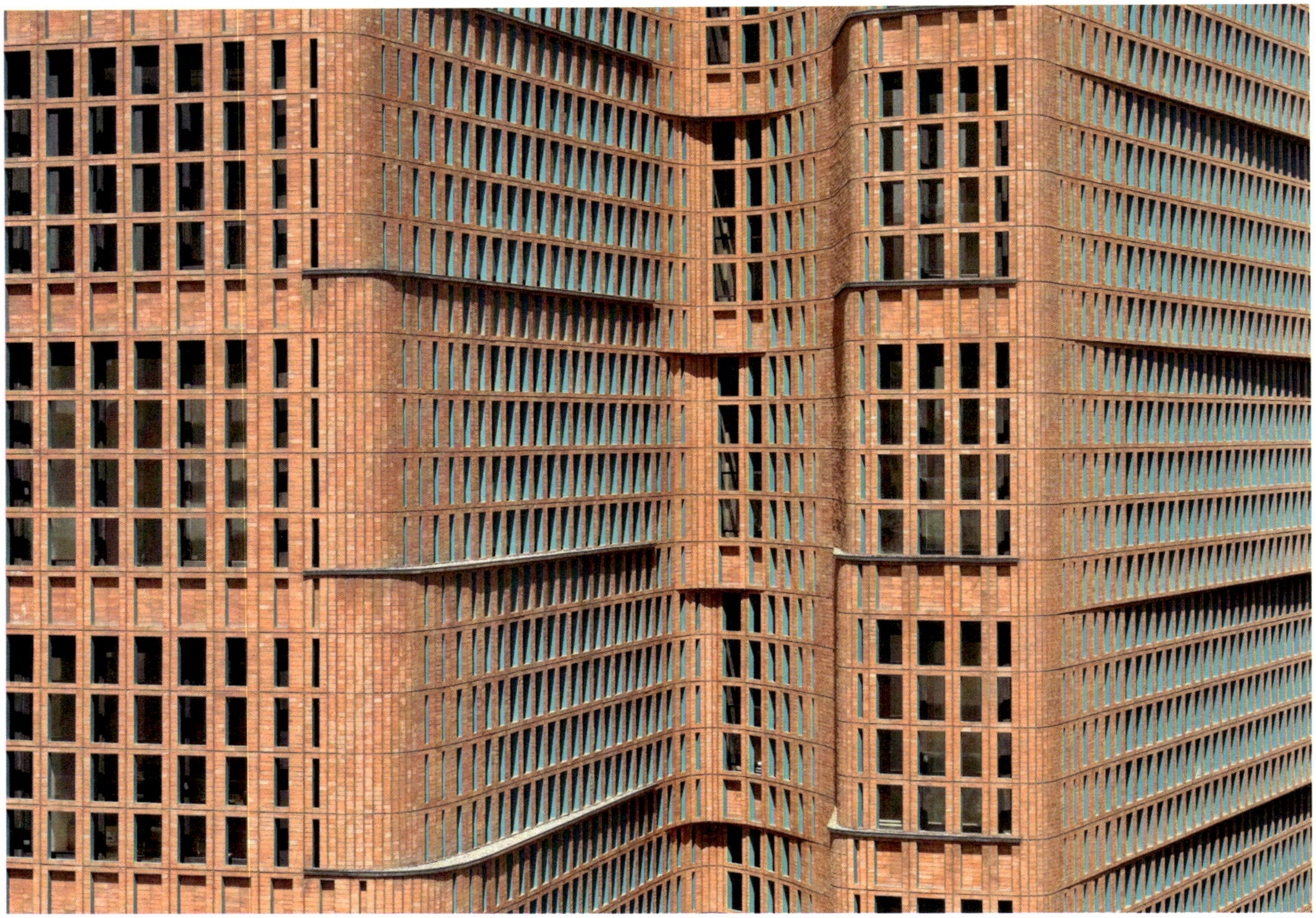

Tochal
Shopping
Center
Hitra Office &
Commercial
Building
Galleria
Shopping
Center
material overload
form overload
visually disturbing elements
color overload

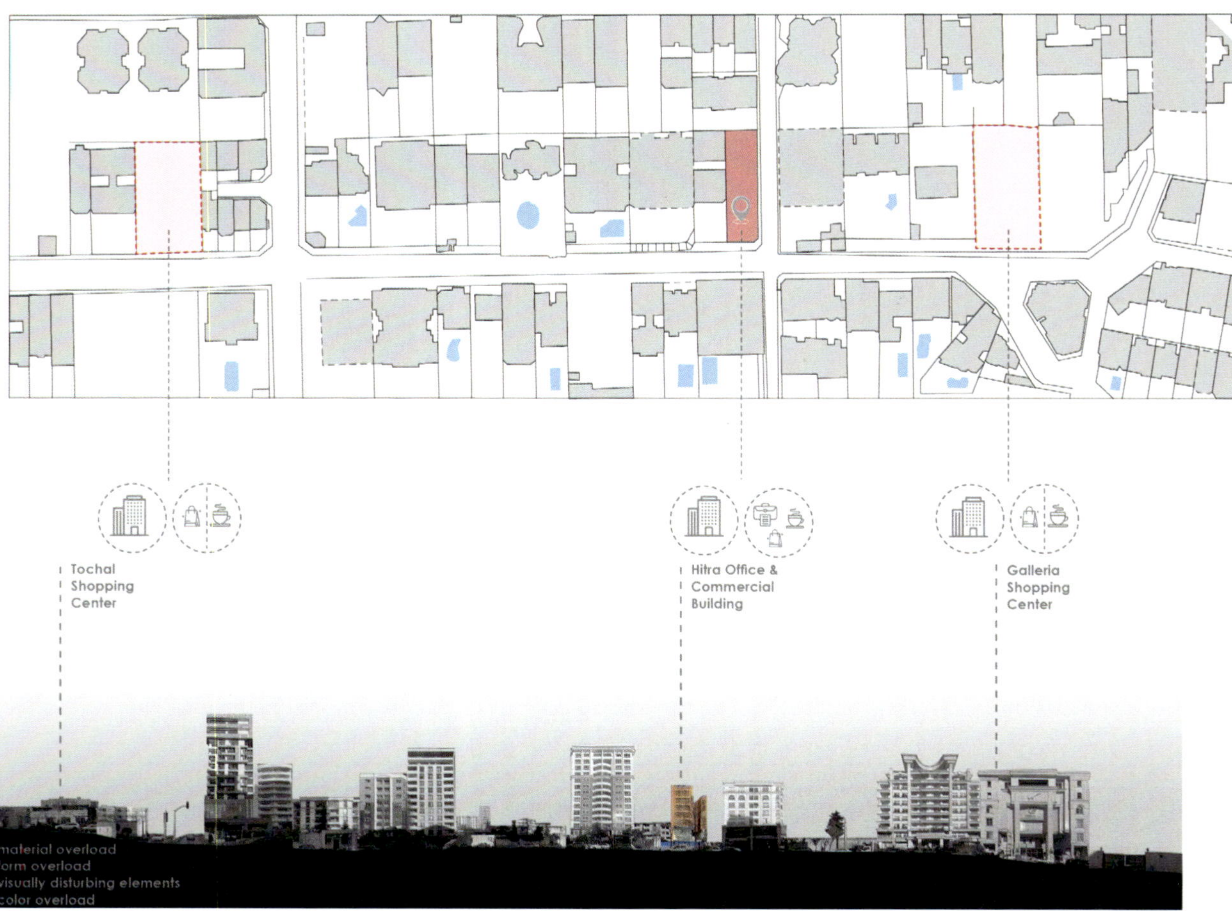

Diagram

حمل با جرثقیل

Hyunjoon Yoo Architects (HYA) is a young architectural practice based in Seoul; South Korea, founded in 2013 by Hyunjoon Yoo (A.I.A), a principal of HYA and a professor at Hongik University. The practice is supported by a team of dedicated architects and designers with diverse experiences, talents, and passions.
HYA has grown and expanded its expertise over the years by actively participating in various projects across the nation, ranging from architectural scale to large scale urban masterplans. Along the way, we have received various global awards.
"Architecture is to Design Relationships" is our motive, creating harmony among people and nature through an innovative architectural approach. We continuously seek the best architectural solutions to make the city smarter, improving its harmonious existence and generating a healthier human-centered living environment for the future.

Hyunjoon Yoo Architects (HYA) est un jeune cabinet d'architecture basé à Séoul ; Corée du Sud, fondé en 2013 par Hyunjoon Yoo (A.I.A), un principal de HYA et un professeur à l'Université Hongik. Le cabinet est soutenu par une équipe d'architectes et de designers dévoués, aux expériences, talents et passions variés.
HYA a développé et étendu son expertise au fil des ans en participant activement à divers projets à travers le pays, allant de l'échelle architecturale aux plans directeurs urbains à grande échelle. En cours de route, nous avons reçu divers prix mondiaux.
" L'architecture consiste à concevoir des relations " est notre motivation, créant une harmonie entre les gens et la nature grâce à une approche architecturale innovante. Nous recherchons en permanence les meilleures solutions architecturales pour rendre la ville plus intelligente, améliorer son existence harmonieuse et générer un environnement de vie plus sain et centré sur l'homme pour l'avenir.

Hyunjoon Yoo Architects (HYA) ist ein junges Architekturbüro mit Sitz in Seoul, Südkorea, das 2013 von Hyunjoon Yoo (A.I.A), einem der Leiter von HYA und Professor an der Hongik University, gegründet wurde. Das Büro wird von einem Team aus engagierten Architekten und Designern mit unterschiedlichen Erfahrungen, Talenten und Leidenschaften unterstützt.
HYA hat sein Fachwissen im Laufe der Jahre durch die aktive Teilnahme an verschiedenen Projekten im ganzen Land, die von architektonischen Maßstäben bis hin zu groß angelegten städtischen Masterplänen reichen, erweitert und ausgebaut. Im Laufe der Zeit haben wir verschiedene globale Auszeichnungen erhalten.
"Architektur ist das Gestalten von Beziehungen" - das ist unser Motiv, um durch einen innovativen architektonischen Ansatz Harmonie zwischen Mensch und Natur zu schaffen. Wir suchen ständig nach den besten architektonischen Lösungen, um die Stadt intelligenter zu machen, ihre harmonische Existenz zu verbessern und ein gesünderes, auf den Menschen ausgerichtetes Lebensumfeld für die Zukunft zu schaffen.

Hyunjoon Yoo Architects (HYA) es un joven estudio de arquitectura con sede en Seúl; Corea del Sur, fundado en 2013 por Hyunjoon Yoo (A.I.A), director de HYA y profesor de la Universidad de Hongik. El estudio está respaldado por un equipo de dedicados arquitectos y diseñadores con diversas experiencias, talentos y pasiones.
HYA ha crecido y ampliado su experiencia a lo largo de los años participando activamente en varios proyectos en todo el país, que van desde la escala arquitectónica hasta los planes maestros urbanos a gran escala. A lo largo del camino, hemos recibido varios premios globales.
"La arquitectura es diseñar relaciones" es nuestro motivo, creando armonía entre las personas y la naturaleza a través de un enfoque arquitectónico innovador. Buscamos continuamente las mejores soluciones arquitectónicas para hacer la ciudad más inteligente, mejorando su existencia armoniosa y generando un entorno de vida más saludable centrado en el ser humano del futuro.

HYUNJOON YOO ARCHITECTS

HYUNJOON YOO

www.hyunjoonyoo.com

THE GARAGE HOUSE

Pangyo-dong, Bundang-gu, Seongnam-si, Gyeonggi-do, South Korea

Program: Residential | *Material:* Brick and Zinc | *Project director:* Hyunjoon Yoo
Leading architect: Jiyoung Jon | *Design team:* Minkyun Kim, Yoomi Chae
Built surface: 127 m² | *Photos:* © Kyungsub Shin

The client of The Garage House is a car lover who dreamed of having a house with a private garage. The key to this design was to meet the client's demand to enjoy hobbies and parties in the garage and courtyard.
The site needed to be setback by 2.5 m from the adjacent land. With a limited amount of space, it was difficult to freely configure the area and shape during the design process. Therefore, individual spaces of the house such as the garage, living room and the kitchen, were designed and expanded around the courtyard.
In order to maximize the use of the site, variable sliding doors were installed toward the setback line to provide flexible expansion of spaces while giving privacy to the user and as a result, a relatively confined space was resolved through visual scalability.

Der Bauherr von The Garage House ist ein Autoliebhaber, der von einem Haus mit einer privaten Garage träumte. Der Schlüssel zu diesem Entwurf lag darin, den Wunsch des Kunden zu erfüllen, in der Garage und im Innenhof Hobbys und Partys zu genießen.
Das Grundstück musste um 2,5 m vom Nachbargrundstück zurückgesetzt werden. Aufgrund des begrenzten Platzes war es schwierig, die Fläche und Form während des Entwurfsprozesses frei zu gestalten. Daher wurden einzelne Bereiche des Hauses, wie die Garage, das Wohnzimmer und die Küche, um den Innenhof herum entworfen und erweitert.
Um die Nutzung des Grundstücks zu maximieren, wurden variable Schiebetüren in Richtung der Rücksprunglinie eingebaut, um eine flexible Erweiterung der Räume zu ermöglichen und gleichzeitig den Nutzern Privatsphäre zu geben, wodurch ein relativ enger Raum durch visuelle Skalierbarkeit aufgelöst wurde.

Le client de The Garage House est un amateur de voitures qui rêvait d'avoir une maison avec un garage privé. La clé de cette conception était de répondre à la demande du client qui souhaitait pratiquer ses loisirs et organiser des fêtes dans le garage et la cour.
Le site devait être en retrait de 2,5 m par rapport au terrain adjacent. Avec un espace limité, il était difficile de configurer librement la surface et la forme pendant le processus de conception. Par conséquent, les espaces individuels de la maison, tels que le garage, le salon et la cuisine, ont été conçus et agrandis autour de la cour.
Afin de maximiser l'utilisation du site, des portes coulissantes variables ont été installées vers la ligne de retrait pour permettre une expansion flexible des espaces tout en assurant l'intimité de l'utilisateur. Ainsi, un espace relativement confiné a été résolu grâce à l'extensibilité visuelle.

El cliente de The Garage House es un amante de los coches que soñaba con tener una casa con garaje privado. La clave de este diseño era satisfacer la demanda del cliente de disfrutar de sus aficiones y fiestas en el garaje y el patio.
Había que retranquearse 2,5 m del terreno adyacente. Con un espacio limitado, era difícil configurar libremente la zona y la forma durante el proceso de diseño. Por lo tanto, los espacios individuales de la casa, como el garaje, el salón y la cocina, se diseñaron y ampliaron alrededor del patio.
Para maximizar el uso del terreno, se instalaron puertas correderas variables hacia la línea de retranqueo para proporcionar una expansión flexible de los espacios y, al mismo tiempo, dar privacidad al usuario; como resultado, se resolvió un espacio relativamente confinado mediante la escalabilidad visual.

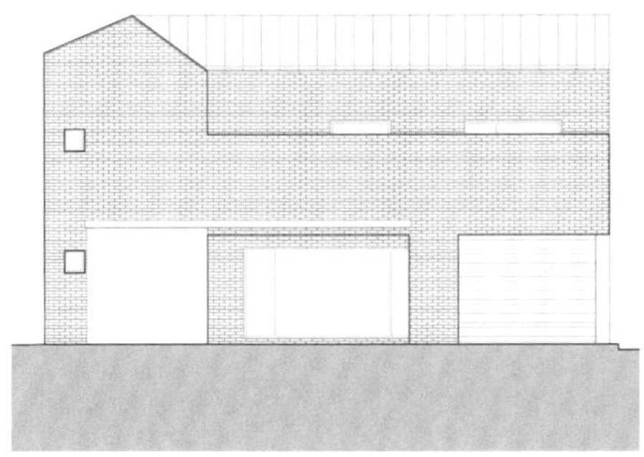

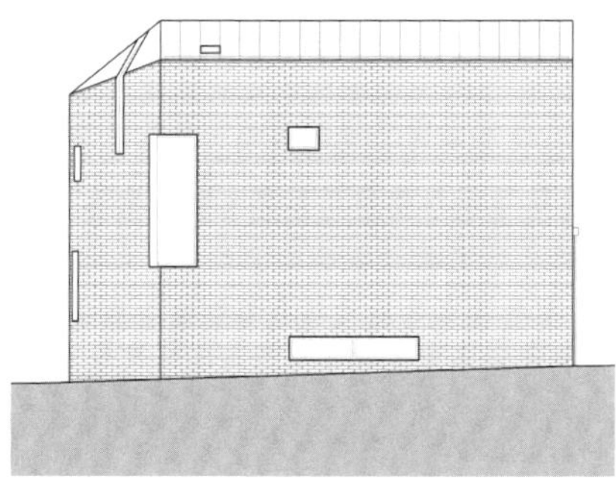

Elevations

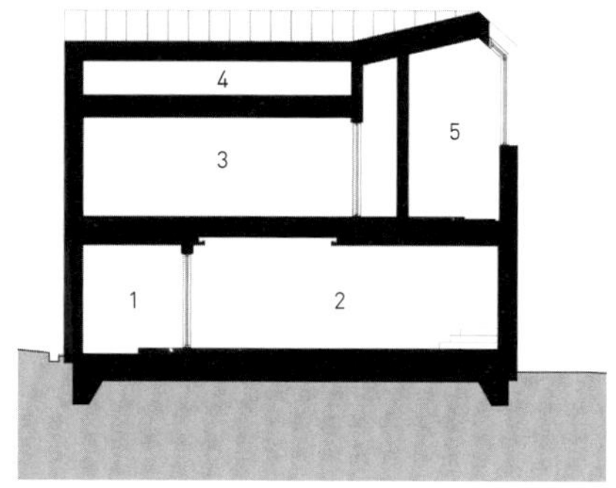

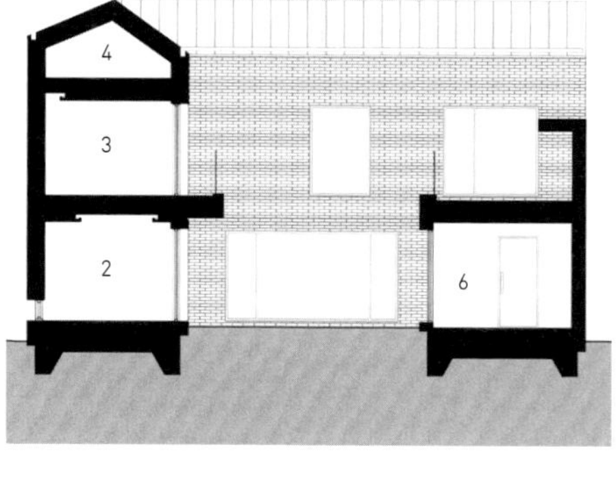

Sections

0 1 3 6m

1. Entrance
2. Living room
3. Room 1
4. Attic room
5. Bathroom 2
6. Garage/Hobby room

4-15

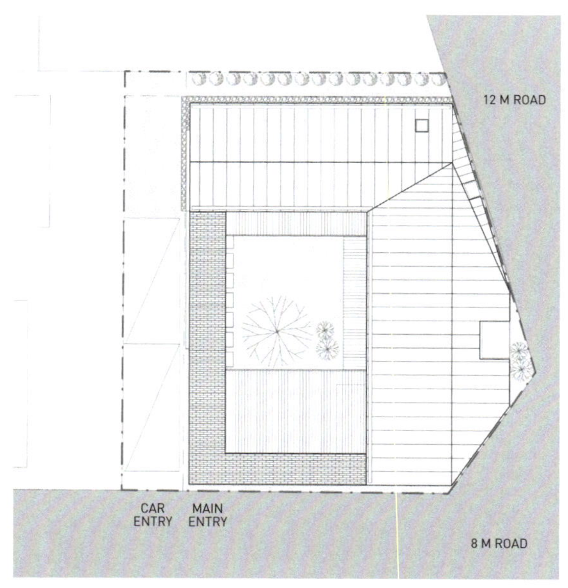

Site plan

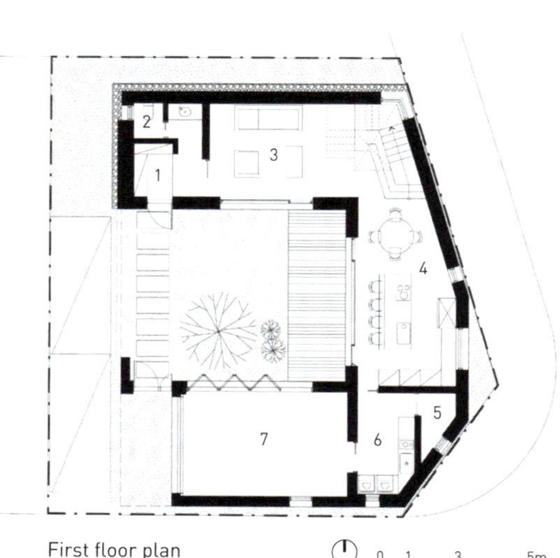

First floor plan

1. Entrance
2. Bathroom
3. Living room
4. Kitchen
5. Storage
6. Sub kitchen
7. Garage/ Hobby room

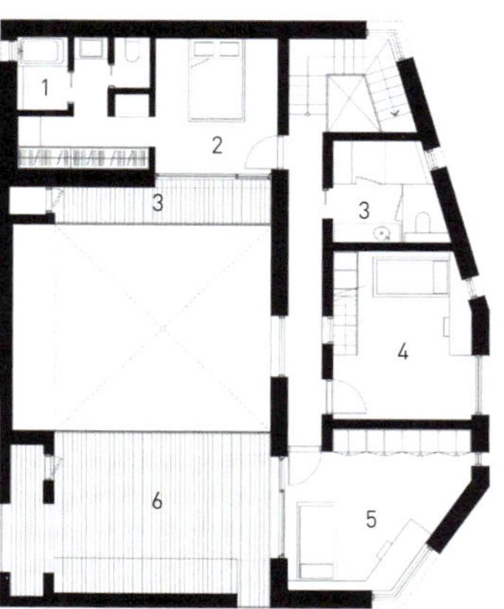

Second floor plan

1. Bathroom 1
2. Room 1
3. Bathroom 2
4. Room 2
5. Room 3
6. Terrace

KANGAROO HOUSE

Baekhyeon-dong, Seongnam-si, Gyeonggi-do, South Korea

Program: Residential | *Material:* Brick and Zinc | *Project director:* Hyunjoon Yoo
Leading architect: Jinsung Heo | *Design team:* Insil Son | *Built surface:* 120 m²
Photos: © Youngchae Park

The client wants to live with their parents in the same "house". So, the son bought the land, and the parent built the house for two families. Combining two houses into one was our approach, and we borrowed the idea of a kangaroo as a design concept. Just like a kangaroo carries its baby in its pouch, the parents' house contains their son's house.
The parents' house is made of black brick, and the son's house is made of wood to give a contrast of being two different houses. Kangaroo House is divided into four parts with a narrow courtyard at the center. The two-story-high courtyard acts as a divider while also being a connector between two houses.
Despite the fact that both generations live on a different floor, managing the relationships between them was one of our top priorities. To create a harmonious relationship, the viewing angle between the spaces in the house was carefully controlled based on the hierarchy of family members.

Der Bauherr möchte mit seinen Eltern im selben „Haus" leben. Also kaufte der Sohn das Grundstück, und die Eltern bauten das Haus für zwei Familien. Unser Ansatz war es, zwei Häuser zu einem zusammenzufassen, und wir haben die Idee eines Kängurus als Designkonzept übernommen. So wie das Känguru sein Baby in seinem Beutel trägt, enthält das Haus der Eltern das Haus des Sohnes.
Das Haus der Eltern ist aus schwarzem Ziegelstein und das Haus des Sohnes aus Holz, um den Kontrast zwischen den beiden Häusern zu verstärken. Das Känguru-Haus ist in vier Teile unterteilt, mit einem schmalen Innenhof in der Mitte. Der zweistöckige Innenhof dient als Trennwand und gleichzeitig als Verbindung zwischen den beiden Häusern.
Trotz der Tatsache, dass beide Generationen auf einer anderen Etage leben, war die Gestaltung der Beziehungen zwischen ihnen eine unserer obersten Prioritäten. Um eine harmonische Beziehung zu schaffen, wurde der Blickwinkel zwischen den Räumen im Haus sorgfältig auf der Grundlage der Hierarchie der Familienmitglieder gesteuert.

Le client souhaite vivre avec ses parents dans la même «maison». Le fils a donc acheté le terrain et le parent a construit la maison pour deux familles. Notre approche a consisté à combiner deux maisons en une seule, et nous avons emprunté l'idée d'un kangourou comme concept de design. Tout comme un kangourou porte son bébé dans sa poche, la maison des parents contient la maison de leur fils.
La maison des parents est faite de briques noires, et celle du fils est en bois pour donner le contraste de deux maisons différentes. La maison Kangourou est divisée en quatre parties avec une cour étroite au centre. La cour, haute de deux étages, fait office de séparation tout en servant de lien entre les deux maisons.
Malgré le fait que les deux générations vivent à un étage différent, la gestion des relations entre elles était l'une de nos principales priorités. Pour créer une relation harmonieuse, l'angle de vue entre les espaces de la maison a été soigneusement contrôlé en fonction de la hiérarchie des membres de la famille.

El cliente quería vivir con sus padres en la misma "casa". Así que el hijo compró el terreno y el padre construyó una casa para dos familias. Combinar dos casas en una fue nuestro enfoque, y tomamos prestada la idea de un canguro como concepto de diseño. Al igual que un canguro lleva a su bebé en su bolsa, la casa de los padres contiene la casa de su hijo.
La casa de los padres es de ladrillo negro, y la del hijo es de madera, a modo de contraste. La Casa Canguro está dividida en cuatro partes con un patio estrecho en el centro, el cual, con sus dos pisos de altura, actúa como divisor y a la vez conector, entre dos casas.
A pesar de que ambas generaciones viven en un piso diferente, gestionar las relaciones entre ellas era una de nuestras principales prioridades. Para crear una relación armoniosa, el ángulo de visión entre los espacios de la casa se controló cuidadosamente en función de la jerarquía de los miembros de la familia.

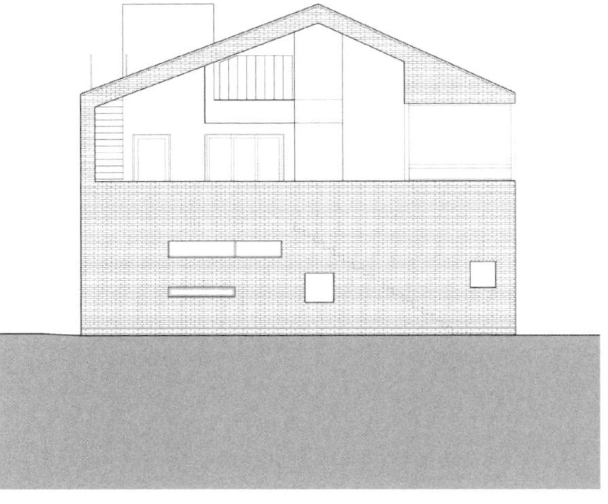

Front elevation

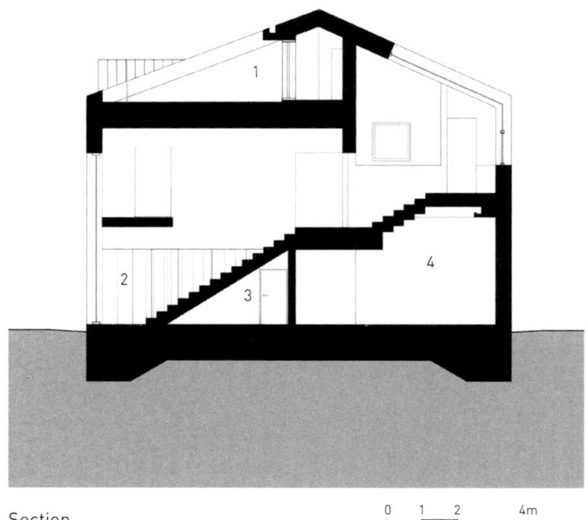

Section

0 1 2 4m

1. Attic
2. Entrance
3. Storage
4. Kitchen

Site plan

0 1 2 4m

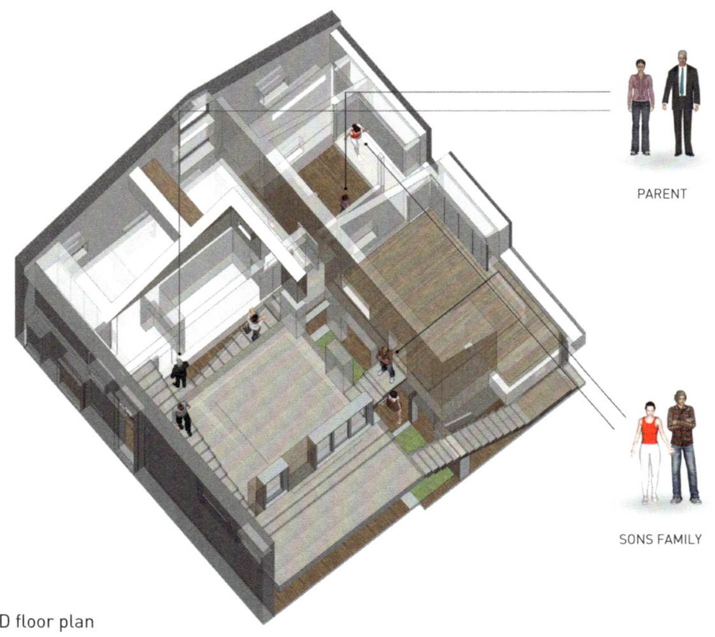

3D floor plan

HAGIDONG HOUSE 2

Hagi-dong, Yuseong-gu, Daejeon-si, South Korea

Program: **Residential** | *Material:* **Brick and Zinc** | *Project director:* **Hyunjoon Yoo**
Leading architect: **Jinsung Heo** | *Design team:* **Jaehong Kim, Hyunseung Lee**
Built surface: **148 m²** | *Photos:* **© Youngchae Park**

Hagidong House 2 sits firmly on the land of a gradual slop in Hagi-dong, Daejeon City. The main design concept was to provide privacy for a family of four and has been developed from the idea of the principle of the Han-Ok (the traditional Korean architecture) landscape: far-distance (borrowing distant scenery), mid-distance (erasing unwanted scenery by a fence) and close-distance (embracing the scenery in the courtyard).
The courtyard adjacent to the main road was raised one level higher, acting as a fence to block the view of the road while maximizing the view of a faraway distant scenery. Despite being a three-story building, two different colored bricks were layered to give the contrast of two masses stacked together. The brick does not only add aesthetics to the design but also allows ease of maintenance.

Das Hagidong House 2 steht auf einem Grundstück mit einem leichten Gefälle in Hagi-dong, Daejeon City. Das Hauptentwurfskonzept bestand darin, einer vierköpfigen Familie Privatsphäre zu bieten, und wurde auf der Grundlage des Prinzips der Han-Ok-Landschaft (der traditionellen koreanischen Architektur) entwickelt: Ferne (Anleihen an entfernte Landschaften), mittlere Entfernung (Auslöschen unerwünschter Landschaften durch einen Zaun) und nahe Entfernung (Umarmung der Landschaften im Innenhof).
Der an die Hauptstraße angrenzende Hof wurde um eine Ebene erhöht und dient als Zaun, der den Blick auf die Straße versperrt und gleichzeitig den Blick auf eine weit entfernte Landschaft maximiert. Obwohl es sich um ein dreistöckiges Gebäude handelt, wurden zwei verschiedenfarbige Ziegelsteine geschichtet, um den Kontrast von zwei aufeinander gestapelten Massen zu erzeugen. Die Ziegelsteine tragen nicht nur zur Ästhetik des Entwurfs bei, sondern ermöglichen auch eine einfache Wartung.

La maison Hagidong 2 est fermement installée sur le terrain d'une pente graduelle à Hagi-dong, dans la ville de Daejeon. Le concept principal de la conception était d'assurer l'intimité d'une famille de quatre personnes et a été développé à partir de l'idée du principe du paysage Han-Ok (l'architecture traditionnelle coréenne) : distance lointaine (emprunter un paysage éloigné), distance moyenne (effacer le paysage indésirable par une clôture) et distance proche (embrasser le paysage dans la cour).
La cour adjacente à la route principale a été surélevée d'un niveau, agissant comme une clôture pour bloquer la vue de la route tout en maximisant la vue d'un paysage lointain. Bien qu'il s'agisse d'un bâtiment de trois étages, deux briques de couleurs différentes ont été superposées pour donner le contraste de deux masses empilées ensemble. La brique n'ajoute pas seulement de l'esthétique à la conception mais permet également un entretien facile.

La Casa Hagidong 2 se asienta firmemente en el terreno de una pendiente gradual en Hagi-dong, en la ciudad de Daejeon. El concepto principal del diseño era proporcionar privacidad a una familia de cuatro miembros y se ha desarrollado a partir de la idea del principio del paisaje Han-Ok (la arquitectura tradicional coreana): distancia lejana (tomar prestado el paisaje lejano), distancia media (borrar el paisaje no deseado mediante una valla) y distancia cercana (abrazar el paisaje en el patio).
El patio adyacente a la carretera principal se elevó un nivel, actuando como una valla para bloquear la vista de la carretera y maximizar la visión de un paisaje lejano. A pesar de ser un edificio de tres plantas, se colocaron ladrillos de dos colores diferentes para conseguir el contraste de dos masas apiladas. El ladrillo no sólo añade estética al diseño, sino que también permite un fácil mantenimiento.

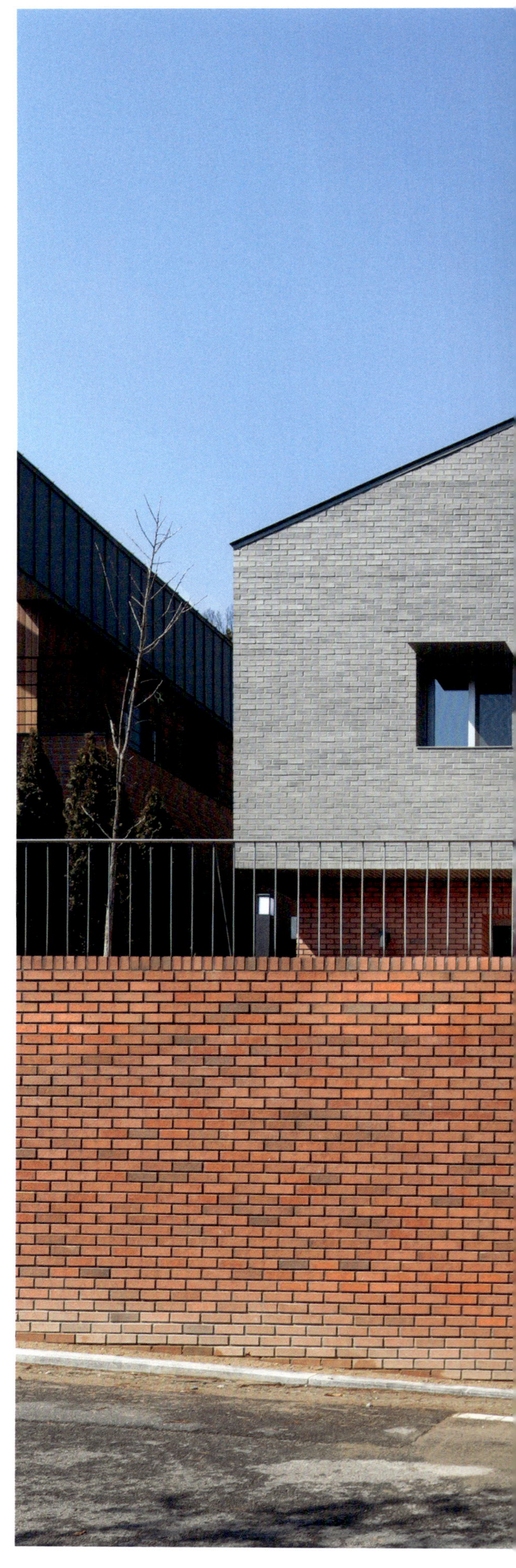

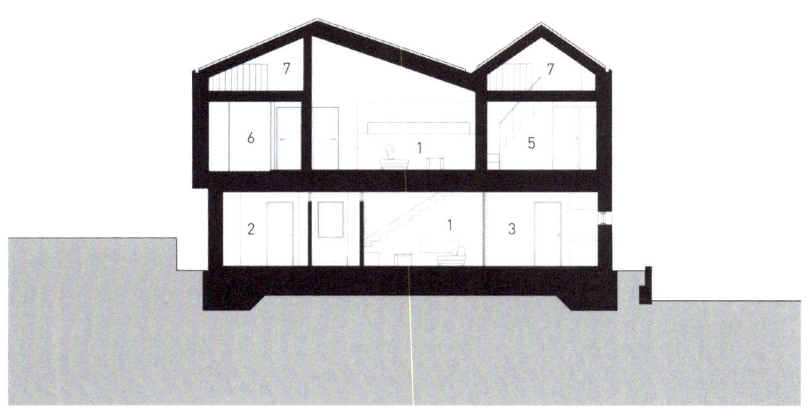

Section 1

1. Living room 1
2. Room 1
3. Kitchen
4. Living room 2
5. Dress room
6. Room 2
7. Attic

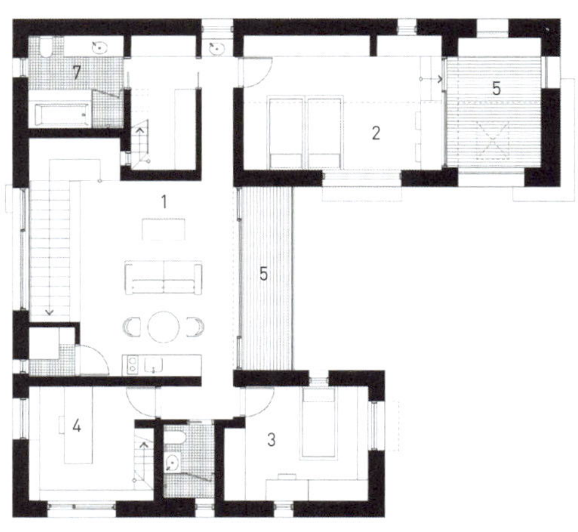

Second floor plan

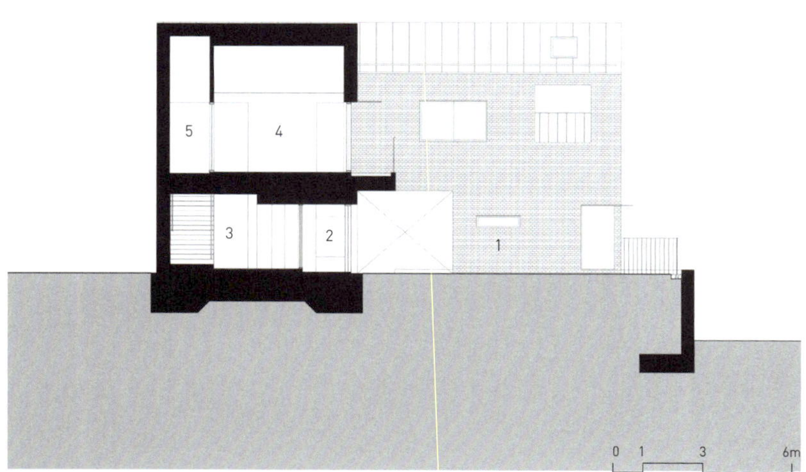

Section 2

1. Garden
2. Entrance
3. Living room 1
4. Living room 2
5. Laundry

First floor plan

1. Entrance
2. Garden
3. Room
4. Study
5. Living room
6. Dining
7. Kitchen

llLab. is a design studio based in Shanghai, Stuttgart and Porto operating within the fields of architecture, design, art, urbanism, research and development. The studio is led by four partners. Their work focuses on using design as a tool to improve social and cultural life through various scales, from urban projects to micro-architecture or installations.
Hanxiao Liu (1985): University of Britich Columbia Bachelor of Applied Science (Mechanical Engineering); University of Pennsylvania, Master of Architecture and Certificate in Landscape Studies
Luís Ricardo (1985): University of Oporto Faculty of Architecture - integrated Master in Architecture, FAUP.
Asst Prof. David Correa (1981); Ryerson University, Bachelor in Architectural Science; University of Calgary, Masters of Architecture; University of Stuttgart, ICD, PhD.
Dr. Taichi Kuma (1985): University of Tokyo, Graduate School; ICD, University of Stuttgart, Guest PhD student; ITECH, University of Stuttgart, Master of Science; University of Tokyo, PhD course.

llLab. est un studio de design basé à Shanghai, Stuttgart et Porto qui opère dans les domaines suivants : l'architecture, le design, l'art, l'urbanisme, la recherche et le développement. Le studio est dirigé par quatre partenaires. Leur travail se concentre sur l'utilisation du design comme outil pour améliorer la vie sociale et culturelle à différentes échelles, des projets urbains à la micro-architecture ou aux installations.
Hanxiao Liu (1985) : Université de Britich Columbia - Licence en sciences appliquées (génie mécanique) ; Université de Pennsylvanie - Maîtrise en architecture et certificat en études paysagères.
Luís Ricardo (1985) : Université de Porto - Faculté d'architecture, maîtrise intégrée en architecture, FAUP.
Professeur adjoint David Correa (1981) : Université Ryerson, licence en sciences de l'architecture ; Université de Calgary, maîtrise en architecture ; Université de Stuttgart, ICD, doctorat.
Taichi Kuma (1985) : Université de Tokyo, Graduate School ; ICD, Université de Stuttgart, doctorant invité ; ITECH, Université de Stuttgart, Master of Science ; Université de Tokyo, cours de doctorat.

llLab. ist ein Designstudio mit Sitz in Shanghai, Stuttgart und Porto, das in den Bereichen: Architektur, Design, Kunst, Urbanismus, Forschung und Entwicklung. Das Studio wird von vier Partnern geleitet. Ihre Arbeit konzentriert sich auf die Verwendung von Design als Werkzeug zur Verbesserung des sozialen und kulturellen Lebens in verschiedenen Maßstäben, von städtischen Projekten bis hin zu Mikroarchitekturen und Installationen.
Hanxiao Liu (1985): Universität Britich-Kolumbien - Bachelor of Applied Science (Maschinenbau); Universität Pennsylvania - Master of Architecture und Zertifikat in Landscape Studies.
Luís Ricardo (1985): Universität von Porto, Fakultät für Architektur, integrierter Master in Architektur, FAUP.
Assist Prof. David Correa (1981): Ryerson University, Bachelor in Architekturwissenschaften; University of Calgary, Master of Architecture; Universität Stuttgart, ICD, Promotion.
Dr. Taichi Kuma (1985): Universität Tokio, Graduiertenschule; ICD, Universität Stuttgart, Gastdoktorand; ITECH, Universität Stuttgart, Master of Science; Universität Tokio, Doktoratsstudium.

llLab. es un estudio de diseño con sede en Shanghái, Stuttgart y Oporto que opera en los campos de arquitectura, diseño, arte, urbanismo, investigación y desarrollo. El estudio está dirigido por cuatro socios. Su trabajo se centra en utilizar el diseño como herramienta para mejorar la vida social y cultural a través de diversas escalas, desde proyectos urbanos hasta micro arquitectura o instalaciones.
Hanxiao Liu (1985): Universidad de Britich Columbia Licenciada en Ciencias Aplicadas (Ingeniería Mecánica); Universidad de Pensilvania - Máster en Arquitectura y Certificado en Estudios de Paisaje
Luís Ricardo (1985): Universidad de Oporto Facultad de Arquitectura, Master integrado en Arquitectura, FAUP.
Profesor Adjunto David Correa (1981): Universidad de Ryerson, Licenciado en Ciencias Arquitectónicas; Universidad de Calgary, Máster en Arquitectura; Universidad de Stuttgart, ICD, Doctorado.
Dr. Taichi Kuma (1985): Universidad de Tokio, Escuela de Postgrado; ICD, Universidad de Stuttgart, estudiante de doctorado invitado; ITECH, Universidad de Stuttgart, Master of Science; Universidad de Tokio, curso de doctorado.

llLab.

HANXIAO LIU, LUÍS RICARDO,
DAVID CORREA, TAICHI KUMA

www.lllab.net

SAN SA VILLAGE

Huairou District, Beijing

Project investor: **2049 Group** | *Construction team:* **San She Inn (Beijing) Cultural Management Co., Ltd.** | *Construction drawings:* **China Electric Design & Research Co., Ltd.** *Civil engineering construction team:* **Yi Wang and his friends** | *Site area:* **around 2,300 m²** *Building area:* **about 1,600 m²** | *Photos:* **© Fernando Guerra/FG+SG**

"San Sa", formerly named as "The Third Hometown", refers to a social space created for an introspective group of people who seek a space away from everyday life to recharge the mind, body, and spirit. The project is situated on a 2,000 m² unused plot, which was originally occupied by a gas station near the Mutianyu Great Wall.
To embed within the design an appreciation for the site's heritage, we extended the existing spatial arrangement of the village, scattering the architectural blocks in-line with the typical village plan, while combining those blocks into an integrated whole. This approach enabled us to create a spatial pattern that blends rather seamlessly into the local built environment. By subverting the stereotypical concept of rural tourism resorts, we hope to create a kind of "village within a village" and to give this piece of land the vitality it deserves.
"San Sa" is a kind of joy to art, an embrace to the five senses, and a respect to regional culture.

„San Sa", früher „The Third Hometown" genannt, bezieht sich auf einen sozialen Raum, der für eine Gruppe von Menschen geschaffen wurde, die einen Raum abseits des Alltags suchen, um Körper, Geist und Seele wieder aufzuladen. Das Projekt befindet sich auf einem 2 000 m² großen, ungenutzten Grundstück, das ursprünglich von einer Tankstelle in der Nähe der Großen Mauer von Mutianyu genutzt wurde.
Um das Erbe des Ortes in den Entwurf einzubeziehen, haben wir die bestehende räumliche Anordnung des Dorfes erweitert, indem wir die architektonischen Blöcke in Anlehnung an den typischen Dorfplan verstreut und gleichzeitig zu einem integrierten Ganzen zusammengefügt haben. Mit diesem Ansatz konnten wir ein räumliches Muster schaffen, das sich ziemlich nahtlos in die örtliche Bebauung einfügt. Indem wir das stereotype Konzept ländlicher Tourismusorte unterlaufen, hoffen wir, eine Art „Dorf im Dorf" zu schaffen und diesem Stück Land die Vitalität zu verleihen, die es verdient.
„San Sa" ist eine Art Freude an der Kunst, eine Umarmung für die fünf Sinne und ein Respekt für die regionale Kultur.

« San Sa », anciennement appelé « The Third Hometown », désigne un espace social créé pour un groupe de personnes introspectives qui recherchent un espace loin de la vie quotidienne pour recharger l'esprit, le corps et l'âme. Le projet est situé sur un terrain inutilisé de 2 000 m², qui était à l'origine occupé par une station-service près de la grande muraille de Mutianyu.
Pour intégrer dans la conception une appréciation du patrimoine du site, nous avons étendu la disposition spatiale existante du village, en dispersant les blocs architecturaux conformément au plan typique du village, tout en combinant ces blocs en un ensemble intégré. Cette approche nous a permis de créer un modèle spatial qui s'intègre plutôt bien à l'environnement bâti local. En renversant le concept stéréotypé des stations de tourisme rural, nous espérons créer une sorte de « village dans le village » et donner à ce terrain la vitalité qu'il mérite.
« San Sa » est une sorte de joie pour l'art, une étreinte pour les cinq sens et un respect pour la culture régionale.

«San Sa», antes llamado «El tercer pueblo», se refiere a un espacio social creado para un grupo introspectivo de personas que buscan un espacio alejado de la vida cotidiana para recargar la mente, el cuerpo y el espíritu. El proyecto está situado en una parcela de 2.000 m² sin uso, que originalmente estaba ocupada por una gasolinera cerca de la Gran Muralla de Mutianyu.
Para integrar en el diseño una apreciación del patrimonio del lugar, ampliamos la disposición espacial existente de la aldea, dispersando los bloques arquitectónicos en línea con el plano típico de la aldea, y combinando al mismo tiempo esos bloques en un todo integrado. Este enfoque nos permitió crear un patrón espacial que se integra perfectamente en el entorno local. Al subvertir el concepto estereotipado de los centros turísticos rurales, esperamos crear una especie de «pueblo dentro de un pueblo» y dar a este terreno la vitalidad que merece.
«San Sa» es una especie de alegría al arte, un abrazo a los cinco sentidos y un respeto a la cultura regional.

General layout

WAAAM

Huairou, Beijing, China

Project status: **Built** | *Project client:* **2049 Investment Group** | *Architectural design:* **llLab.**
Project partners: **Hanxiao Liu, Luis Ricardo** | *Project leads:* **Henry D'Ath, Yihui Zhao**
Project team: **Lingkong Yin, Fei Chen, Lexian Hu, Yujun Yan, Lingling Liu, Camilo Espitia**
Photos: **© Arch-Exist Photography**

China's landscape and cities have undergone big transformation in the last decades. However, the Beigou Village, which is located in the Huairou District, on the outskirts of Beijing, maintains its traditional appearance.
The most recent project in Beigou, WAAAM (originally named the Glazed-Tile Art Architecture Museum), is a testament to the broad impact that rural revitalization has brought to the community.
The concept of the WAAAM is based on the history of the site, the villagers' lives and the integration of traditional crafts. The museum takes a critical approach to local materials by positioning them in a new light, expressing their features in a more contemporary sensibility.
The space is a platform for communication between the permanence of Beigou and the ever-changing avant-garde consciousness of their people. The building records the context of the past, the ambitions of the present while embracing the uncharted territory of the future.

Chinas Landschaften und Städte haben sich in den letzten Jahrzehnten stark gewandelt. Das Dorf Beigou im Huairou-Bezirk am Stadtrand von Peking hat jedoch sein traditionelles Aussehen bewahrt. Das jüngste Projekt in Beigou, das WAAAM (ursprünglich Glazed-Tile Art Architecture Museum), ist ein Beweis für die weitreichenden Auswirkungen, die die Wiederbelebung des ländlichen Raums auf die Gemeinde gehabt hat.
Das Konzept des WAAAM basiert auf der Geschichte des Ortes, dem Leben der Dorfbewohner und der Integration des traditionellen Handwerks. Das Museum setzt sich kritisch mit den lokalen Materialien auseinander, indem es sie in ein neues Licht rückt und ihre Eigenschaften in einer zeitgenössischen Sensibilität zum Ausdruck bringt.
Der Raum ist eine Plattform für die Kommunikation zwischen der Beständigkeit von Beigou und dem sich ständig wandelnden avantgardistischen Bewusstsein seiner Bewohner. Das Gebäude nimmt den Kontext der Vergangenheit und die Ambitionen der Gegenwart auf, während es gleichzeitig das unerforschte Territorium der Zukunft umarmt.

Les paysages et les villes de Chine ont subi de grandes transformations au cours des dernières décennies. Cependant, le village de Beigou, qui se trouve dans le district de Huairou, à la périphérie de Pékin, conserve son aspect traditionnel.
Le projet le plus récent de Beigou, le WAAAM (initialement appelé Glazed-Tile Art Architecture Museum), témoigne du large impact de la revitalisation rurale sur la communauté.
Le concept du WAAAM est basé sur l'histoire du site, la vie des villageois et l'intégration de l'artisanat traditionnel. Le musée adopte une approche critique des matériaux locaux en les positionnant sous un nouveau jour, exprimant leurs caractéristiques dans une sensibilité plus contemporaine.
L'espace est une plate-forme de communication entre la permanence de Beigou et la conscience avant-gardiste en constante évolution de ses habitants. Le bâtiment enregistre le contexte du passé, les ambitions du présent tout en embrassant le territoire inexploré de l'avenir.

El paisaje y las ciudades de China han sufrido grandes transformaciones en las últimas décadas. Sin embargo, el pueblo de Beigou, situado en el distrito de Huairou, en las afueras de Pekín, mantiene su aspecto tradicional.
El proyecto más reciente de Beigou, el WAAAM (originalmente llamado Museo de Arquitectura de Arte de Azulejos), es un testimonio del amplio impacto que la revitalización rural ha traído a la comunidad.
El concepto del WAAAM se basa en la historia del lugar, la vida de los aldeanos y la integración de la artesanía tradicional. El museo adopta un enfoque crítico de los materiales locales al situarlos bajo una nueva luz, expresando sus características con una sensibilidad más contemporánea.
El espacio es una plataforma de comunicación entre la permanencia de Beigou y la siempre cambiante conciencia vanguardista de sus gentes. El edificio registra el contexto del pasado y las ambiciones del presente, a la vez que abraza el territorio inexplorado del futuro.

Sketches

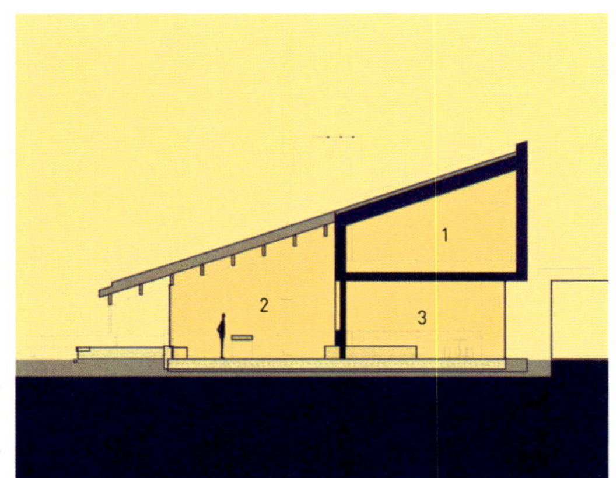

East to west section

1. Event space
2. Cafe
3. Resting space

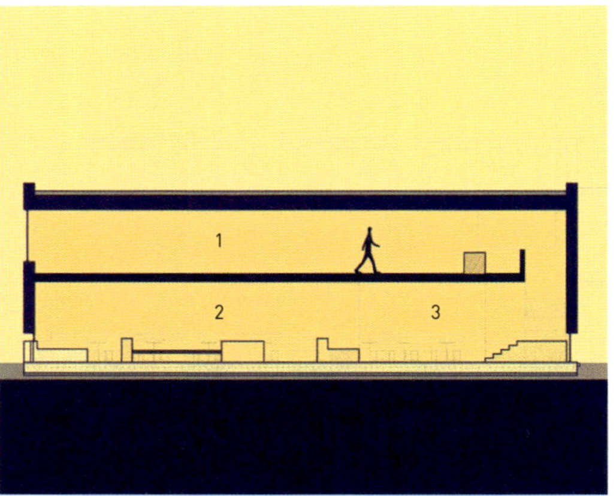

North hall south to north section

1. Event space
2. Main exhibition
3. Resting space

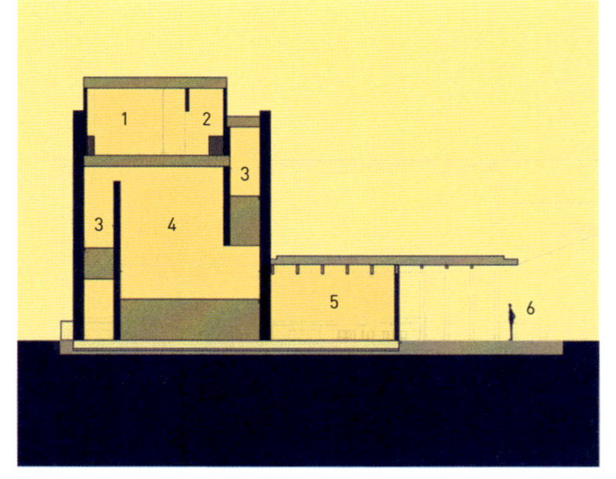

South to north section

1. Great wall dining
2. Preparation
3. Narrow gallery
4. Main hall stair
5. Cafe
6. Outdoor seating

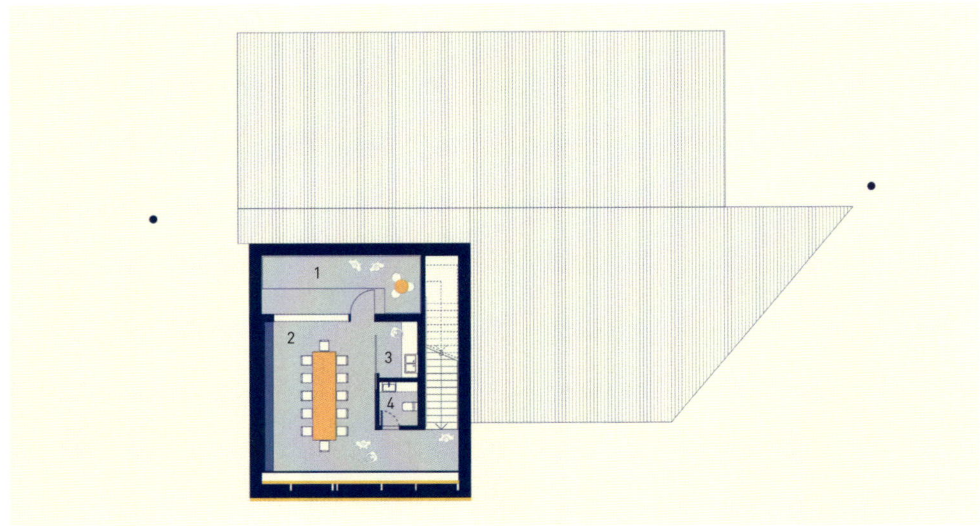

1. Rooftop terrace
2. Great wall dining
3. Preparation
4. Toilet

Third floor plan

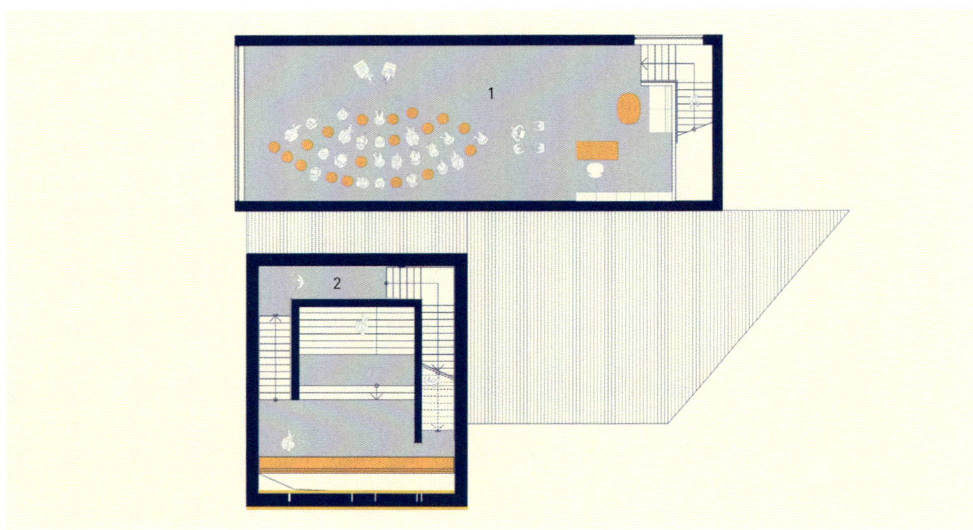

1. Event space
2. Narrow gallery

Second floor plan

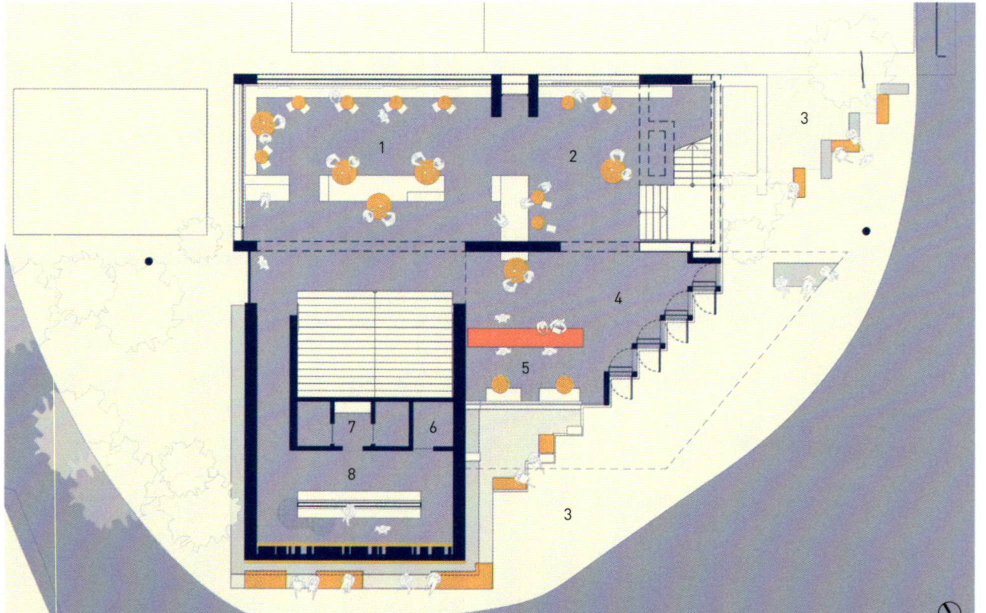

1. Main exhibition space
2. Resting space
3. Outdoor seating
4. Community space
5. Cafe
6. Storage
7. Toilet
8. Exhibition/meditation space

First floor plan

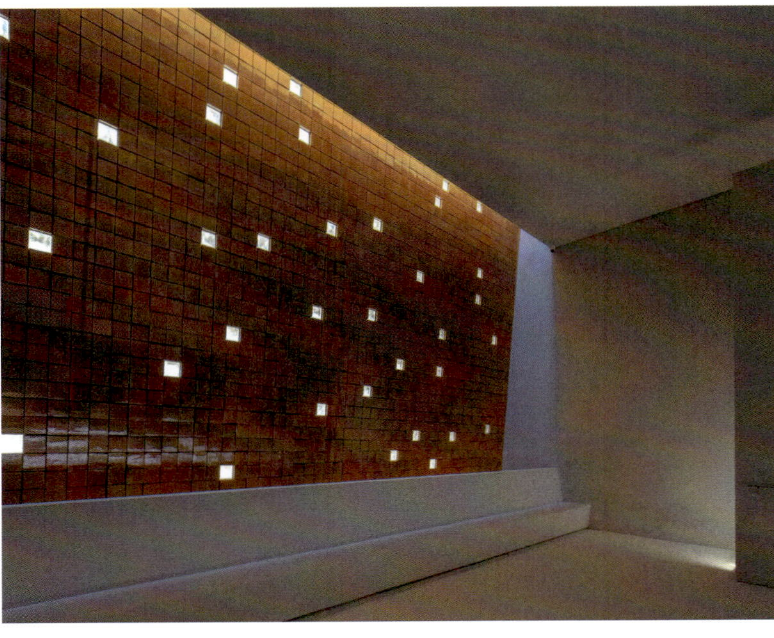

Kaminsky Arkitektur consists of 60 employees with offices in Stockholm and Gothenburg. Together we create sustainable architecture with an artistic dimension.
We are recognized for our strong positioning on sustainability, where we are an active voice. For far too long, architecture has been perceived as surface, decorations that can be added at the end of a process, instead of using it as a powerful tool that can improve our world. We want to design buildings that make people happy and have a minimal ecological footprint.
Joakim Kaminsky has been awarded the Carl Larsson Scholarship and Young Swedish Form. He has a background as an architect at UN-Studio and Wingårdhs. Joakim teaches regularly at Chalmers Arkitektur. The office was founded in 2007 by Fredrik Kjellgren and Joakim Kaminsky as Kjellgren Kaminsky Architects and today it is run by Joakim Kaminsky under the name Kaminsky Arkitektur.

Kaminsky Arkitektur est composé de 60 employés avec des bureaux à Stockholm et à Göteborg. Ensemble, nous créons une architecture durable avec une dimension artistique.
Nous sommes reconnus pour notre positionnement fort en matière de durabilité, où nous sommes une voix active. Pendant trop longtemps, l'architecture a été perçue comme une surface, des décorations que l'on peut ajouter à la fin d'un processus, au lieu de l'utiliser comme un outil puissant qui peut améliorer notre monde. Nous voulons concevoir des bâtiments qui rendent les gens heureux et qui ont une empreinte écologique minimale.
Joakim Kaminsky a reçu la bourse Carl Larsson et le prix Young Swedish Form. Il a travaillé comme architecte à UN-Studio et Wingårdhs. Joakim enseigne régulièrement à Chalmers Arkitektur. Le bureau a été fondé en 2007 par Fredrik Kjellgren et Joakim Kaminsky sous le nom de Kjellgren Kaminsky Architects et est aujourd'hui dirigé par Joakim Kaminsky sous le nom de Kaminsky Arkitektur.

Kaminsky Arkitektur besteht aus 60 Mitarbeitern mit Büros in Stockholm und Göteborg. Gemeinsam schaffen wir nachhaltige Architektur mit einer künstlerischen Dimension.
Wir sind bekannt für unsere starke Positionierung im Bereich der Nachhaltigkeit, wo wir eine aktive Stimme sind. Viel zu lange wurde Architektur als Oberfläche wahrgenommen, als Dekoration, die am Ende eines Prozesses hinzugefügt werden kann, anstatt sie als mächtiges Werkzeug zu nutzen, das unsere Welt verbessern kann. Wir wollen Gebäude entwerfen, die Menschen glücklich machen und einen minimalen ökologischen Fußabdruck haben.
Joakim Kaminsky wurde mit dem Carl-Larsson-Stipendium und der Young Swedish Form ausgezeichnet. Er hat eine Ausbildung als Architekt bei UN-Studio und Wingårdhs absolviert. Joakim unterrichtet regelmäßig an der Chalmers Arkitektur. Das Büro wurde 2007 von Fredrik Kjellgren und Joakim Kaminsky als Kjellgren Kaminsky Architects gegründet und wird heute von Joakim Kaminsky unter dem Namen Kaminsky Arkitektur geführt.

Kaminsky Arkitektur cuenta con 60 empleados con oficinas en Estocolmo y Gotemburgo. Juntos creamos arquitectura sostenible con una dimensión artística.
Somos reconocidos por nuestro fuerte posicionamiento en materia de sostenibilidad, donde somos una voz activa. Durante demasiado tiempo, la arquitectura se ha percibido como algo superficial, adornos que se pueden añadir al final de un proceso, en lugar de utilizarla como una poderosa herramienta que puede mejorar nuestro mundo. Queremos diseñar edificios que hagan felices a las personas y tengan una huella ecológica mínima.
Joakim Kaminsky ha recibido la beca Carl Larsson y el premio Young Swedish Form. Tiene experiencia como arquitecto en UN-Studio y Wingårdhs. Joakim da clases regularmente en Chalmers Arkitektur. El despacho fue fundado en 2007 por Fredrik Kjellgren y Joakim Kaminsky como Kjellgren Kaminsky Architects y hoy lo dirige Joakim Kaminsky bajo el nombre de Kaminsky Arkitektur.

KAMINSKY ARKITEKTUR

JOAKIM KAMINSKY

www.kaminsky.se

TOWNHOUSES IN GUSTAVSLUND

Gustavslund, Sweden

Team: **Joakim Kaminsky, Fredrik Kjellgren, Eduard Boisse, Francesca Suaria, Jakob Danckwardt-Lillieström** | *Photos:* **© Kalle Sanner, Mathilda Ahlbäck**

Townhouses in Gustavslund designed and developed by the architect.
Brick is one of the cornerstones of Helsingborg's development and prosperity, both as an export commodity and a visual element in the cityscape. The new terraced houses in Gustavslund builds on that tradition - both in form and choice of materials. Dark brown bricks dominate the exterior and protect against strong winds. Even the balcony railings are ingeniously made of brick. Each house is L-shaped and has its own atrium courtyard in a sunny west facing position.
The houses have been designed so that each home opens onto a private wind-protected atrium courtyard while the street façade is more closed. Around the west-facing atrium courtyard, daily life is taking place, protected from insight. The best projects need time to develop, for these twelve townhouses in Gustavslund we have had the opportunity to refine our design for two years and can proudly state that the result has been accordingly.

Stadthäuser in Gustavslund, entworfen und entwickelt vom Architekten.
Backstein ist einer der Eckpfeiler der Entwicklung und des Wohlstands von Helsingborg, sowohl als Exportgut als auch als visuelles Element im Stadtbild. Die neuen Reihenhäuser in Gustavslund knüpfen an diese Tradition an - sowohl in der Form als auch in der Wahl der Materialien. Dunkelbraune Ziegel dominieren das Äußere und schützen vor starkem Wind. Selbst die Balkongeländer sind auf raffinierte Weise aus Ziegeln gefertigt. Jedes Haus ist L-förmig und hat einen eigenen Atriumhof in sonniger Westlage.
Die Häuser wurden so konzipiert, dass sich jedes Haus zu einem privaten, windgeschützten Atriumhof hin öffnet, während die Straßenfassade eher geschlossen ist. Rund um den nach Westen ausgerichteten Atriumhof spielt sich das tägliche Leben ab, geschützt vor Einblicken. Die besten Projekte brauchen Zeit, um sich zu entwickeln. Für diese zwölf Stadthäuser in Gustavslund hatten wir zwei Jahre lang die Gelegenheit, unseren Entwurf zu verfeinern und können mit Stolz sagen, dass das Ergebnis entsprechend ist.

Maisons de ville à Gustavslund conçues et développées par l'architecte.
La brique est l'une des pierres angulaires du développement et de la prospérité de Helsingborg, à la fois comme produit d'exportation et comme élément visuel du paysage urbain. Les nouvelles maisons mitoyennes de Gustavslund s'appuient sur cette tradition, tant dans leur forme que dans le choix des matériaux. Des briques brun foncé dominent l'extérieur et protègent des vents violents. Même les balustrades des balcons sont ingénieusement faites de briques. Chaque maison est en forme de L et possède sa propre cour en atrium, ensoleillée et orientée à l'ouest.
Les maisons ont été conçues de manière à ce que chacune d'entre elles s'ouvre sur une cour atrium privée protégée du vent, tandis que la façade sur rue est plus fermée. Autour de la cour atrium orientée vers l'ouest, la vie quotidienne se déroule à l'abri des regards. Les meilleurs projets ont besoin de temps pour se développer. Pour ces douze maisons de ville à Gustavslund, nous avons eu l'occasion d'affiner notre conception pendant deux ans et nous pouvons fièrement affirmer que le résultat est à la hauteur.

Casas adosadas en Gustavslund diseñadas y desarrolladas por el arquitecto.
El ladrillo es una de las piedras angulares del desarrollo y la prosperidad de Helsingborg, tanto como producto de exportación como elemento visual del paisaje urbano. Las nuevas casas adosadas se basan en esa tradición, tanto en la forma como en la elección de los materiales. Los ladrillos de color marrón oscuro dominan el exterior y protegen de los fuertes vientos. Incluso las barandillas de los balcones están ingeniosamente hechas de ladrillo. Cada casa tiene forma de L y cuenta con su propio patio en una posición soleada orientada al oeste.
Las casas se han diseñado de forma que cada una de ellas se abre a un atrio privado protegido del viento, mientras que la fachada de la calle es más cerrada. Alrededor del patio orientado al oeste se desarrolla la vida cotidiana, protegida de la vista. Los mejores proyectos necesitan tiempo para desarrollarse; para estas doce casas adosadas en Gustavslund hemos tenido la oportunidad de perfeccionar nuestro diseño durante dos años y podemos afirmar con orgullo que el resultado ha sido el adecuado.

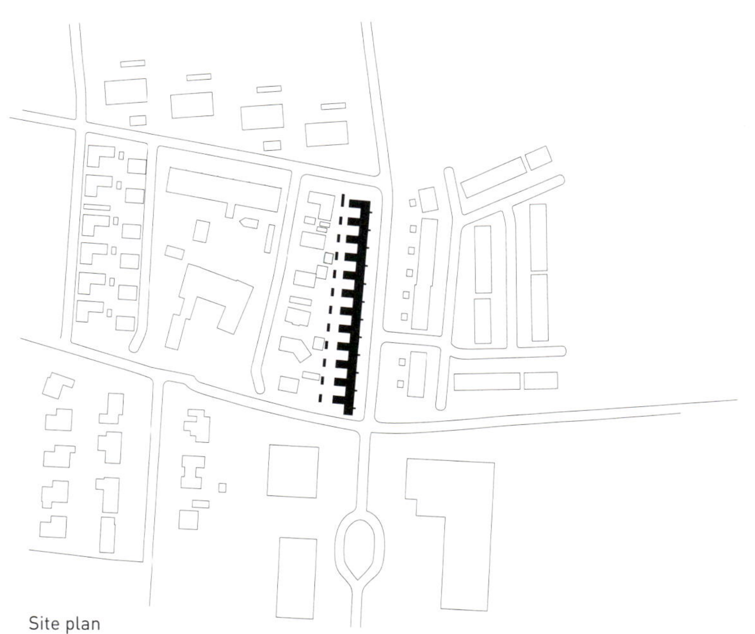

Site plan

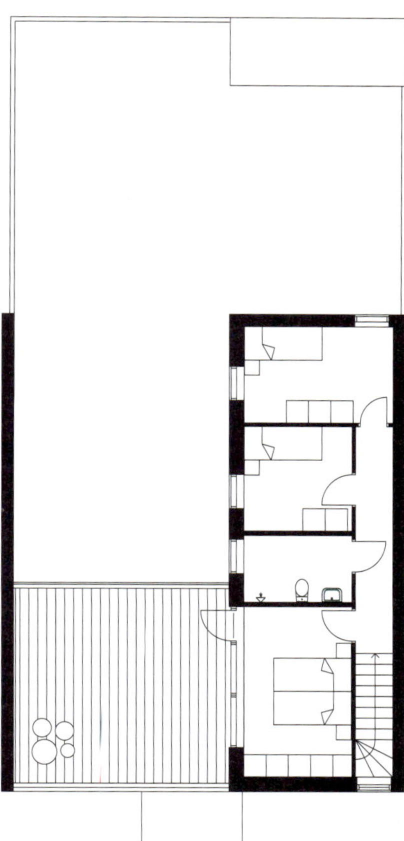

First floor plan

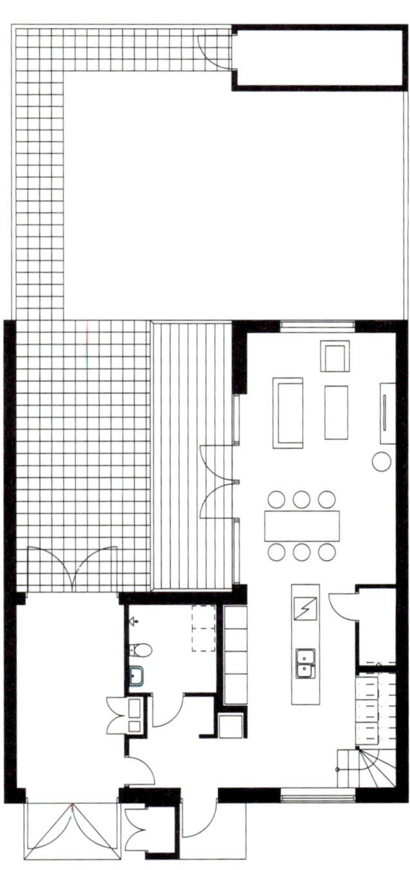

Ground floor plan

OCEANKAJEN

Helsingborg, Sweden

Team: **Fredrik Kjellgren, Joakim Kaminsky, Sandra Nygren, Erik Andersson, Edouard Boisse, Annie Andersson, Nevida Myrtaj** | *Photos:* **© Kalle Sanner**

First row.
With the best location in Oceanhamnen in Helsingborg, Kaminsky Arkitektur has built a residential complex with the starting point of creating an environment characterized by diversity, innovation and sustainability. Oceankajen is an innovative housing project with a focus on social sustainability, which is in the first stage of the H + urban development project in Helsingborg. Kaminsky Arkitektur won the project in a land allocation competition, together with Riksbyggen with the motto "a smorgasbord of bricks", and the result does live up to those expectations. The house's brick facades are a natural and durable material with local anchoring. Color and masonry technique are varied for each staircase length, which gives a variation in expression. The building is designed as a low-energy house and the project tests a number of innovative technical solutions for the resource flows energy, water, sewage and waste according to the City of Helsingborg's program "Smart systems and clever solutions."

Erste Reihe.
In bester Lage in Oceanhamnen in Helsingborg hat Kaminsky Arkitektur einen Wohnkomplex gebaut, dessen Ausgangspunkt die Schaffung einer von Vielfalt, Innovation und Nachhaltigkeit geprägten Umgebung ist. Oceankajen ist ein innovatives Wohnungsbauprojekt mit Schwerpunkt auf sozialer Nachhaltigkeit, das sich in der ersten Phase des Stadtentwicklungsprojekts H + in Helsingborg befindet. Kaminsky Arkitektur hat das Projekt im Rahmen eines Grundstücksvergabe-Wettbewerbs zusammen mit Riksbyggen unter dem Motto „ein Sammelsurium von Ziegeln" gewonnen, und das Ergebnis wird diesen Erwartungen gerecht. Die Ziegelfassaden des Hauses sind ein natürliches und dauerhaftes Material mit lokaler Verankerung. Farbe und Mauerwerkstechnik sind für jede Treppenlänge unterschiedlich, was zu einer Variation des Ausdrucks führt. Das Gebäude ist als Niedrigenergiehaus konzipiert, und das Projekt testet eine Reihe innovativer technischer Lösungen für die Ressourcenströme Energie, Wasser, Abwasser und Abfall im Rahmen des Programms „Intelligente Systeme und clevere Lösungen" der Stadt Helsingborg.

Première rangée.
Bénéficiant du meilleur emplacement à Oceanhamnen à Helsingborg, Kaminsky Arkitektur a construit un complexe résidentiel avec pour point de départ la création d'un environnement caractérisé par la diversité, l'innovation et la durabilité. Oceankajen est un projet de logement innovant axé sur la durabilité sociale, qui constitue la première étape du projet de développement urbain H + à Helsingborg. Kaminsky Arkitektur a remporté le projet lors d'un concours d'attribution de terrains, avec Riksbyggen, avec pour devise « un buffet de briques », et le résultat est à la hauteur de ces attentes. Les façades en briques de la maison sont un matériau naturel et durable avec un ancrage local. La couleur et la technique de maçonnerie varient pour chaque longueur d'escalier, ce qui donne une variation d'expression. Le bâtiment est conçu comme une maison à faible consommation d'énergie et le projet teste un certain nombre de solutions techniques innovantes pour les flux de ressources en énergie, eau, eaux usées et déchets, conformément au programme de la ville d'Helsingborg « Systèmes intelligents et solutions intelligentes ».

Primera fila.
Con la mejor ubicación en Oceanhamnen, en Helsingborg, Kaminsky Arkitektur ha construido un complejo residencial con el punto de partida de crear un entorno caracterizado por la diversidad, la innovación y la ecología. Oceankajen es un innovador proyecto de viviendas centrado en la sostenibilidad social, que se encuentra en la primera fase del proyecto de desarrollo urbano H+ en Helsingborg. Kaminsky Arkitektur ganó el proyecto en un concurso de adjudicación de terrenos, junto con Riksbyggen, con el lema «un *smorgasbord* de ladrillos», un típico plato de la cocina sueca. El resultado está a la altura de las expectativas. Las fachadas de ladrillo de la casa son un material natural y duradero con anclaje local. El color y la técnica de albañilería son variados para cada longitud de escalera, lo que ofrece una variedad de expresiones. El edificio está diseñado como una casa de bajo consumo energético y el proyecto pone a prueba una serie de soluciones técnicas innovadoras para los flujos de recursos de energía, agua, alcantarillado y residuos de acuerdo con el programa de la ciudad de Helsingborg «Sistemas inteligentes y soluciones inteligentes».

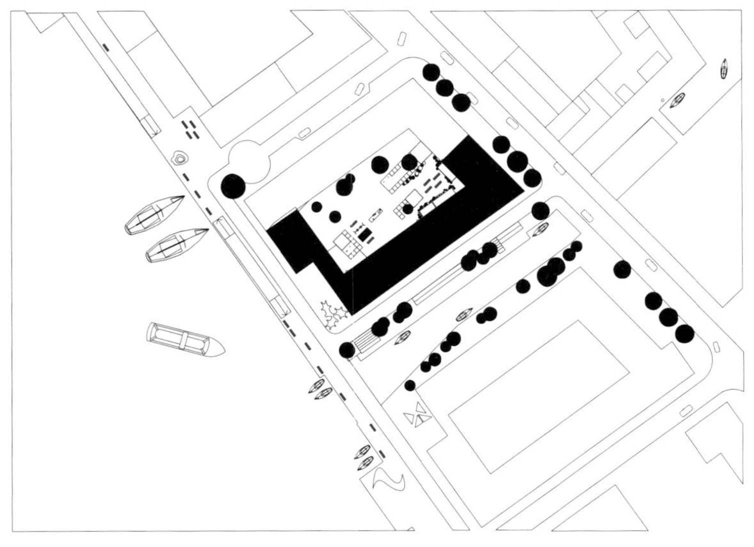

Site plan

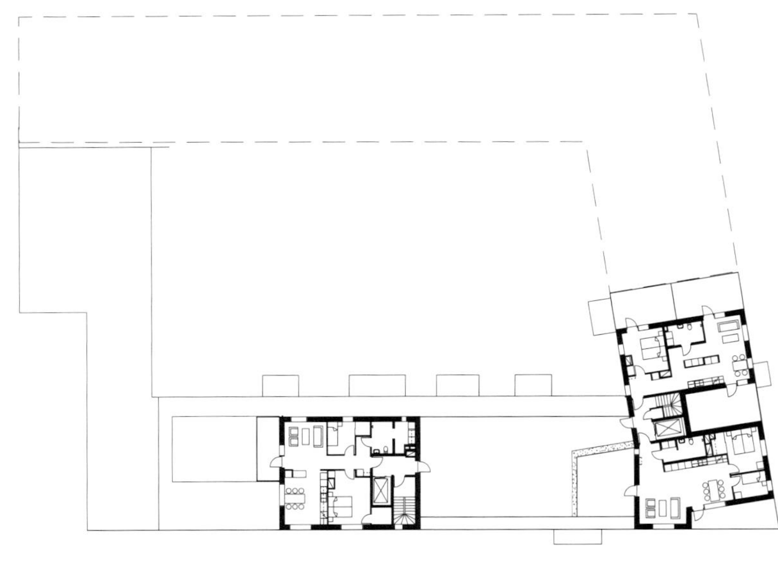

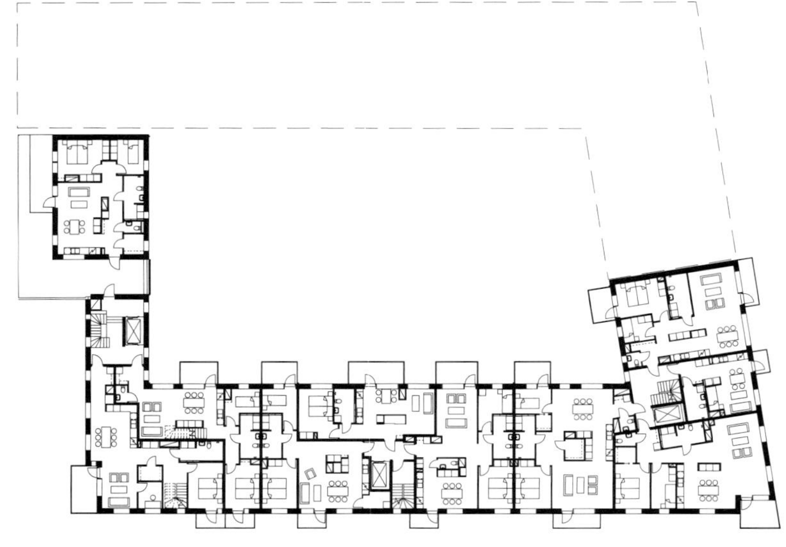

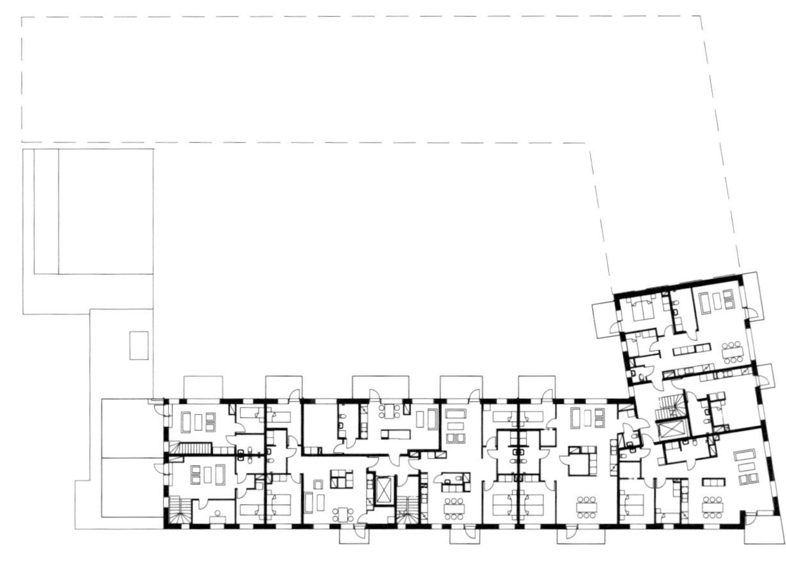

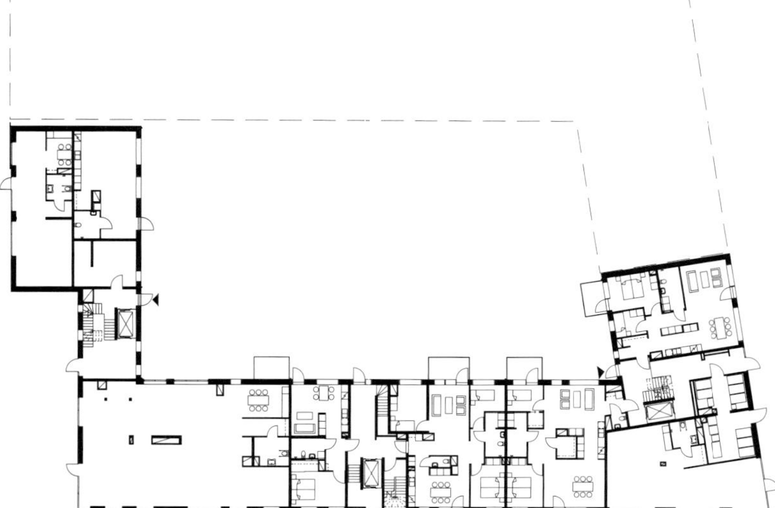

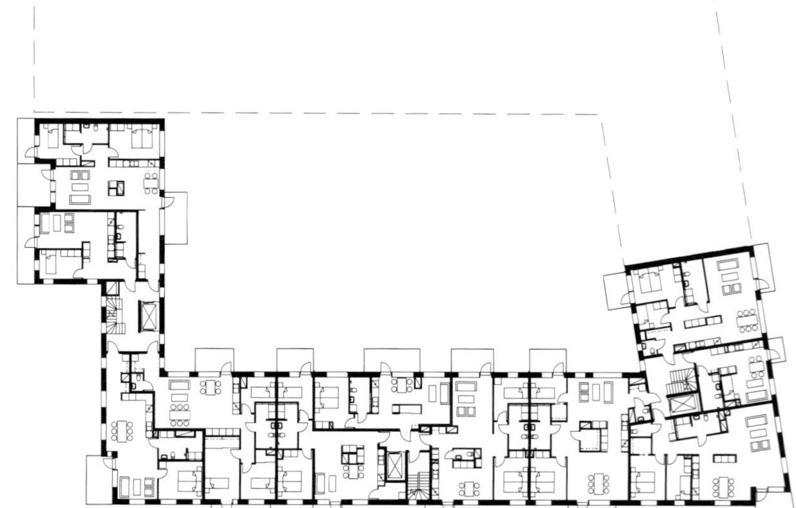

Floor plans

Kaunitz Yeung Architecture is an internationally recognised practice founded by the husband and wife team of David Kaunitz and Ka Wai Yeung. It combines their extensive commercial experience with David's knowledge of living in and working with communities. The result is architecture that places people at its centre.
David Kaunitz: Director and co-founder, Kaunitz Yeung Architecture | Speaker | LecturerConsultation, collaboration and time are the three ingredients David Kaunitz adds to his architectural practice that transforms a design from a building into a place.
Ka Wai Yeung: Director and co-founder, Kaunitz Yeung Architecture | Lecturer | AuthorExceptional client engagement, resourcefulness and close attention to detail are the specialties Ka Wai Yeung combines in her architectural practice, elevating a design from aesthetic functionality to innovative placemaking.

Kaunitz Yeung Architecture est un cabinet de renommée internationale fondé par l'équipe mari et femme de David Kaunitz et Ka Wai Yeung. Il associe leur vaste expérience commerciale à la connaissance qu'a David de la vie et du travail au sein des communautés. Le résultat est une architecture qui place les gens au centre.
David Kaunitz : Directeur et cofondateur, Kaunitz Yeung Architecture | Conférencier | Chargé de coursLa consultation, la collaboration et le temps sont les trois ingrédients que David Kaunitz ajoute à sa pratique architecturale pour transformer un projet de bâtiment en un lieu.
Ka Wai Yeung : Directeur et cofondateur, Kaunitz Yeung Architecture | Conférencier | AuteurUn engagement exceptionnel envers le client, de l'ingéniosité et une attention particulière aux détails sont les spécialités que Ka Wai Yeung combine dans sa pratique architecturale, élevant une conception de la fonctionnalité esthétique à la création d'un lieu innovant.

Kaunitz Yeung Architecture ist ein international anerkanntes Büro, das von dem Ehepaar David Kaunitz und Ka Wai Yeung gegründet wurde. Es verbindet ihre umfassende Erfahrung im kommerziellen Bereich mit Davids Wissen über das Leben in und die Arbeit mit Gemeinschaften. Das Ergebnis ist eine Architektur, die den Menschen in den Mittelpunkt stellt.
David Kaunitz: Direktor und Mitbegründer, Kaunitz Yeung Architecture | Referent | DozentBeratung, Zusammenarbeit und Zeit sind die drei Zutaten, die David Kaunitz in sein Architekturbüro einbringt und die einen Entwurf von einem Gebäude in einen Ort verwandeln.
Ka Wai Yeung: Direktorin und Mitbegründerin, Kaunitz Yeung Architecture | Dozentin | AutorinAußergewöhnliches Engagement für den Kunden, Einfallsreichtum und Liebe zum Detail sind die Spezialitäten, die Ka Wai Yeung in ihrem Architekturbüro vereint und die einen Entwurf von ästhetischer Funktionalität zu innovativer Ortsgestaltung machen.

Kaunitz Yeung Architecture es un estudio internacionalmente reconocido, fundado por el matrimonio David Kaunitz y Ka Wai Yeung. Combinan su amplia experiencia comercial con los conocimientos de David sobre la vida en las comunidades y el trabajo con ellas. El resultado es una arquitectura que sitúa a las personas en el centro de los proyectos.
David Kaunitz: Director y cofundador de Kaunitz Yeung Architecture | Ponente | Conferenciante-Consultor, colaboración y tiempo son los tres ingredientes que David Kaunitz añade a su práctica arquitectónica y que transforman un diseño de un edificio en un lugar.
Ka Wai Yeung: Director y cofundador de Kaunitz Yeung Architecture | Conferenciante | Autor, un compromiso excepcional con el cliente, la inventiva y la atención al detalle son las especialidades que Ka Wai Yeung combina en su práctica arquitectónica, elevando un diseño desde la funcionalidad estética hasta la creación de un lugar innovador.

KAUNITZ YEUNG ARCHITECTURE

DAVID KAUNITZ, KA WAI YEUNG

www. kaunitzyeung.com

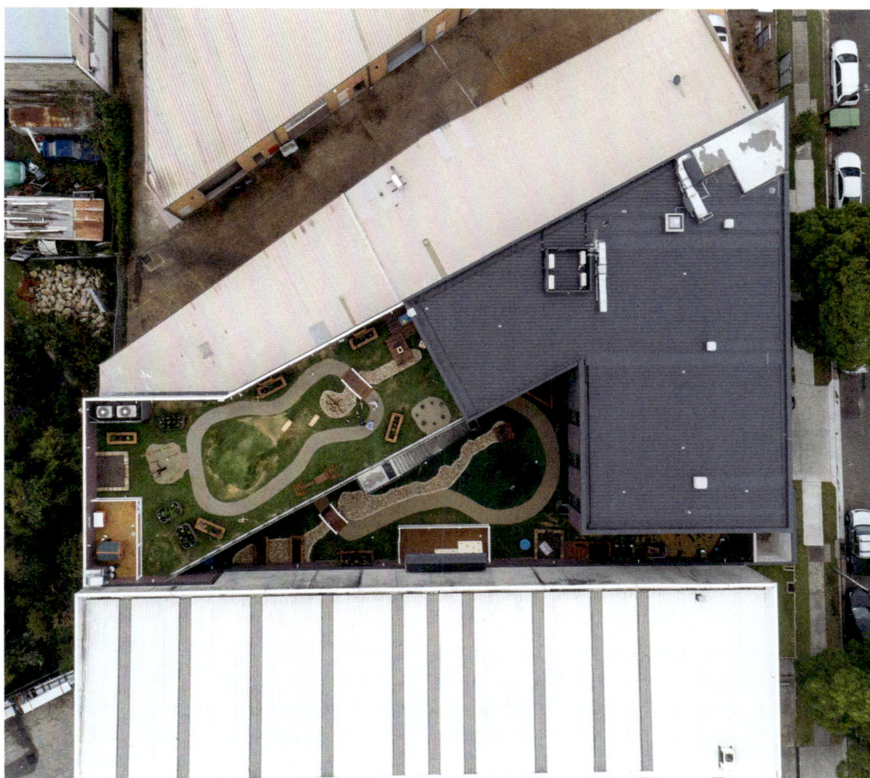

MULTI STOREY CHILDCARE

Brookvale, New South Wales, Australia

Client: Private + Paisley Park Childcare | *Awards:* 2019 Good Design - Winner Commercial and Residential Architecture | *Photos:* © Brett Boardman

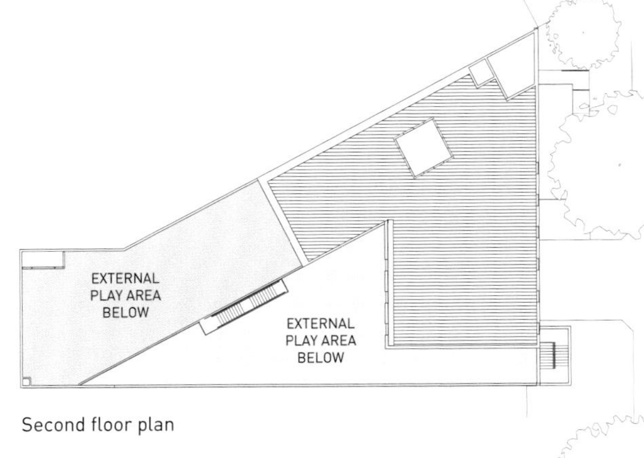

Second floor plan

The brief was to create a learning oasis within an urban environment, with the capacity to accommodate 120 children. Paisley Park Childcare Brookvale, New South Wales, redefines commercial childcare by creating a learning oasis that lifts children out of the highly industrialised environment. The three-storey centre raises the children above ground level with the roof of one level becoming the outdoor space of the next, maximising natural light and ventilation whilst providing direct access to high quality outdoor space.
The design sets a new standard in childcare. Indoor/outdoor spaces that are protected and filled with natural light provide the perfect environment for children to thrive. This high-quality learning environment, combined with our resources and curriculum, are industry-leading and support the children's learning while helping fuel their imagination.

Die Aufgabe bestand darin, eine Lernoase in einer städtischen Umgebung zu schaffen, die Platz für 120 Kinder bietet. Paisley Park Childcare Brookvale, New South Wales, definiert die kommerzielle Kinderbetreuung neu, indem es eine Lernoase schafft, die die Kinder aus der stark industrialisierten Umgebung heraushebt. Das dreistöckige Zentrum erhebt die Kinder über den Boden, wobei das Dach einer Etage zum Außenbereich der nächsten wird, wodurch natürliches Licht und Belüftung maximiert werden und ein direkter Zugang zu einem hochwertigen Außenbereich entsteht.
Der Entwurf setzt einen neuen Standard in der Kinderbetreuung. Geschützte und lichtdurchflutete Innen- und Außenbereiche bieten die perfekte Umgebung für die Entwicklung von Kindern. Diese qualitativ hochwertige Lernumgebung in Kombination mit unseren Ressourcen und Lehrplänen ist branchenführend und unterstützt das Lernen der Kinder, indem sie ihre Fantasie anregt.

L'objectif était de créer une oasis d'apprentissage dans un environnement urbain, avec une capacité d'accueil de 120 enfants. Paisley Park Childcare Brookvale, en Nouvelle-Galles du Sud, redéfinit les services de garde d'enfants commerciaux en créant une oasis d'apprentissage qui sort les enfants d'un environnement hautement industrialisé. Le centre de trois étages élève les enfants au-dessus du niveau du sol, le toit d'un niveau devenant l'espace extérieur du niveau suivant, maximisant la lumière et la ventilation naturelles tout en fournissant un accès direct à un espace extérieur de haute qualité.
Cette conception établit une nouvelle norme en matière de garde d'enfants. Des espaces intérieurs/extérieurs protégés et remplis de lumière naturelle constituent l'environnement idéal pour l'épanouissement des enfants. Cet environnement d'apprentissage de haute qualité, associé à nos ressources et à notre programme, est à la pointe du secteur et favorise l'apprentissage des enfants tout en contribuant à alimenter leur imagination.

El encargo consistía en crear un oasis de aprendizaje dentro de un entorno urbano, con capacidad para acoger a 120 niños. Paisley Park Childcare Brookvale, Nueva Gales del Sur, redefine la atención infantil creando un oasis de aprendizaje que saca a los niños del entorno altamente industrializado. El centro de tres plantas eleva a los niños por encima del nivel del suelo y el techo de un nivel se convierte en el espacio exterior del siguiente, maximizando la luz natural y la ventilación y proporcionando al mismo tiempo un acceso directo al espacio exterior.
El diseño establece un nuevo estándar en el cuidado de los niños. Los espacios interiores y exteriores protegidos y llenos de luz natural proporcionan el entorno perfecto para que prosperen. Este entorno de aprendizaje de alta calidad, combinado con nuestros recursos y planes de estudio, son líderes en el sector y apoyan el aprendizaje a la vez que ayudan a alimentar su imaginación.

Second floor plan

1. Fire stairs
2. Lobby
3. Accesible toiler + laundry
4. Cool room
5. Kitchen
6. Pre school WC
7. Pre school room 1
8. Pre school room 2

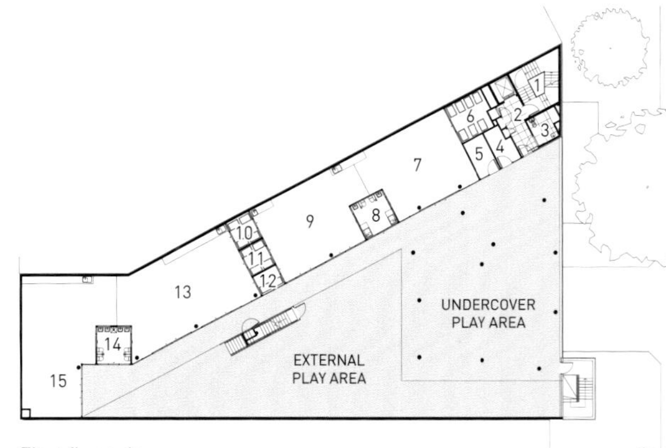

First floor plan

1. Fire stairs
2. Lobby
3. Accesible toiler + laundry
4. Parent's room
5. Director's office
6. Cot room 1
7. Baby playroom 1
8. Baby WC
9. Baby playroom 2
10. Cot room 2
11. Cot room 3
12. Cot room 4
13. Toddler playroom
14. Toddler WC
15. Toddler playroom

Paisley Park
Early Learning Centres
1800 724 753
www.paisleypark.com.au

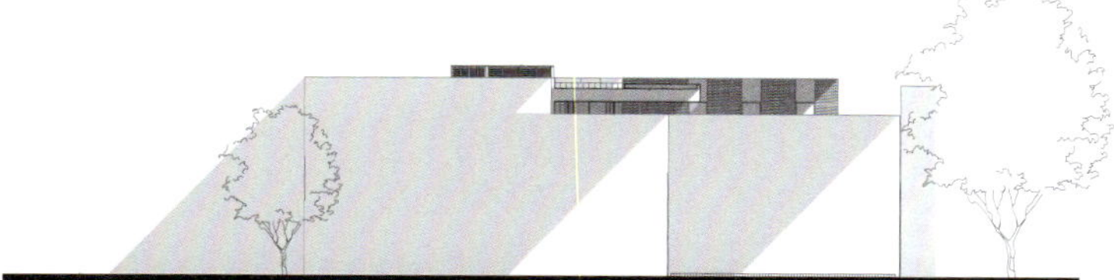

North elevation

East elevation

West elevation

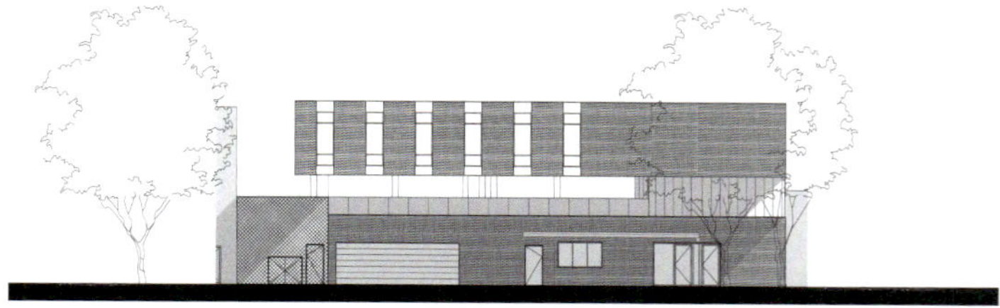

South elevation

35

Kosloff Architecture was founded in 2017 by Stephanie Bullock and Julian Kosloff, growing rapidly to a team of 22. The practice was founded based on a sustainable and ethical business in line with the BCorp charter. Accordingly, we have been carbon neutral since our inception and we achieved BCorp certification in 2019. We believe that in order to build a highly engaged practice culture, we need to challenge existing ideas regarding ownership, planning, career trajectories and modes of working. Our commitment to quality includes ISO certification in the provision of architectural services, occupational health and safety and environmental management. Public work has always been our focus with high aspirations regarding what it can deliver to its stakeholders, its cultural context and the broader community. We are driven by three core values: Aspiration, Collaboration and Impact.

Kosloff Architecture a été fondé en 2017 par Stephanie Bullock et Julian Kosloff, se développant rapidement pour atteindre une équipe de 22 personnes. Le cabinet a été fondé sur la base d'une activité durable et éthique, conformément à la charte BCorp. En conséquence, nous sommes neutres en carbone depuis notre création et nous avons obtenu la certification BCorp (2019). Nous pensons que pour construire une culture de cabinet très engagée, nous devons remettre en question les idées existantes concernant la propriété, la planification, les trajectoires de carrière et les modes de travail. Notre engagement envers la qualité comprend la certification ISO pour la prestation de services architecturaux, la santé et la sécurité au travail et la gestion environnementale. Le travail communautaire a toujours été au centre de nos préoccupations, avec des aspirations élevées quant à ce qu'il peut apporter à ses parties prenantes, à son contexte culturel et à la communauté au sens large. Nous sommes animés par trois valeurs fondamentales : Aspiration, Collaboration et Impact.

Kosloff Architecture wurde 2017 von Stephanie Bullock und Julian Kosloff gegründet und wuchs schnell auf ein Team von 22 Mitarbeitern an. Das Büro wurde auf der Grundlage eines nachhaltigen und ethischen Geschäfts im Einklang mit der BCorp-Charta gegründet. Dementsprechend sind wir seit unserer Gründung klimaneutral und haben die BCorp-Zertifizierung (2019) erhalten.Wir sind davon überzeugt, dass wir für den Aufbau einer hoch engagierten Praxiskultur bestehende Vorstellungen von Eigenverantwortung, Planung, Karriereverläufen und Arbeitsweisen in Frage stellen müssen. Unser Engagement für Qualität umfasst die ISO-Zertifizierung für die Erbringung von Architekturdienstleistungen, Gesundheit und Sicherheit am Arbeitsplatz sowie Umweltmanagement. Die Arbeit für die Gemeinschaft war schon immer unser Schwerpunkt, und wir haben hohe Ansprüche an das, was sie für ihre Interessengruppen, ihr kulturelles Umfeld und die breitere Gemeinschaft leisten kann. Wir lassen uns von drei Grundwerten leiten: Streben, Zusammenarbeit und Wirkung.

Kosloff Architecture fue fundado en 2017 por Stephanie Bullock y Julian Kosloff, creciendo rápidamente hasta contar con un equipo de 22 personas. El estudio se fundó basándose en un negocio sostenible y ético en línea con la carta BCorp. En consecuencia, somos neutros en carbono desde nuestros inicios y conseguimos la certificación BCorp (2019). Creemos que para construir una cultura de práctica altamente comprometida, tenemos que desafiar las ideas existentes con respecto a la propiedad, la planificación, las trayectorias profesionales y los modos de trabajo. Nuestro compromiso con la calidad incluye la certificación ISO en la prestación de servicios de arquitectura, seguridad y salud laboral y gestión medioambiental. El trabajo comunitario ha sido siempre nuestro centro de atención, con grandes aspiraciones respecto a lo que puede aportar a sus interesados, su contexto cultural y la comunidad en general. Nos impulsan tres valores fundamentales: Aspiración, Colaboración e Impacto.

KOSLOFF ARCHITECTURE

www.kosloffarchitecture.com

PASCOE VALE PRIMARY SCHOOL

Victoria, Australia

Built surface: **496 m² new, 1,211 m² refurbishment** | *Photos:* **© Derek Swalwell**

Pascoe Vale Primary School is home to a fine example of neo-classical school design, a two-storey heritage listed building designed by the Chief Architect of the Public Works Department, E. Evan Smith. Since its construction in 1929, the original listed building had undergone minimal to no re - furbishment works and was comprised of 12 traditionally enclosed classrooms that did not provide the flexible and adaptable 21st Century learning spaces needed to support the school's curriculum. The project includes the renovation of the existing heritage listed building, and an extension to this building to create a new school entry, administration, and staff facilities. The latter has been designed to support the development of teacher's assessment practices, a priority for the school, and the original building has been extensively refurbished to provide 21st century learning spaces throughout.

Die Pascoe Vale Primary School beherbergt ein schönes Beispiel für neoklassizistisches Schuldesign, ein zweistöckiges, denkmalgeschütztes Gebäude, das vom Chefarchitekten des Public Works Department, E. Evan Smith, entworfen wurde. Seit seiner Erbauung im Jahr 1929 wurde das ursprüngliche denkmalgeschützte Gebäude nur minimal oder gar nicht renoviert und bestand aus 12 traditionell geschlossenen Klassenräumen, die nicht die flexiblen und anpassungsfähigen Lernräume des 21. Jahrhunderts boten, die für den Lehrplan der Schule erforderlich sind. Das Projekt umfasst die Renovierung des bestehenden denkmalgeschützten Gebäudes und einen Anbau an dieses Gebäude, um einen neuen Schuleingang, eine Verwaltung und Personalräume zu schaffen. Letztere wurden so konzipiert, dass sie die Entwicklung von Beurteilungspraktiken für Lehrer unterstützen, eine Priorität der Schule, und das ursprüngliche Gebäude wurde umfassend renoviert, um überall Lernräume des 21.

L'école primaire de Pascoe Vale abrite un bel exemple de conception d'école néoclassique, un bâtiment classé de deux étages conçu par l'architecte en chef du département des travaux publics, E. Evan Smith. Depuis sa construction en 1929, le bâtiment classé d'origine n'avait subi que peu ou pas de travaux de rénovation et était composé de 12 salles de classe traditionnellement fermées qui n'offraient pas les espaces d'apprentissage flexibles et adaptables du 21e siècle nécessaires pour soutenir le programme scolaire de l'école. Le projet comprend la rénovation du bâtiment existant, classé patrimoine, et une extension de ce bâtiment pour créer une nouvelle entrée de l'école, une administration et des installations pour le personnel. Ces dernières ont été conçues pour soutenir le développement des pratiques d'évaluation des enseignants, une priorité pour l'école, et le bâtiment d'origine a été largement rénové pour fournir des espaces d'apprentissage du 21ème siècle.

La Escuela Primaria Pascoe Vale es un buen ejemplo de diseño escolar neoclásico, un edificio de dos plantas catalogado como patrimonio, diseñado por el arquitecto jefe del Departamento de Obras Públicas, E. Evan Smith. Desde su construcción en 1929, el edificio original, protegido por la ley, había sido objeto de una renovación mínima o nula y constaba de 12 aulas tradicionalmente cerradas que no ofrecían los espacios de aprendizaje flexibles y adaptables del siglo XXI necesarios para apoyar el plan de estudios de la escuela. El proyecto incluye la renovación del edificio existente, protegido por el patrimonio, y una ampliación del mismo para crear una nueva entrada a la escuela, la administración y las instalaciones para el personal. Estas últimas han sido diseñadas para apoyar el desarrollo de las prácticas de evaluación de los profesores, una prioridad para la escuela, y el edificio original ha sido ampliamente reformado para proporcionar espacios de aprendizaje del siglo XXI en su totalidad.

P S

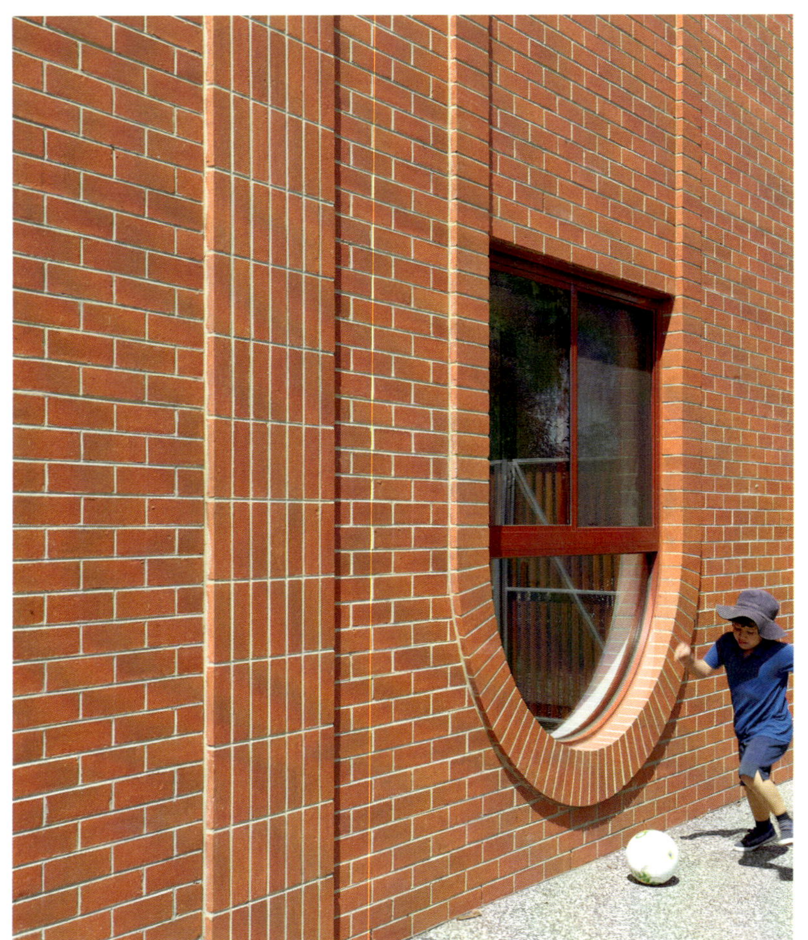

Site plan

1. Playground
2. BER building
3. Community hub
4. Relocatable
5. Building B
6. Buinding A (extension)
7. Building A (existing)

P V

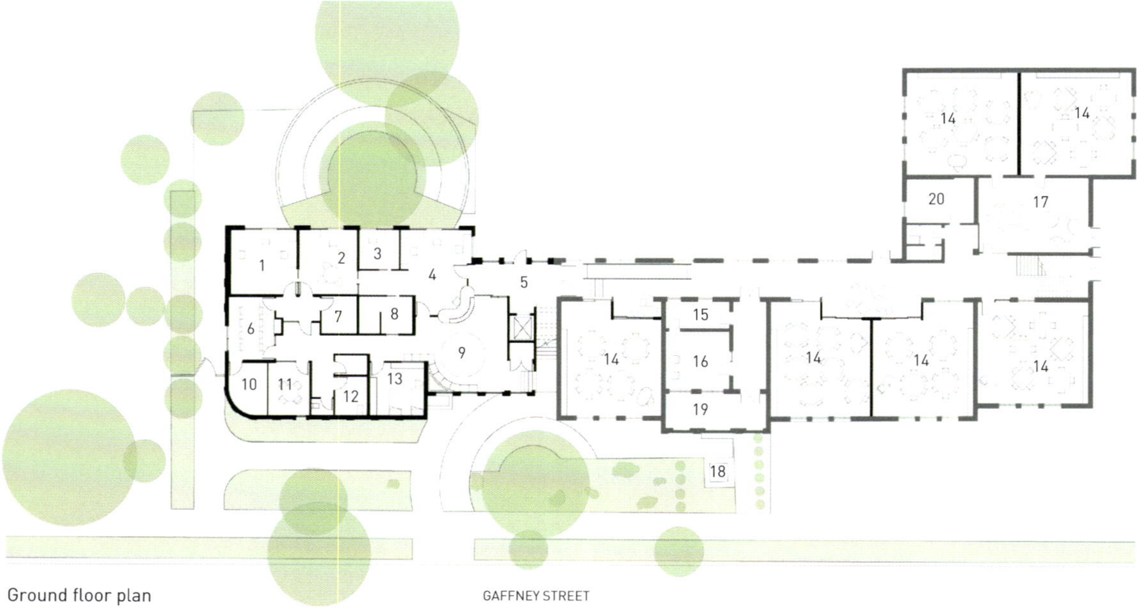

Ground floor plan

1. Senior leadership
2. Principal
3. Business and finance
4. Admin and reception
5. Circulation
6. Meeting and conference
7. Store
8. Resource
9. Foyer
10. Storage
11. Student welfare
12. WC
13. First aid
14. Classroom
15. Server room
16. IT workroom
17. Maker space ground
18. Cenotaph
19. Porch
20. Office

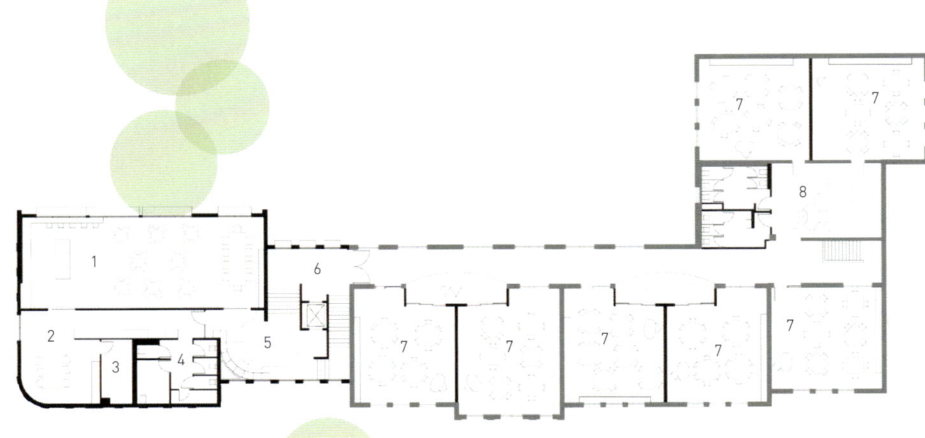

1. Staff lounge
2. Staff work
3. Storage
4. WC
5. Informal breakout
6. Circulation
7. Classroom
8. Maker space

First floor plan

ADMINISTRATION

The founder of Le House Company is the architect Le Hung Trong (19/11/1983): before of the establishment in 2015, it took him nine years to get an Archviz Artist position in an architecture firm after he graduated from Van Lang University - Architecture Design.
In the next seven years, he was alone on his way to look for the differences in how to conceive design. When he realized completely that he had enough confidence to start up his own company based on his passions and experiences, he decided to do it with those wishing to contribute to Le House's creativity to present the image of Viet Nam's architecture internationally.
"To be creative is forgetting the definitions of what is already in your mind".

Le fondateur de Le House Company est l'architecte Le Hung Trong (19/11/1983) : avant la création en 2015, il lui a fallu neuf ans pour obtenir un poste d'Archviz Artist dans un cabinet d'architecture après avoir été diplômé de l'Université Van Lang - Architecture Design.
Au cours des sept années suivantes, il était seul sur son chemin à la recherche des différences dans la façon de concevoir le design. Lorsqu'il s'est rendu compte qu'il avait suffisamment confiance en lui pour créer sa propre entreprise en s'appuyant sur ses passions et ses expériences, il a décidé de le faire avec ceux qui souhaitent contribuer à la créativité de Le House pour présenter l'image de l'architecture vietnamienne à l'échelle internationale.
« Être créatif, c'est oublier les définitions de ce qui est déjà dans votre esprit ».

Der Gründer von Le House Company ist der Architekt Le Hung Trong (19.11.1983): Vor der Gründung im Jahr 2015 brauchte er neun Jahre, um nach seinem Abschluss an der Van Lang University - Architecture Design - eine Stelle als Archviz Artist in einem Architekturbüro zu bekommen.
In den folgenden sieben Jahren war er allein auf der Suche nach den Unterschieden in der Art und Weise, wie man Design konzipiert. Als er feststellte, dass er genug Selbstvertrauen hatte, um sein eigenes Unternehmen auf der Grundlage seiner Leidenschaften und Erfahrungen zu gründen, beschloss er, dies gemeinsam mit denjenigen zu tun, die zur Kreativität von Le House beitragen wollten, um das Image der vietnamesischen Architektur international zu präsentieren.
„Kreativ zu sein bedeutet, die Definitionen dessen, was man bereits im Kopf hat, zu vergessen".

El fundador de Le House Company es el arquitecto Le Hung Trong (19/11/1983): antes de la creación en 2015, tardó nueve años en conseguir un puesto de Artista en un estudio de arquitectura tras graduarse en la Universidad Van Lang - Diseño de Arquitectura.
En los siguientes siete años, se concentró en su camino para buscar las diferencias en la forma de concebir el diseño. Cuando se dio cuenta por completo de que tenía la suficiente confianza para crear su propia empresa basada en sus pasiones y experiencias, decidió hacerlo con quienes deseaban contribuir a la creatividad de Le House para presentar la imagen de la arquitectura de Vietnam a nivel internacional.
«Ser creativo es olvidar las definiciones de lo que ya está en tu mente».

LE HOUSE

LE HUNG TRONG

www.le-house.vn

CO DAM VEGETARIAN RESTAURANT

Ha Noi, Viet Nam

Project director: Le Hung Trong | *Design team:* Arch. Le Hung Trong, Tran Nhat Phi
Engineering: Vo Van Ly | *Built surface:* 680 m^2 | *Photos:* © Trieu Chien

We are connected through the spirit of Buddhism by the breath of people in search of "beauty". The simplicity of the project comes from the red brick that is the main material, creating the temple arches that transport to the "Heaven" of the mysterious Champa culture, a place that has hidden secrets for many years.
The solution to renovate this mysterious space consisted of a steel paving system.
The door simulates the entrance to the Champa temple, following a series of meticulous calculation techniques. As far as the lighting is concerned, the dark tone will allow it to resemble a temple as much as possible.
The place dazzles by the exclusive presence of candles. The earthenware of ancient patterns and reliefs are built by Ninh Thuan craftsmen.This is the first time we have seen a combination of terracotta and stainless steel, creating a perfect harmony.The whole project, in addition to being outstanding, is hidden under the shade of the trees, without being disturbing.

Wir sind durch den Geist des Buddhismus mit dem Atem der Menschen auf der Suche nach „Schönheit" verbunden. Die Einfachheit des Projekts ergibt sich aus dem roten Ziegelstein, der das Hauptmaterial ist und die Tempelbögen bildet, die in den „Himmel" der mysteriösen Champa-Kultur führen, einem Ort, der seit vielen Jahren Geheimnisse birgt.
Die Lösung zur Renovierung dieses geheimnisvollen Raums bestand in einem Stahlpflastersystem.
Die Tür simuliert den Eingang des Champa-Tempels, wobei eine Reihe von sorgfältigen Berechnungstechniken angewandt wurde. Was die Beleuchtung betrifft, so wird der dunkle Farbton es ermöglichen, einem Tempel so weit wie möglich zu ähneln.
Der Ort wird durch die ausschließliche Anwesenheit von Kerzen geblendet. Die Tongefäße mit alten Mustern und Reliefs werden von Handwerkern aus Ninh Thuan hergestellt. Es ist das erste Mal, dass wir eine Kombination aus Terrakotta und rostfreiem Stahl sehen, die eine perfekte Harmonie bildet. Das gesamte Projekt ist nicht nur außergewöhnlich, sondern auch im Schatten der Bäume versteckt, ohne zu stören.

Nous sommes reliés par l'esprit du bouddhisme par le souffle de personnes en quête de « beauté ». La simplicité du projet vient de la brique rouge qui est le matériau principal, créant les arches du temple qui transportent au « Paradis » de la mystérieuse culture Champa, un lieu qui a caché des secrets pendant de nombreuses années.
La solution pour rénover cet espace mystérieux a consisté en un système de pavage en acier.
La porte simule l'entrée du temple Champa, en suivant une série de techniques de calcul méticuleuses. En ce qui concerne l'éclairage, le ton sombre permet de ressembler le plus possible à un temple.
Le lieu éblouit par la présence exclusive de bougies. Les faïences aux motifs et reliefs anciens sont réalisées par des artisans de Ninh Thuan. C'est la première fois que nous voyons une combinaison de terre cuite et d'acier inoxydable, créant une harmonie parfaite. L'ensemble du projet, en plus d'être remarquable, est caché à l'ombre des arbres, sans être dérangeant.

Estamos conectados a través del espíritu del budismo por el aliento de la gente en búsqueda de la «belleza». La simplicidad del proyecto viene del ladrillo rojo que es el material principal, creando los arcos del templo que transportan al «Cielo» de la misteriosa cultura Champa, lugar que ha escondido secretos durante muchos años.
La solución para renovar este espacio misterioso consistió en un sistema de pavimento de acero.
La puerta simula la entrada del templo de Champa, siguiendo una serie de técnicas de cálculo meticuloso. En lo referente a la iluminación, la oscuridad del tono permitirá que se asemeje lo mas posible a un templo.
El lugar deslumbra por la presencia exclusiva de velas. La loza de los patrones antiguos y los relieves están construidas por los artesanos de Ninh Thuan.Es la primera vez que se observa una combinación entre la terracota y el acero inoxidable, aportando una armonía perfecta. El conjunto del proyecto, ademas de sobresaliente, se esconde bajo la sombra de los árboles, sin que resulte molesto.

CỔ ĐÀM

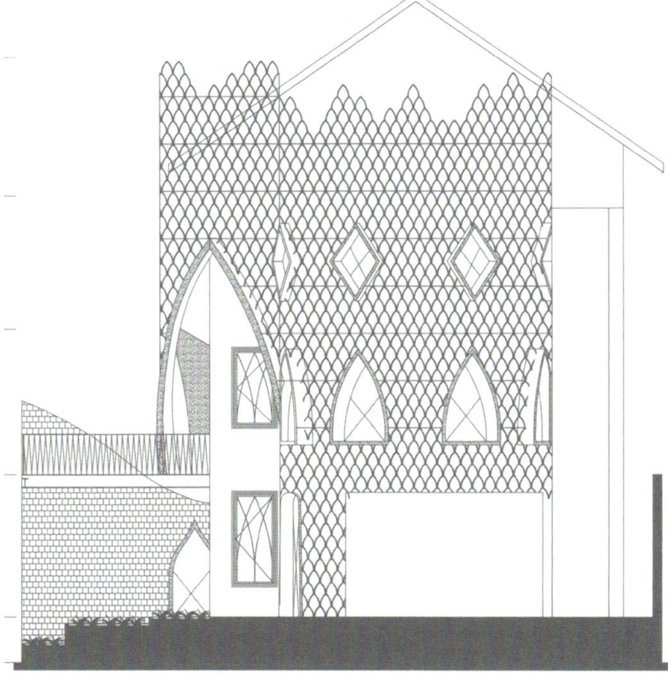

Elevations

Sketch

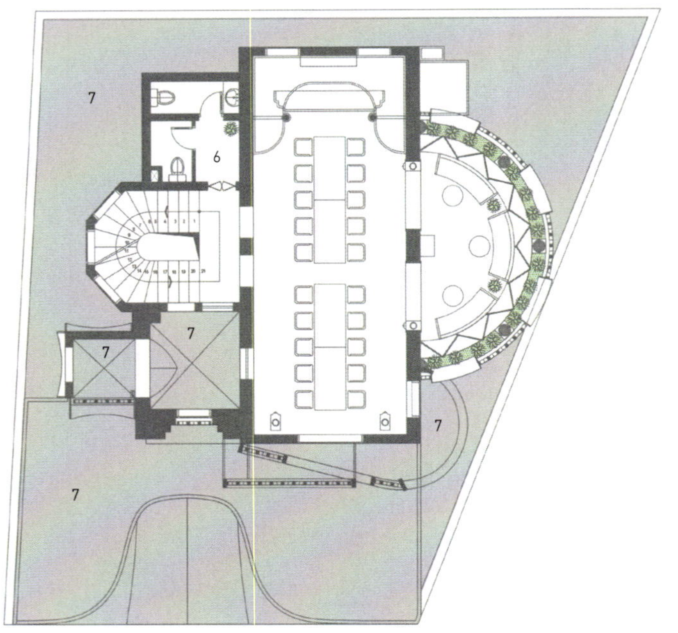

Third floor plan

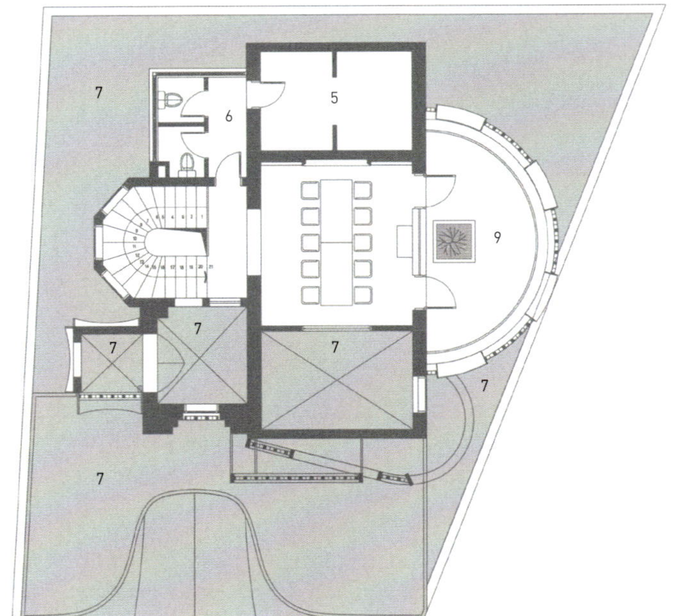

Second floor plan

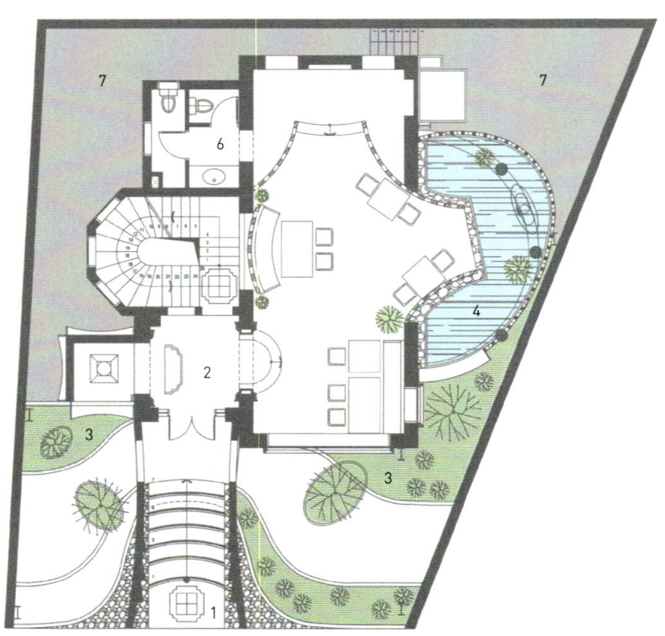

First floor plan

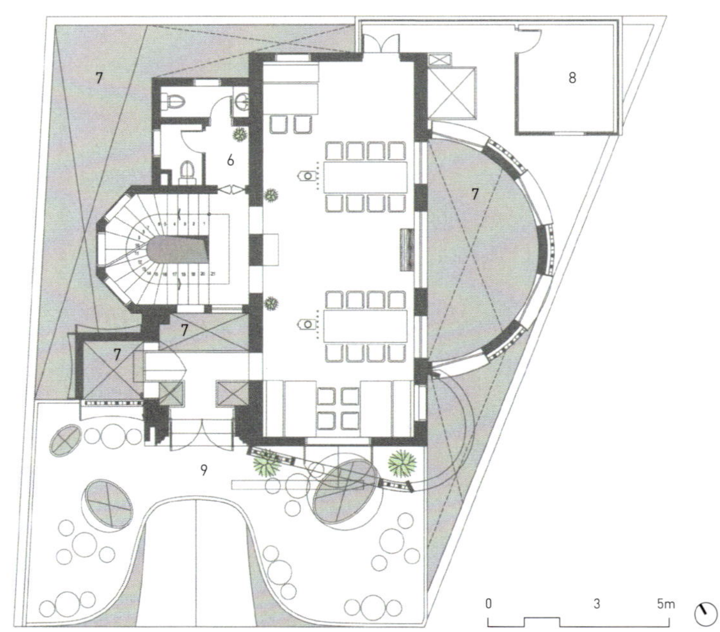

Second floor plan

1. Entrance
2. Lobby
3. Grasses and tree zone
4. Lake
5. Storage
6. WC
7. Cascades
8. Kitchen
9. Balcony

We believe that design is immaterial, that it must respond to a need, and that each place must have its own relevance. We are insistent, in constant search for the avant-garde. We are convinced that architecture is ineffable and we are aware that each project arises from the need to challenge ourselves.
We are an architectural studio, a collective of ideas, a workshop of architects in continuous transformation; we design sensations and we think about living.

Nous pensons que le design est immatériel, qu'il doit répondre à un besoin, et que chaque lieu doit avoir sa propre pertinence. Nous sommes insistants, à la recherche constante de l'avant-garde. Nous sommes convaincus que l'architecture est ineffable et nous sommes conscients que chaque projet naît du besoin de nous remettre en question.
Nous sommes un studio d'architecture, un collectif d'idées, un atelier d'architectes en transformation continue ; nous concevons des sensations et nous pensons à vivre.

Wir glauben, dass Design immateriell ist, dass es auf ein Bedürfnis reagieren muss und dass jeder Ort seine eigene Bedeutung haben muss. Wir sind beharrlich, auf der ständigen Suche nach der Avantgarde. Wir sind davon überzeugt, dass Architektur unaussprechlich ist, und wir sind uns bewusst, dass jedes Projekt aus dem Bedürfnis heraus entsteht, uns selbst herauszufordern.
Wir sind ein Architekturbüro, ein Ideenkollektiv, eine Werkstatt von Architekten in ständiger Veränderung; wir entwerfen Sensationen und wir denken über das Leben nach.

Creemos que el diseño es inmaterial, debe responder a una necesidad, y que cada lugar debe tener su propia pertinencia; Somos insistentes, en constante búsqueda por la vanguardia. Estamos convencidos de que la arquitectura es inefable y somos conscientes de que cada proyecto surge de la necesidad de retarnos a nosotros mismos.
Somos un estudio de arquitectura, un colectivo de ideas, un taller de artífices en transformación continua; Diseñamos sensaciones y pensamos el habitar.

OA+

www.oamas.co

GP BUILDING

Medellín, Antioquia, Colombia

Program: **Offices** | *Lead architects:* **Danny Rozo, Juan Diego Carvajal, Susana Arroyave**
Built surface: **989.56 m^2** | *Photos:* **© Mateo Soto**

GP is located in the traditional neighbourhood of La Aguacatala in the city of Medellín and it is the reinterpretation of that lifestyle. In its façades we find brick, concrete and metal; the relationship of masonry with the domestic is intentional, and arises from the need to rescue traditional construction systems, Medellín is the colour of brick. The project is made up of a series of overlapping volumes, displaced in plan to build planters; the vegetation becomes then the fourth material.
The programmatic distribution is logical: a first floor with the lobby and common spaces and the private offices and a rooftop located on the upper floor. The layout of conventional offices goes in the opposite direction of the lessons that the pandemic has taught us, we are now digital nomads and the interior design seeks to be welcoming and domestic: terracotta colours, noble materials and giving a leading role to its metal structure. The building seeks to be constructively, programmatically and socially efficient.

GP befindet sich im traditionellen Viertel La Aguacatala in der Stadt Medellín und ist die Neuinterpretation dieses Lebensstils. In seinen Fassaden finden wir Ziegel, Beton und Metall; die Beziehung des Mauerwerks zum Wohnbereich ist beabsichtigt und ergibt sich aus der Notwendigkeit, traditionelle Bausysteme zu retten, denn Medellín ist die Farbe des Ziegels. Das Projekt besteht aus einer Reihe von sich überschneidenden Volumen, die im Grundriss verschoben sind, um Pflanzgefäße zu bauen; die Vegetation wird so zum vierten Material.
Die programmatische Aufteilung ist logisch: ein erstes Stockwerk mit der Lobby und den Gemeinschaftsräumen und die privaten Büros und eine Dachterrasse im oberen Stockwerk. Das Layout der konventionellen Büros geht in die entgegengesetzte Richtung zu den Lektionen, die uns die Pandemie gelehrt hat, wir sind jetzt digitale Nomaden, und die Inneneinrichtung versucht, einladend und häuslich zu sein: Terrakottafarben, edle Materialien und eine Hauptrolle für die Metallstruktur. Das Gebäude soll konstruktiv, programmatisch und sozial effizient sein.

GP est situé dans le quartier traditionnel de La Aguacatala dans la ville de Medellín et il est la réinterprétation de ce style de vie. Dans ses façades, nous trouvons de la brique, du béton et du métal ; la relation de la maçonnerie avec le domestique est intentionnelle, et découle de la nécessité de sauver les systèmes de construction traditionnels, Medellín est la couleur de la brique. Le projet est constitué d'une série de volumes superposés, déplacés en plan pour construire des jardinières ; la végétation devient alors le quatrième matériau.
La distribution programmatique est logique : un premier étage avec le lobby et les espaces communs et les bureaux privés et un rooftop situés à l'étage supérieur. La disposition des bureaux conventionnels va à l'encontre des leçons que la pandémie nous a enseignées, nous sommes désormais des nomades numériques et l'aménagement intérieur se veut accueillant et domestique : couleurs terre cuite, matériaux nobles et donnant un rôle prépondérant à sa structure métallique. Le bâtiment se veut constructif, programmatique et socialement efficace.

GP está ubicado en el tradicional barrio de La Aguacatala en la ciudad de Medellín y es la reinterpretación de ese estilo de vida. En sus fachadas encontramos ladrillo, hormigón y metal; la relación de la mampostería con lo doméstico es intencional y surge de la necesidad de rescatar los sistemas constructivos tradicionales, Medellín es el color del ladrillo. El proyecto se compone de una serie de volúmenes superpuestos, desplazados en planta para construir jardineras; la vegetación se convierte entonces en el cuarto material.
La distribución programática es lógica: una primera planta con el vestíbulo y los espacios comunes y las oficinas privadas y una azotea situadas en la planta superior. La distribución de las oficinas convencionales va en dirección contraria a las lecciones que la pandemia nos ha enseñado, ahora somos nómadas digitales y el diseño interior busca ser acogedor y doméstico: colores terracota, materiales nobles que dan protagonismo a la estructura metálica. El edificio busca ser constructivo, programático y socialmente eficiente.

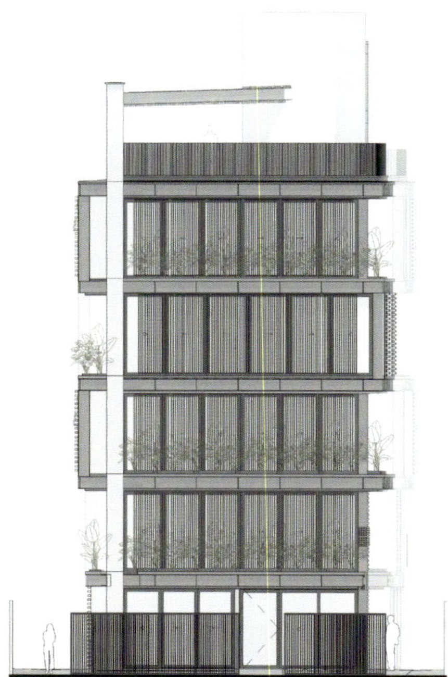

East elevation - Main facade

South elevation

Longitudinal section

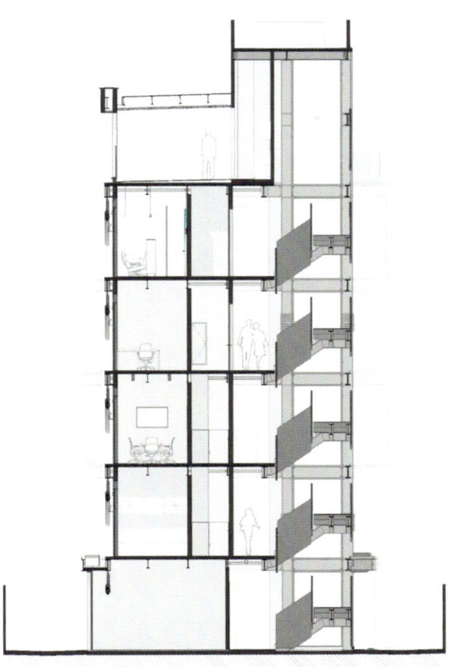

Cross section

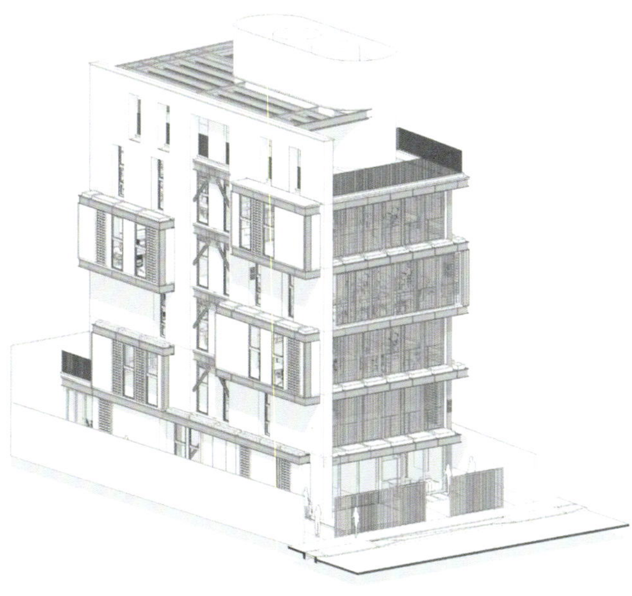

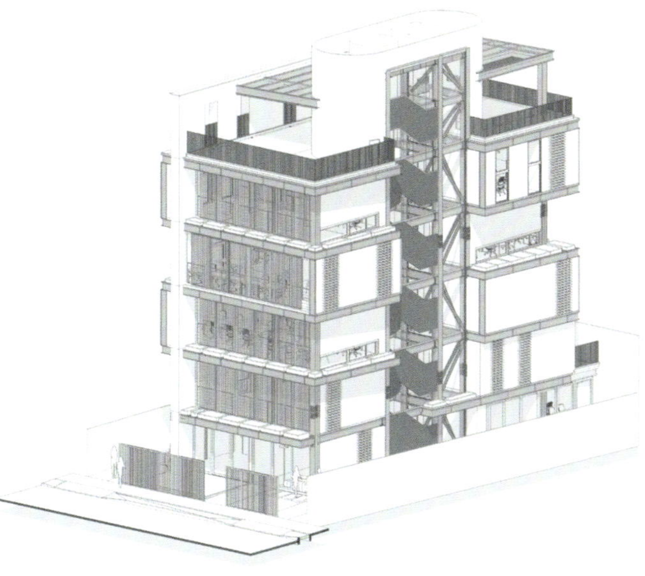

Axonometries

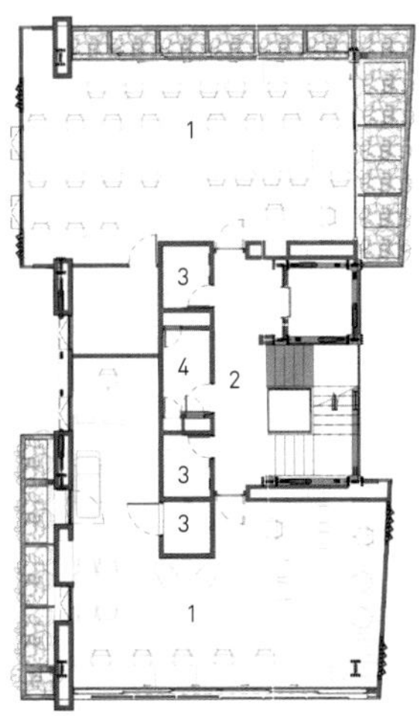

Fourth floor plan

1. Oficina
2. Lobby
3. Baños
4. Cuarto técnico

Fifth floor plan

1. Oficina
2. Lobby
3. Baños
4. Cuarto técnico
5. Sala de reuniones
6. Archivo

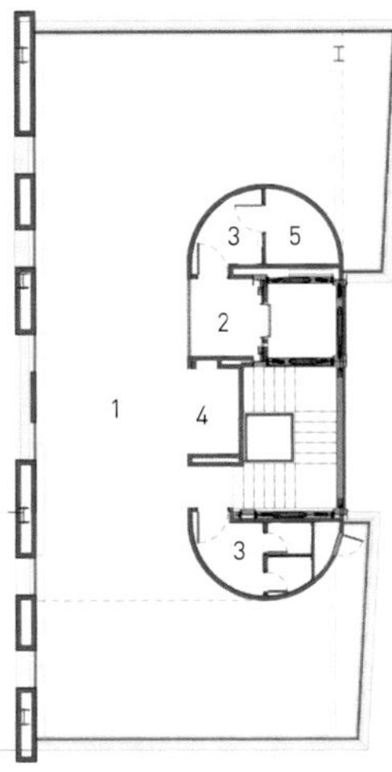

Terrace plan

1. Terraza
2. Lobby
3. Baños
4. Cocineta
5. Cuarto técnico

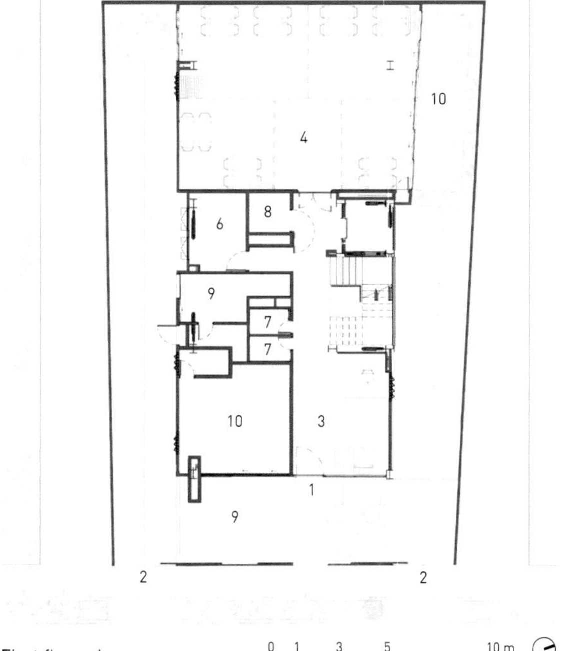

First floor plan

1. Acceso principal
2. Acceso vehicular
3. Lobby
4. Auditorio
5. Local
6. Oficina
7. Baños
8. Cuarto técnico
9. Cuarto basuras
10. Deck

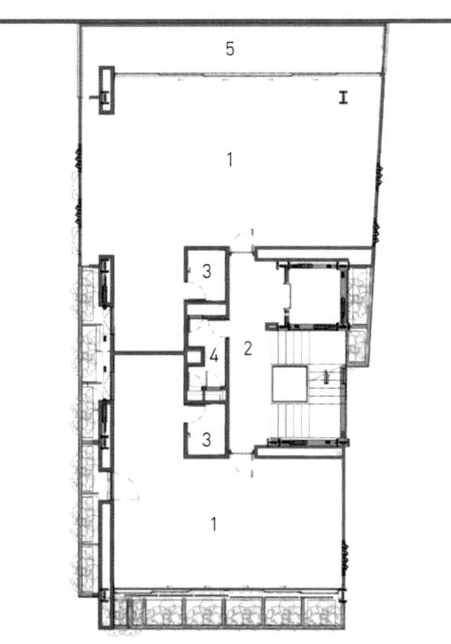

Second floor plan

1. Oficina
2. Lobby
3. Baños
4. Cuarto técnico
5. Terraza

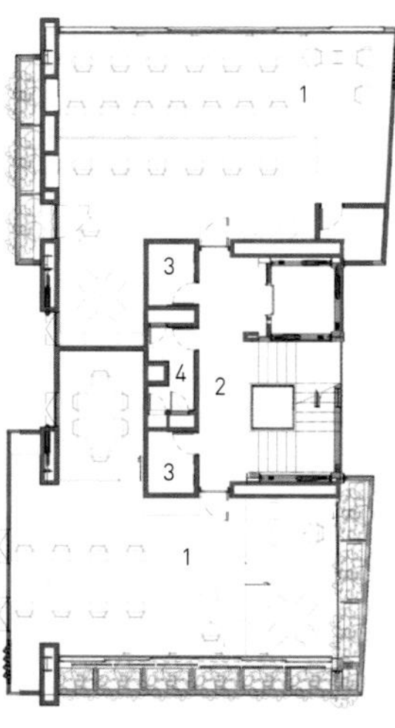

Third floor plan

1. Oficina
2. Lobby
3. Baños
4. Cuarto técnico

We believe in "architecture-appropriate" that evolves from the physical and cultural context of its locality, by the programmatic essentials extracted from client's brief and the design choices they make, and by being informed by rational experience, history and tradition, nevertheless all of it illuminated by architectural insight. The balancing of these priorities is not formulaic, just as we like to think that our work never is, as it varies widely from project to project, and is often honestly messy. But in the end we believe, it is very much essential to creating better architecture. Our main concern in a project is not to merely resolve the planning of functional adjacencies, but to seek and render its architecture with a perceivable dimension of appropriateness rather than exercising in formal and ideological arbitrariness, by grounding it in the concrete reality of its context.

Nous croyons en une « architecture appropriée », qui évolue à partir de son propre contexte physique, des éléments essentiels du programme formulés à partir du briefing du client et des choix de conception qu'il fait, informés par l'expérience/l'histoire et éclairés par la perspicacité. L'équilibre de ces priorités n'est jamais une formule, tout comme nous pensons que leur travail ne l'est jamais, car il varie largement d'un projet à l'autre et est souvent honnêtement désordonné ; mais en fin de compte, nous pensons qu'il est essentiel à une meilleure architecture. Pour résumer, notre principale préoccupation dans le projet n'est pas de résoudre simplement les diverses fonctions qui prennent place, mais de rendre son architecture avec une dimension d'adéquation plutôt que d'arbitraire en l'ancrant dans la réalité de son contexte.

Wir glauben an eine „angemessene Architektur", die sich aus ihrem eigenen physischen Kontext entwickelt, an die Programmgrundlagen, die aus dem Auftrag des Kunden und den von ihm getroffenen Designentscheidungen formuliert werden, die durch Erfahrung/Geschichte informiert und durch Erkenntnisse erhellt werden. Die Ausgewogenheit dieser Prioritäten ist niemals formelhaft, so wie wir auch der Meinung sind, dass ihre Arbeit niemals formelhaft ist, da sie von Projekt zu Projekt stark variiert und oft ehrlich gesagt chaotisch ist; aber letztendlich glauben wir, dass sie für eine bessere Architektur sehr wichtig ist. Zusammenfassend lässt sich sagen, dass unser Hauptanliegen bei diesem Projekt nicht die bloße Lösung der verschiedenen Funktionen ist, sondern die Architektur mit einer Dimension der Angemessenheit und nicht der Beliebigkeit auszustatten, indem sie in der Realität des Kontextes verankert wird.

Creemos en una «arquitectura apropiada», que evoluciona a partir de su propio contexto físico, de los elementos esenciales del programa formulados a partir de las instrucciones del cliente y de las opciones de diseño que éste toma, informadas por la experiencia/historia e iluminadas por la perspicacia. El equilibrio de estas prioridades nunca es una fórmula, al igual que pensamos que su trabajo nunca lo es, ya que varía mucho de un proyecto a otro y a menudo es honestamente desordenado; pero al final creemos que es muy esencial para una mejor arquitectura. En resumen, nuestra principal preocupación en el proyecto no es simplemente resolver las diversas funciones que se llevan a cabo, sino dotar a su arquitectura de una dimensión de adecuación y no de arbitrariedad al basarla en la realidad de su contexto.

ROY ANTONY ARCHITECTS

ROY ANTONY

royantonyarchitects.com

ALANKAR RESIDENCE

Changanassery, Kottayam, Kerala

Project team: **Sainath Kadavil, Shyam Prasad, Vaishnavi Aneesh, Aswathi Shajan, Casia Maria John, Dhiya Anna Charley, Jinju Ann Johnson, Karoline Morera, Mohammed Shibin K., Neha Miria Ninan, Vinu Elias Jacob (architects), Anju Rajan, Isam Khan, Jose J Kottoor** | *Photos:* **© Shyam Sreeshylam**

Alankar Residence for Mr. Shahabudeen is one of the recently completed projects by our firm. It is located within 4 km of the Changanassery town-centre, in a residential neighborhood. Situated on a 410 m^2 property, with an average site elevation of 1.2 m, the total building area occupies 456.12 m^2. The client approached us with a simple request that the house should have 5 bedrooms giving us freedom to conceive the building and choose its architectural form. What we have attempted in Alankar Residence is a harmonious reconciliation of the diverse design factors that are part of any architectural project.

Alankar Residence is a retrospective exploration of the notion of dwelling: looking back at the traditional practice of Kerala which is rich in craft and symbolic significance, retrieving its valid lessons, redefining its constitutive elements, and bringing them to bear concretely in the present by integrating them in the project.

Die Alankar Residence für Herrn Shahabudeen ist eines der kürzlich abgeschlossenen Projekte unseres Büros. Es befindet sich 4 km vom Stadtzentrum von Changanassery entfernt in einem Wohnviertel. Es befindet sich auf einem 410 m^2 großen Grundstück mit einer durchschnittlichen Geländehöhe von 1,2 m. Die Gesamtfläche des Gebäudes beträgt 456,12 m^2.

Der Bauherr trat an uns mit dem einfachen Wunsch heran, dass das Haus 5 Schlafzimmer haben sollte, was uns die Freiheit gab, das Gebäude zu konzipieren und seine architektonische Form zu wählen. Was wir mit der Alankar Residence versucht haben, ist eine harmonische Versöhnung der verschiedenen Designfaktoren, die Teil eines jeden Architekturprojekts sind.

Alankar Residence ist eine retrospektive Erkundung des Begriffs des Wohnens: ein Rückblick auf die traditionelle Praxis in Kerala, die reich an handwerklicher und symbolischer Bedeutung ist, ein Wiederaufgreifen ihrer gültigen Lehren, eine Neudefinition ihrer konstitutiven Elemente und ihre konkrete Umsetzung in der Gegenwart, indem sie in das Projekt integriert werden.

La résidence Alankar pour M. Shahabudeen est l'un des projets récemment achevés par notre cabinet. Elle est située à moins de 4 km du centre ville de Changanassery, dans un quartier résidentiel. Situé sur une propriété de 410 m^2, avec une élévation moyenne du site de 1,2 m, la surface totale du bâtiment occupe 456,12 m^2.

Le client nous a approchés avec une demande simple : la maison devait avoir 5 chambres à coucher, ce qui nous a donné la liberté de concevoir le bâtiment et de choisir sa forme architecturale. Ce que nous avons tenté dans la résidence Alankar est une conciliation harmonieuse des divers facteurs de conception qui font partie de tout projet architectural.

La résidence Alankar est une exploration rétrospective de la notion d'habitation : nous nous sommes penchés sur la pratique traditionnelle du Kerala, riche en signification artisanale et symbolique, pour en tirer des leçons valables, redéfinir ses éléments constitutifs et les mettre en œuvre concrètement dans le présent en les intégrant au projet.

La Residencia Alankar para el Sr. Shahabudeen es uno de los proyectos recientemente realizados por nuestra empresa. Está situada a 4 km del centro de la ciudad de Changanassery, en un barrio residencial. Situado en una propiedad de 410 m^2, con una elevación media del terreno de 1,2 m, la superficie total del edificio ocupa 456,12 m^2.

El cliente se dirigió a nosotros con la simple petición de que la casa tuviera 5 dormitorios, dándonos libertad para concebir el edificio y elegir su forma arquitectónica. Lo que hemos intentado en la Residencia Alankar es una reconciliación armoniosa de los diversos factores de diseño que forman parte de cualquier proyecto arquitectónico.

La Residencia Alankar es una exploración retrospectiva de la noción de vivienda: volver la vista atrás a la práctica tradicional de Kerala, rica en significado artesanal y simbolismo, recuperar sus lecciones válidas, redefinir sus elementos constitutivos y traerlos concretamente al presente integrándolos en el proyecto.

Section

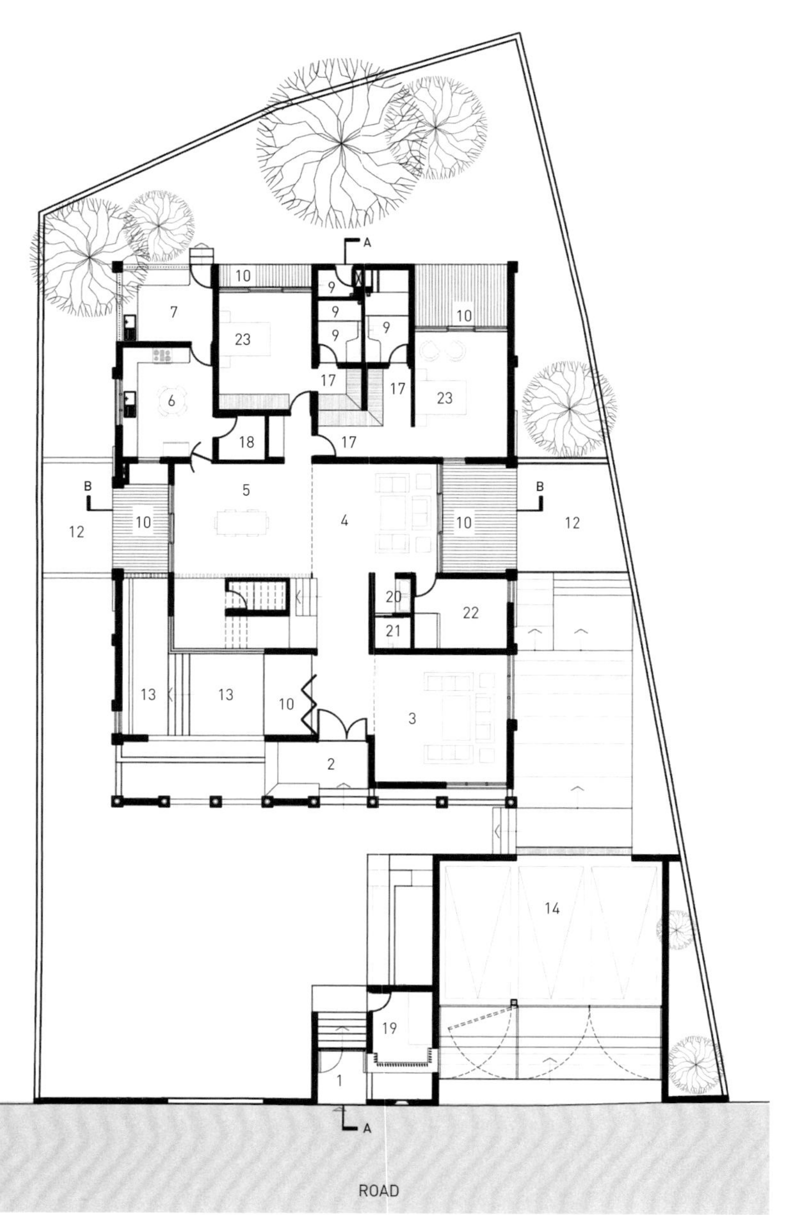

Ground floor plan

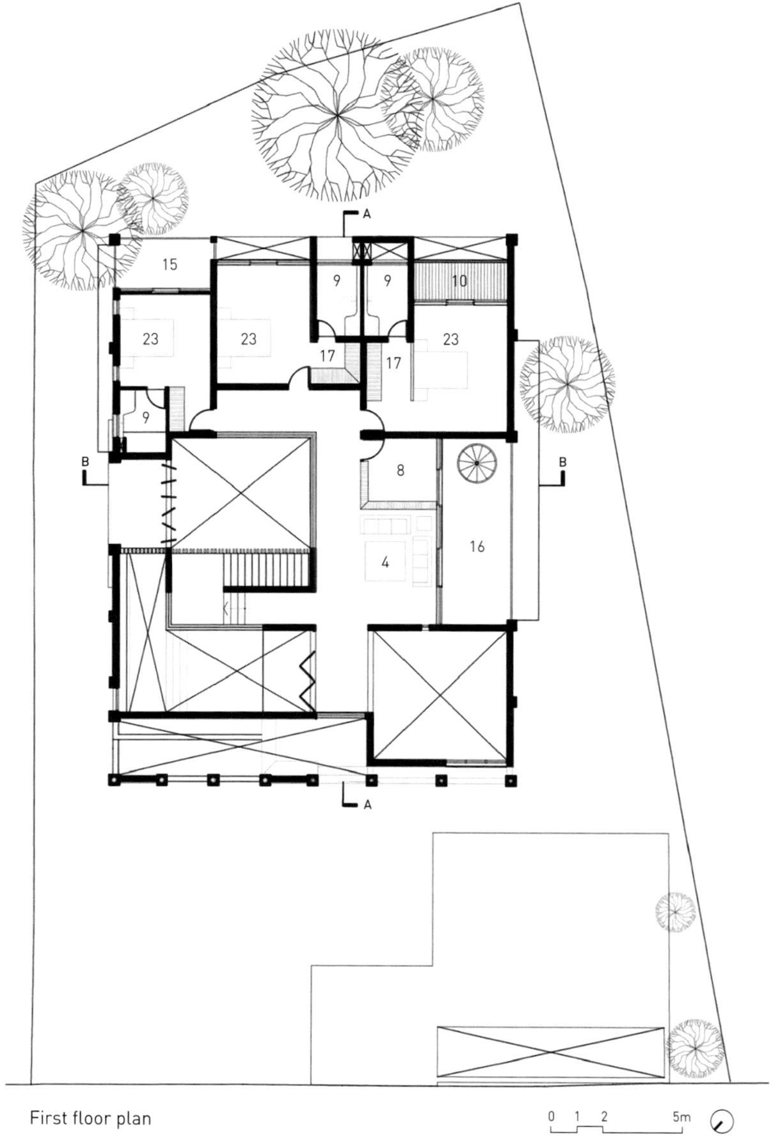

First floor plan

1. Entrance
2. Sitout
3. Living space
4. Family living
5. Dining space
6. Kitchen
7. Work area
8. Utility
9. Toilet
10. Deck
11. Passage
12. Landscape
13. Waterbody
14. Porch
15. Balcony
16. Terrace
17. Dress area
18. Store
19. Security
20. Wash area
21. Powder room
22. Prayer room
23. Bedroom

Nguyen Huu Son Duong, founder of SILAA Architects, was born in the city of Hue, Vietnam. He graduated from Ha Noi University of Architecture. In 2012 he joined the Vo Trong Nghia Architects studio as a senior architect, where he worked for two years until 2014. In 2017 he founded SILAA Architects, a Vietnamese architecture studio, based in the city of Hue, focusing mainly on residential and hotel projects.

Nguyen Huu Son Duong, fondateur de SILAA Architects, est né dans la ville de Hue, au Vietnam. Il est diplômé de l'université d'architecture de Ha Noi. En 2012, il a rejoint le studio Vo Trong Nghia Architects en tant qu'architecte principal, où il a travaillé pendant deux ans jusqu'en 2014.
En 2017, il a fondé SILAA Architects, un studio d'architecture vietnamien, basé dans la ville de Hue, se concentrant principalement sur des projets résidentiels et hôteliers.

Nguyen Huu Son Duong, der Gründer von SILAA Architects, wurde in der Stadt Hue in Vietnam geboren. Er machte seinen Abschluss an der Ha Noi University of Architecture. Im Jahr 2012 trat er als leitender Architekt in das Büro Vo Trong Nghia Architects ein, wo er bis 2014 zwei Jahre lang arbeitete.
Im Jahr 2017 gründete er SILAA Architects, ein vietnamesisches Architekturbüro mit Sitz in der Stadt Hue, das sich hauptsächlich auf Wohn- und Hotelprojekte konzentriert.

Nguyen Huu Son Duong, fundador de SILAA Architects, nació en la ciudad de Hue (Vietnam). Se graduó en la Universidad de Arquitectura de Ha Noi. En 2012 se incorporó al estudio Vo Trong Nghia Architects como arquitecto senior, donde trabajó durante dos años hasta 2014.
En 2017 fundó SILAA Architects, un estudio de arquitectura vietnamita, con sede en la ciudad de Hue, centrado principalmente en proyectos residenciales y hoteleros.

SILAA ARCHITECTS

NGUYEN HUU SON DUONG

www.facebook.com/Silaaarchitects

HACHI HOMESTAY & SPA / HACHI POMELO HOUSE

Thuy Bieu Village, Hue City, Vietnam

Program: Homestay | *Lead architect:* Nguyen Huu Son Duong | *Gross built area:* 735 m²
Photos: © Hoang Le

Located in Hue,Vietnam, this 2 storey house welcomes the guests from all over the world to enjoy their days in a lush garden full of pomelo trees. The U-shaped plan allows all the activities take place around a swimming pool in the center.
The open ground floor serves as a common area. The bedrooms are lifted on an exposed concrete frame, one separated to the other, creating a play of interesting voids. The connection between ground and first level is established through many small spaces on the upper floor as well as the open space in the center of the pool.
A 500 m² sloping roof covers the U-shaped plan and protects the space underneath from the harsh tropical climate. The use of reclaimed wood for all the wooden structure, doors, windows and furniture is one of the highlight of this house.The expression of the old wood together with the exposed concrete, brick, stone and terrazzo brings a cosy atmosphere.

Dieses zweistöckige Haus in Hue, Vietnam, heißt Gäste aus aller Welt willkommen, die ihre Tage in einem üppigen Garten voller Pampelmusenbäume genießen. Der U-förmige Grundriss ermöglicht es, dass sich alle Aktivitäten um einen zentralen Swimmingpool herum abspielen.
Das offene Erdgeschoss dient als Gemeinschaftsraum. Die Schlafzimmer sind auf einer Sichtbetonstruktur aufgeständert und voneinander getrennt, so dass ein interessantes Spiel von Leerräumen entsteht. Die Verbindung zwischen dem Erdgeschoss und der ersten Etage wird durch viele kleine Räume im Obergeschoss sowie durch die Freifläche im Poolbereich hergestellt.
Ein 500 m² großes Schrägdach überdeckt den U-förmigen Grundriss und schützt den unteren Bereich vor dem rauen tropischen Klima. Die Verwendung von wiedergewonnenem Holz für die gesamte Holzstruktur, Türen, Fenster und Möbel ist einer der Höhepunkte dieses Hauses, und der Ausdruck von altem Holz zusammen mit Sichtbeton, Ziegel, Stein und Terrazzo schafft eine einladende Atmosphäre.

Située à Hue, au Viêt Nam, cette maison à deux étages accueille des clients du monde entier pour passer des journées agréables dans un jardin luxuriant planté de pamplemoussiers. Le plan en U permet à toutes les activités de se dérouler autour d'une piscine centrale.
Le rez-de-chaussée ouvert sert d'espace commun. Les chambres sont surélevées sur une structure en béton apparent, séparées les unes des autres, créant un jeu de vides intéressant. Le lien entre le rez-de-chaussée et le premier niveau est établi par de nombreux petits espaces à l'étage supérieur, ainsi que par l'espace ouvert de la zone de la piscine.
Un toit en pente de 500 m² couvre le plan en U et protège l'espace inférieur du rude climat tropical. L'utilisation de bois récupéré pour l'ensemble de la structure en bois, les portes, les fenêtres et le mobilier est l'un des points forts de cette maison. L'expression du vieux bois associée au béton apparent, à la brique, à la pierre et au terrazzo crée une atmosphère chaleureuse.

Situada en Hue,Vietnam, esta casa de dos plantas acoge a los huéspedes de todo el mundo para que disfruten de sus días en un exuberante jardín lleno de pomelos.La planta en forma de U permite que todas las actividades tengan lugar alrededor de una piscina central.
La planta baja abierta sirve de zona común. Los dormitorios se levantan sobre una estructura de hormigón visto, uno separado del otro, creando un juego de interesantes vacíos. La conexión entre la planta baja y el primer nivel se establece a través de muchos espacios pequeños en la planta superior, así como el espacio abierto en la zona de la piscina.
Una cubierta inclinada de 500 m² cubre la planta en forma de U y protege el espacio inferior del duro clima tropical. El uso de madera recuperada para toda la estructura de madera, las puertas, las ventanas y los muebles es uno de los aspectos más destacados de esta casa.La expresión de la madera antigua junto con el hormigón visto, el ladrillo, la piedra y el terrazo aporta un ambiente acogedor.

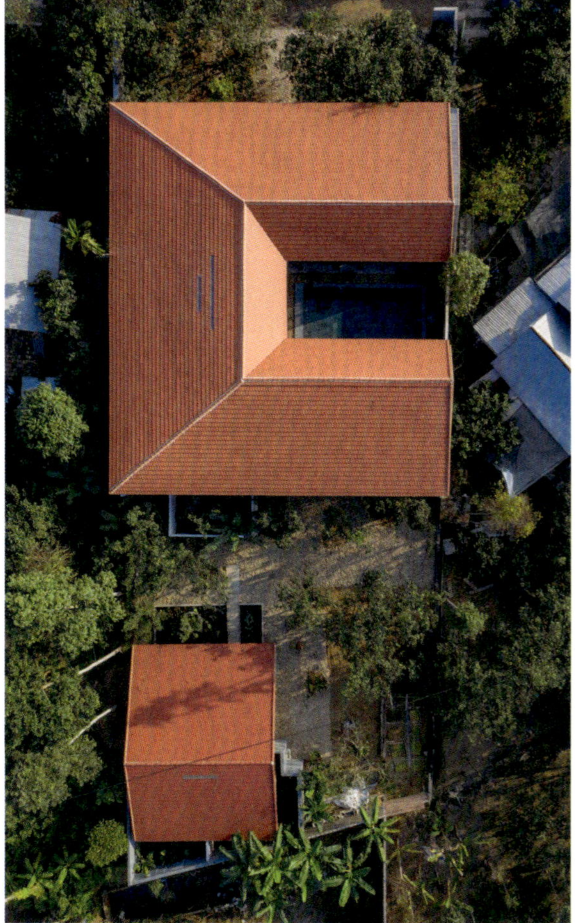

Site plan

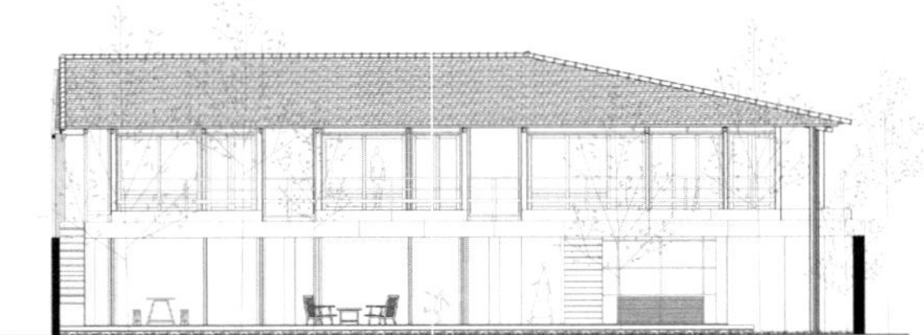
Front elevation

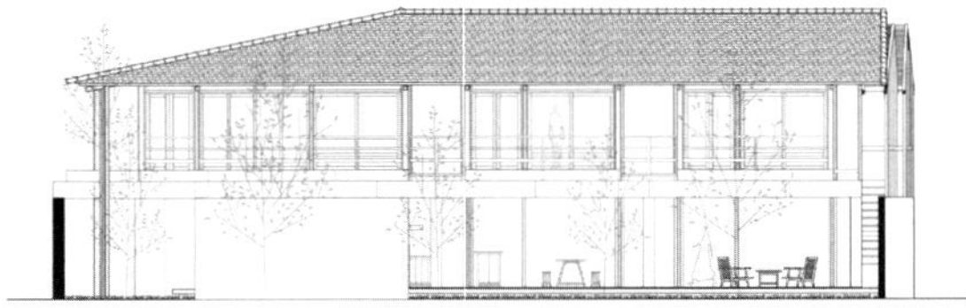
Back elevation

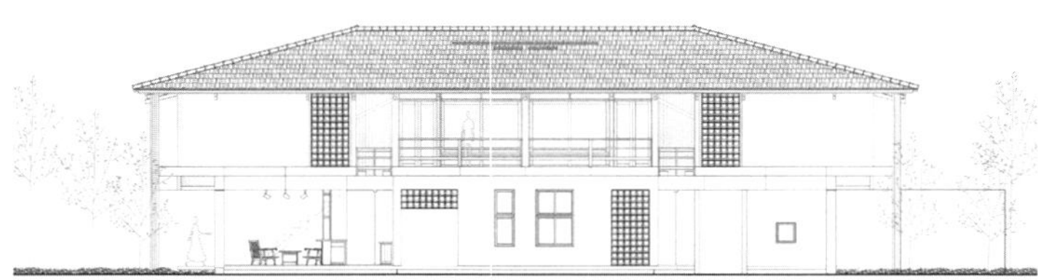
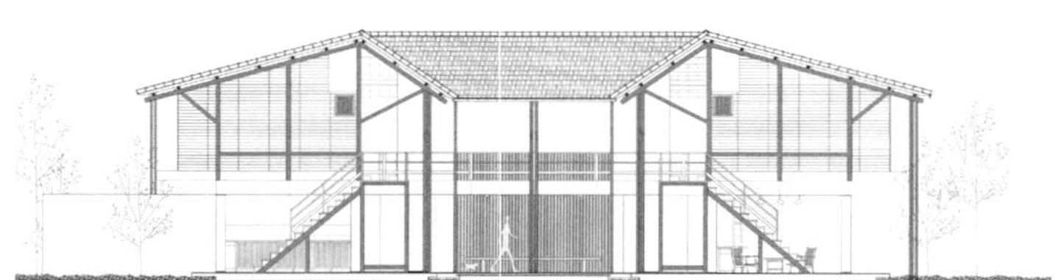
Side elevations

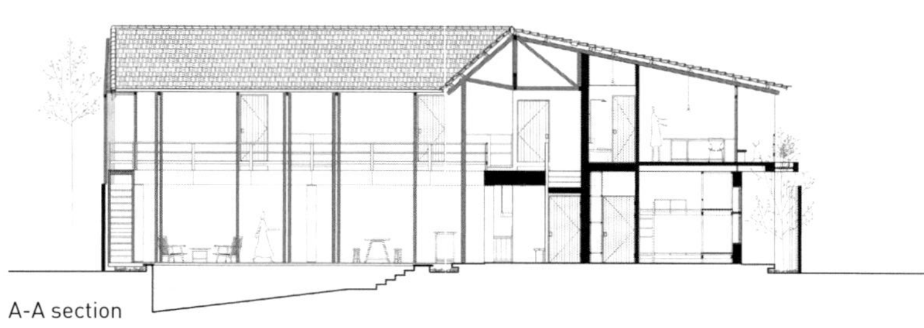
A-A section

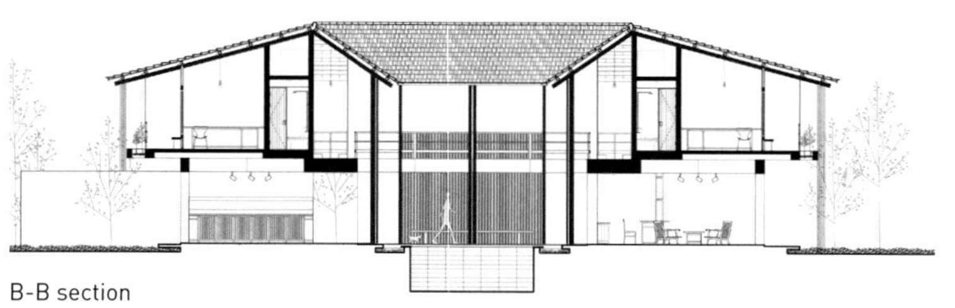
B-B section

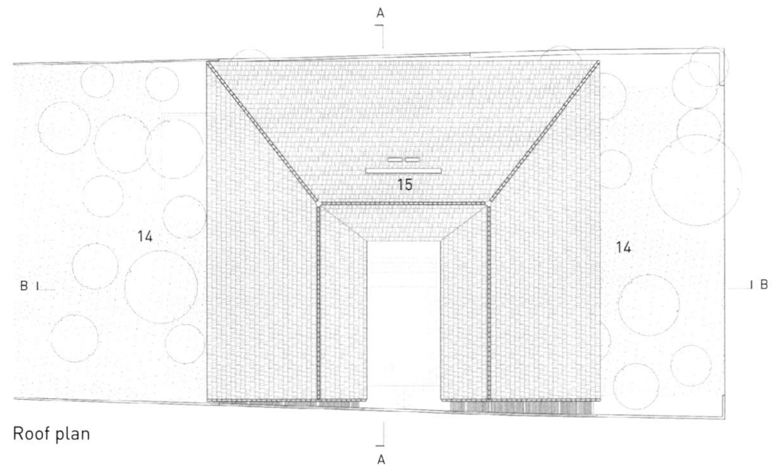
Roof plan

Upper floor plan

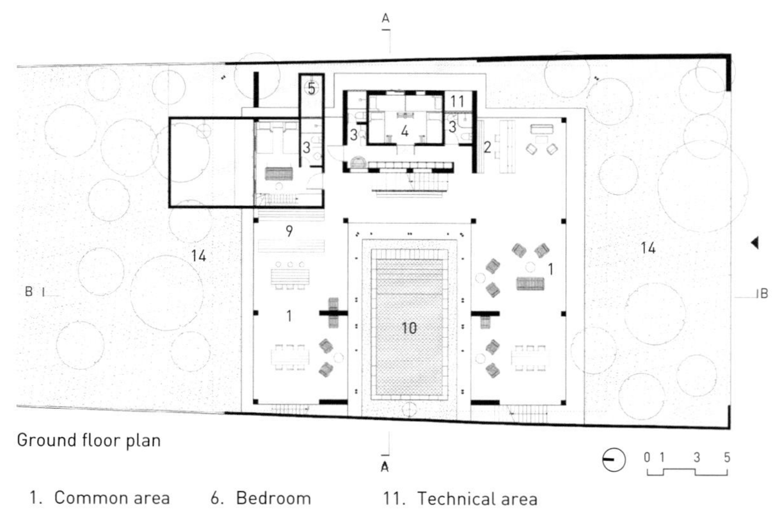
Ground floor plan

1. Common area
2. Reception
3. Restroom
4. Dormitory
5. Outdoor shower
6. Bedroom
7. Terrace
8. Inner garden
9. Kitchenette
10. Swimming pool
11. Technical area
12. Hallway
13. Loggia
14. Pomelo garden
15. Skylight

Studiohoon, founded by Hoon.Lee in 2018, is a design studio based in Seoul, South Korea. He studied architecture and interior design at Kyunghee University in South Korea and a master's in interior design at the Royal College of Art in London and Istituto Europeo di Design in Milan. Also, he has an experience as a contemporary artist in MMCA Changdong residency in South Korea after finishing his master's degree. His design is based on perspectives about the context of the object. Through careful observation, he reads the context of the space, the context of the behaviour, and the context of the shape/material, and unravels the selected contexts from this observation to reconnect them in contrast.

Studiohoon wurde 2018 von Hoon.Lee gegründet und ist ein Designstudio mit Sitz in Seoul, Südkorea. Er studierte Architektur und Innenarchitektur an der Kyunghee University in Südkorea und absolvierte einen Master in Innenarchitektur am Royal College of Art in London und am Istituto Europeo di Design in Mailand. Außerdem hat er nach Abschluss seines Masterstudiums Erfahrungen als zeitgenössischer Künstler im MMCA Changdong in Südkorea gesammelt. Sein Design basiert auf der Betrachtung des Kontextes eines Objekts. Durch sorgfältige Beobachtung liest er den Kontext des Raums, den Kontext des Verhaltens und den Kontext der Form/des Materials und entwirrt die ausgewählten Kontexte aus dieser Beobachtung, um sie im Kontrast neu zu verbinden.

Studiohoon, fondé par Hoon.Lee en 2018, est un studio de design basé à Séoul, en Corée du Sud. Il a étudié l'architecture et le design d'intérieur à l'université de Kyunghee en Corée du Sud et un master en design d'intérieur au Royal College of Art de Londres et à l'Istituto Europeo di Design de Milan. Il a également acquis une expérience en tant qu'artiste contemporain dans le cadre de la résidence du MMCA Changdong en Corée du Sud après avoir terminé sa maîtrise. Son design est basé sur les perspectives du contexte de l'objet. Par une observation attentive, il lit le contexte de l'espace, le contexte du comportement et le contexte de la forme/du matériau, et démêle les contextes sélectionnés à partir de cette observation pour les reconnecter par contraste.

Studiohoon, fundado por Hoon.Lee en 2018, es un estudio de diseño con sede en Seúl, Corea del Sur. Estudió arquitectura y diseño de interiores en la Universidad Kyunghee de Corea del Sur y un máster en diseño de interiores en el Royal College of Art de Londres y en el Istituto Europeo di Design de Milán. Además, tiene una experiencia como artista contemporáneo en la residencia MMCA Changdong, en Corea del Sur, tras finalizar su máster. Su diseño se basa en perspectivas sobre el contexto del objeto. A través de una cuidadosa observación, lee el contexto del espacio, del comportamiento y de la forma/material, y desentraña las soluciones a partir de esta observación para reconectarlos en forma de contraste.

STUDIOHOON

HOON. LEE

studiohoon.com

MOMENTO BREWERS

Gangnam-gu, Seoul, South Korea

Program: **Momento Brewers** | *Project director:* **Hoon. Lee** | *Leading architect:* **Hoon. Lee**
Design team: **Hoon. Lee** | *Built surface:* **47 m²** | *Photos:* **© Hoon. Lee, Beezy Studio**

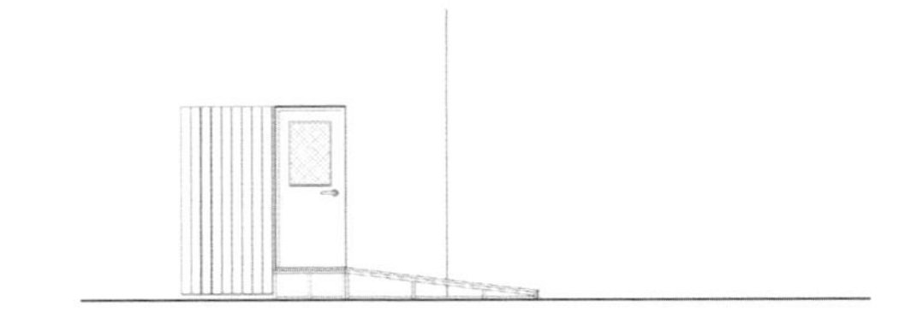

Momento Brewers is not a brand that simply experiences a high-quality coffee or a beautiful space, but it is designed by defining the entire activity there as a brand. Momento Brewers was designed as a standing bar that limits seating and instead provides open space.
The interior of the shop is divided into two spaces. A bar space where you can chat with a barista and an empty space where you can drink coffee and appreciate the space and exhibition works. Those two spaces are separated by concrete walls, and both are connected to outer space through the windows on the brick wall.
All materials are processed so that users can comfortably experience their original beauty. The decoration of the outer wall and inside flooring is removed, so the structure is shown as it is. Rough cement bricks and concrete parts are painted to maintain their shape and enjoy the texture.

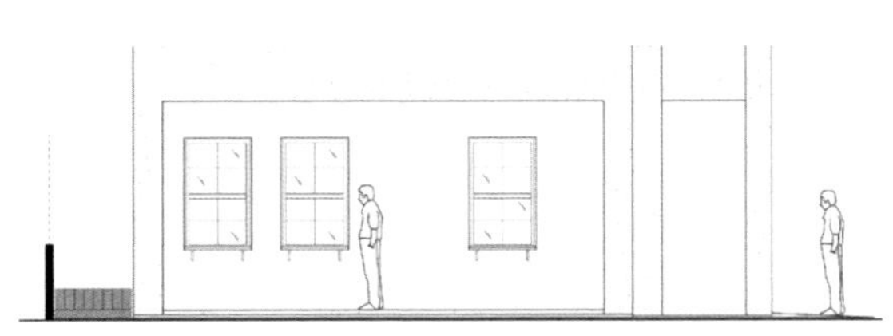

Momento Brewers ist keine Marke, die einfach nur einen hochwertigen Kaffee oder einen schönen Raum erlebt, sondern sie ist so konzipiert, dass sie die gesamte Aktivität dort als Marke definiert. Momento Brewers wurde als Stehbar konzipiert, die nur wenige Sitzplätze bietet und stattdessen einen offenen Raum.
Das Innere des Ladens ist in zwei Bereiche unterteilt. Einen Barbereich, in dem man sich mit einem Barista unterhalten kann, und einen leeren Raum, in dem man Kaffee trinken und den Raum und die Ausstellungsstücke betrachten kann. Diese beiden Räume sind durch Betonwände voneinander getrennt, und beide sind durch die Fenster in der Backsteinmauer mit dem Außenraum verbunden.
Alle Materialien sind so verarbeitet, dass die Nutzer ihre ursprüngliche Schönheit bequem erleben können. Die Dekoration der Außenwand und der Innenböden wurde entfernt, so dass die Struktur so gezeigt wird, wie sie ist. Raue Zementziegel und Betonteile werden gestrichen, um ihre Form zu erhalten und die Textur zu genießen.

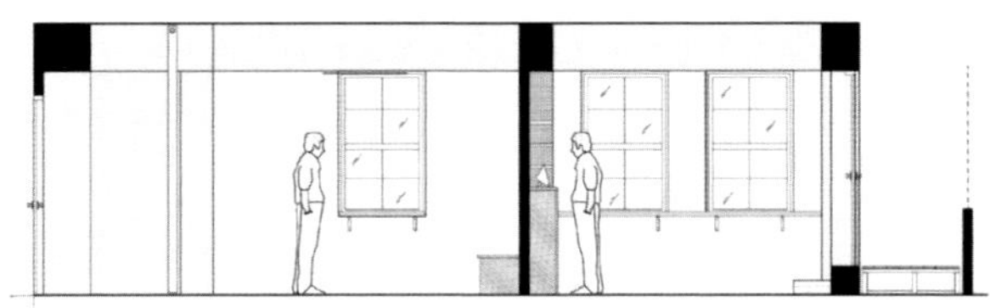

Momento Brewers n'est pas une marque qui se contente de faire l'expérience d'un café de haute qualité ou d'un bel espace, mais elle est conçue en définissant toute l'activité qui s'y déroule comme une marque. Momento Brewers a été conçu comme un bar debout qui limite les places assises et offre plutôt un espace ouvert.
L'intérieur de la boutique est divisé en deux espaces. Un espace bar où vous pouvez discuter avec un barista et un espace vide où vous pouvez boire un café et apprécier l'espace et les œuvres de l'exposition. Ces deux espaces sont séparés par des murs en béton, et tous deux sont reliés à l'espace extérieur par les fenêtres du mur de briques.
Tous les matériaux sont traités de manière à ce que les utilisateurs puissent confortablement faire l'expérience de leur beauté originale. La décoration du mur extérieur et du sol intérieur est supprimée, de sorte que la structure est présentée telle quelle. Les briques en ciment brut et les parties en béton sont peintes pour conserver leur forme et apprécier leur texture.

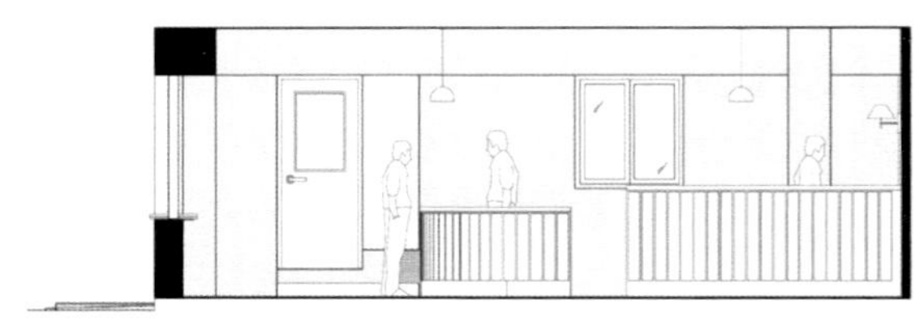

Momento Brewers no es una marca que simplemente experimenta un café de alta calidad o un espacio hermoso, sino que se diseña definiendo la actividad como marca. Momento Brewers se diseñó como un bar de pie que limita los asientos y, en cambio, ofrece un espacio abierto.
El interior de la tienda se divide en dos espacios. Un espacio de bar en el que se puede charlar con un barista y un espacio vacío en el que se puede beber café y apreciar el espacio y las obras de la exposición. Estos dos espacios están separados por muros de hormigón, y ambos están conectados con el espacio exterior a través de las ventanas de la pared de ladrillo.
Todos los materiales están procesados para que los usuarios puedan experimentar cómodamente su belleza original. Se elimina la decoración de la pared exterior y del suelo interior, de modo que la estructura se muestra tal cual. Los ladrillos de cemento y las piezas de hormigón se pintan para mantener su forma y disfrutar de su textura.

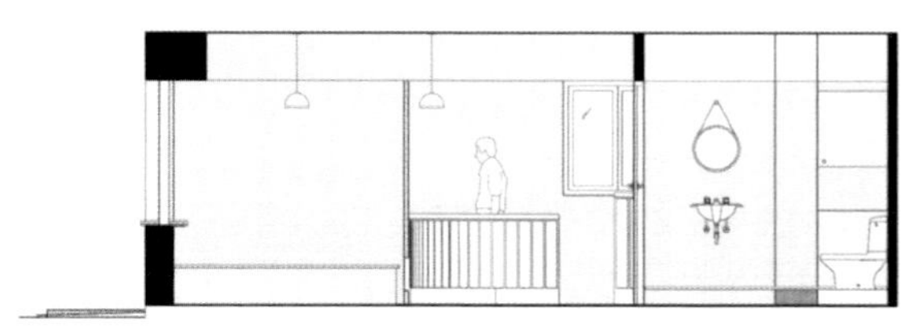

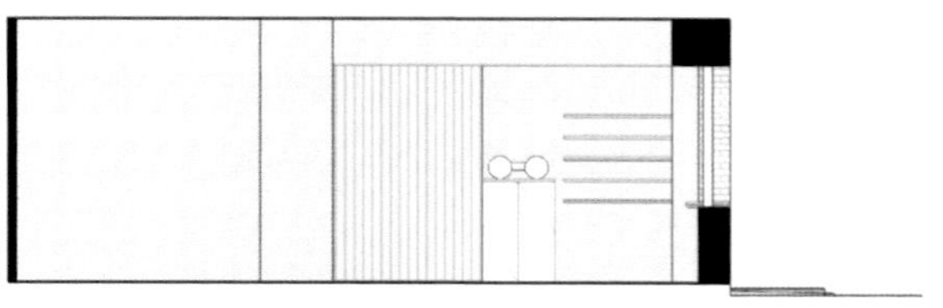

Elevations

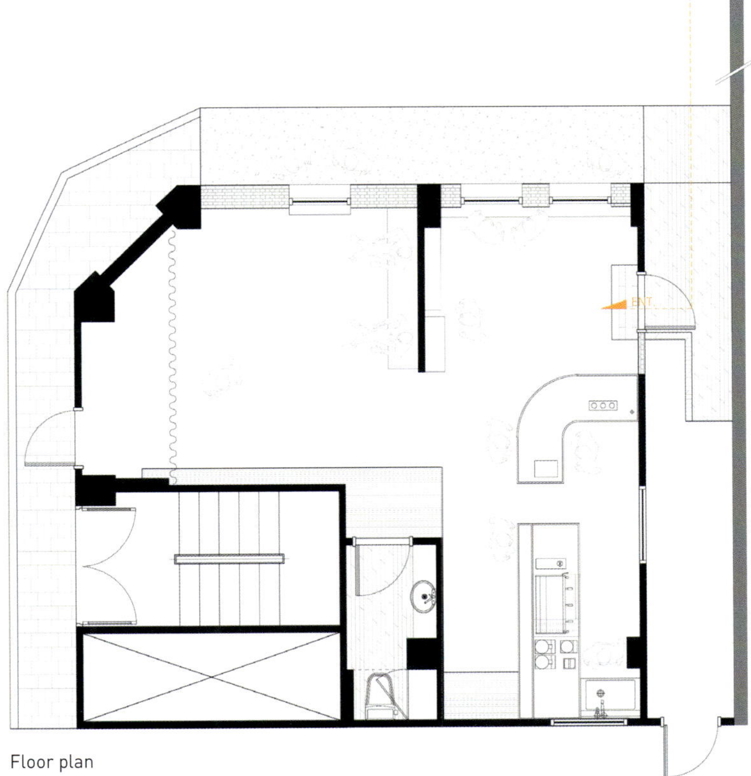

Floor plan

Market
Lane
Coffee

Founded in 1993 by Pierre-Louis Taillandier, Taillandier Architectes Associés (TAA) is an architecture and urbanism agency based in Toulouse, France. TAA is an open-minded studio, working side by side with private and public partners.
The people at TAA give their best to develop architectural solutions. Regardless of the nature of the project, the answer has to improve the quality of life of the end user and the direct environment. Every project designed by Taillandier Architectes Associés solves a series of equations blending program, user and environmental specifics. To achieve a truly obvious architectural and urban solution, Pierre-Louis Taillandier set up a rational and efficient methodology splitting the project into five dimensions: contextual, intellectual, technical, financial and sensitive.

Fondée en 1993 par Pierre-Louis Taillandier, Taillandier Architectes Associés (TAA) est une agence d'architecture et d'urbanisme basée à Toulouse, en France. TAA est un cabinet à l'esprit ouvert, qui travaille en étroite collaboration avec des partenaires privés et publics.
Le personnel de TAA fait de son mieux pour développer des solutions architecturales. Quelle que soit la nature du projet, la réponse doit améliorer la qualité de vie de l'utilisateur final et de l'environnement direct. Chaque projet conçu par Taillandier Architectes Associés résout une série d'équations qui mêlent les spécificités du programme, de l'utilisateur et de l'environnement. Pour parvenir à une solution architecturale et urbaine qui s'impose d'elle-même, Pierre-Louis Taillandier a établi une méthodologie rationnelle et efficace qui divise le projet en cinq dimensions : contextuelle, intellectuelle, technique, financière et sensible.

Das 1993 von Pierre-Louis Taillandier gegründete büro Taillandier Architectes Associés (TAA) ist ein Architektur - und Stadtplanungsbüro mit sitz in Toulouse, Frankreich. TAA ist ein aufgeschlossenes studio, das eng mit privaten und öffentlichen partnern zusammenarbeitet.
Die mitarbeiter von TAA geben ihr bestes, um architektonische lösungen zu entwickeln. Unabhängig von der art des projekts muss die antwort die lebensqualität des endnutzers und der unmittelbaren umgebung verbessern. Jedes von Taillandier Architectes Associés entworfene projekt löst eine reihe von gleichungen, die die besonderheiten des programms, des nutzers und der umgebung berücksichtigen. Um eine wirklich selbstverständliche architektonische und städtebauliche lösung zu erreichen, hat Pierre-Louis Taillandier eine rationale und effiziente methodik entwickelt, die das projekt in fünf dimensionen unterteilt: kontextuell, intellektuell, technisch, finanziell und sensibel.

Fundada en 1993 por Pierre-Louis Taillandier, Taillandier Architectes Associés (TAA) es una agencia de arquitectura y urbanismo con sede en Toulouse, Francia. TAA es un estudio de mentalidad abierta, que trabaja codo con codo con socios privados y públicos.
El personal de TAA da lo mejor de sí mismo para desarrollar soluciones arquitectónicas. Independientemente de la naturaleza del proyecto, la respuesta tiene que mejorar la calidad de vida del usuario final y el entorno directo. Cada proyecto diseñado por Taillandier Architectes Associés resuelve una serie de ecuaciones que mezclan las especificidades del programa, del usuario y del entorno. Para lograr una solución arquitectónica y urbana realmente evidente, Pierre-Louis Taillandier estableció una metodología racional y eficaz que divide el proyecto en cinco dimensiones: contextual, intelectual, técnica, financiera y sensible.

TAILLANDIER ARCHITECTES ASSOCIÉS

PIERRE-LOUIS TAILLANDIER

www.taa.archi

RÉSIDENCE LE 16

Toulouse, France

Program: **new construction of 16 collective housing and 2 houses** | *Project director:* **Pierre-Louis Taillandier** | *Leading architect:* **Laurie Corrocher** | *Built surface:* **979 m²**
Photos: **© Nicolas Da Silva Lucas**

The 18 new dwellings of "Le 16" are split over two buildings. On one side Building A, a four-story apartment block creating an urban façade on the roundabout, and, on the other side, Building B, an intermediate two-story volume that creates a harmonious transition between the collective buildings and the single-family houses.
Building A holds 16 dwellings. The construction is aligned on the edge of the plot and rises to four stories as well as an attic. On the ground floor, the main entrance hall is positioned at the angle of the building whilst the rest of the floor contains parking and services. The apartments are located on the upper floors and are all south-facing with loggias opening towards the inner garden. The façades occupy the sharp corner of the plot and create a focal point on rue de Cugnaux. They are clad in brick laid horizontally on most of the façade except on horizontal strips where the bricks are laid vertically. Building B is built up against the existing neighboring house along the shared border of the plot.

Die 18 neuen Wohnungen von „Le 16" sind auf zwei Gebäude aufgeteilt. Auf der einen Seite Gebäude A, ein viergeschossiger Wohnblock, der eine städtische Fassade am Kreisverkehr bildet, und auf der anderen Seite Gebäude B, ein zweigeschossiger Zwischenbau, der einen harmonischen Übergang zwischen den Kollektivbauten und den Einfamilienhäusern schafft.
Das Gebäude A beherbergt 16 Wohnungen. Der Bau ist am Rand des Grundstücks ausgerichtet und erstreckt sich über vier Stockwerke sowie ein Dachgeschoss. Im Erdgeschoss befindet sich die Haupteingangshalle im Winkel des Gebäudes, während der Rest des Stockwerks Parkplätze und Dienstleistungen enthält. Die Wohnungen befinden sich in den oberen Stockwerken und sind alle nach Süden ausgeric htet, wobei sich die Loggien zum Innengarten hin öffnen. Die Fassaden befinden sich an der spitzen Ecke des Grundstücks und bilden einen Blickpunkt in der Rue de Cugnaux. Sie sind mit Ziegeln verkleidet, die auf dem größten Teil der Fassade horizontal verlegt sind, mit Ausnahme der horizontalen Streifen, wo die Ziegel vertikal verlegt sind und jedes Stockwerk des Gebäudes markieren. Das Gebäude B ist entlang der gemeinsamen Grundstücksgrenze an das bestehende Nachbarhaus angebaut.

Les 18 nouveaux logements de « Le 16 » sont répartis sur deux bâtiments. D'un côté le bâtiment A, un immeuble collectif de quatre étages créant une façade urbaine sur le rond-point, et, de l'autre côté, le bâtiment B, un volume intermédiaire de deux étages qui crée une transition harmonieuse entre les bâtiments collectifs et les maisons individuelles.
Le bâtiment A accueille 16 logements. La construction est alignée sur le bord de la parcelle et s'élève à quatre étages ainsi qu'un attique. Au rez-de-chaussée, le hall d'entrée principal est positionné à l'angle du bâtiment tandis que le reste de l'étage contient le parking et les services. Les appartements sont situés aux étages supérieurs et sont tous orientés au sud avec des loggias s'ouvrant sur le jardin intérieur. Les façades occupent l'angle vif de la parcelle et créent un point focal sur la rue de Cugnaux. Elles sont revêtues de briques posées horizontalement sur la majeure partie de la façade sauf sur les bandes horizontales où les briques sont posées verticalement marquant chaque niveau de plancher du bâtiment. Le bâtiment B est adossé à la maison voisine existante le long de la limite commune de la parcelle.

Las 18 nuevas viviendas de «Le 16» se reparten en dos edificios. Por un lado, el edificio A, un bloque de apartamentos de cuatro plantas que crea una fachada urbana en la rotonda, y, por otro lado, el edificio B, un volumen intermedio de dos plantas que crea una transición armoniosa entre los edificios colectivos y las viviendas unifamiliares.
El edificio A alberga 16 viviendas. La construcción está alineada en el borde de la parcela y se eleva hasta cuatro plantas, además de un ático. En la planta baja, el vestíbulo principal se sitúa en el ángulo del edificio, mientras que el resto de la planta contiene el aparcamiento y los servicios. Los apartamentos se sitúan en las plantas superiores y están todos orientados al sur con logias que se abren hacia el jardín interior. Las fachadas ocupan el ángulo agudo de la parcela y crean un punto focal en la calle de Cugnaux. Están revestidas de ladrillo colocado horizontalmente en la mayor parte de la fachada, excepto en las franjas horizontales, donde los ladrillos se colocan en vertical, marcando cada nivel del edificio. El edificio B está construido contra la casa vecina a lo largo del límite compartido de la parcela.

TRAMWAY

Site plan

TRAMWAY
CÉDEZ LE PASSAGE

North east elevation

North west elevation

Cross sections

South east elevation

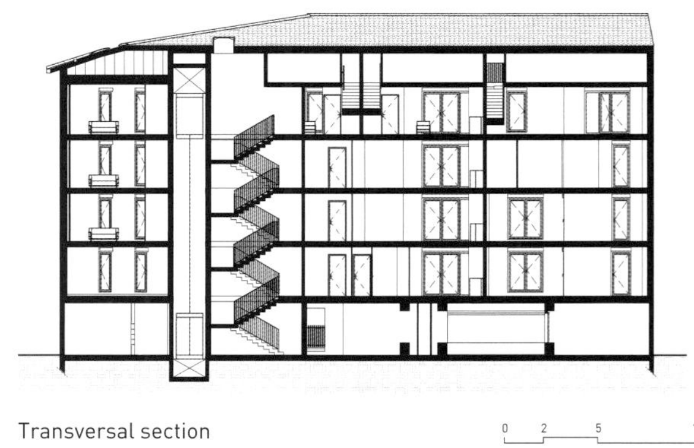

Transversal section

0 2 5 10

South elevation

0 2 5 10

Third floor plan

Fourth floor plan

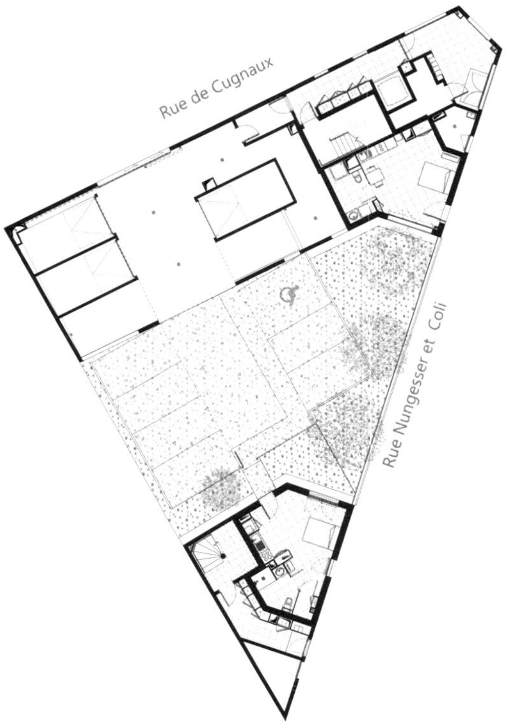

Rue de Cugnaux

Rue Nungesser et Coli

Ground floor plan

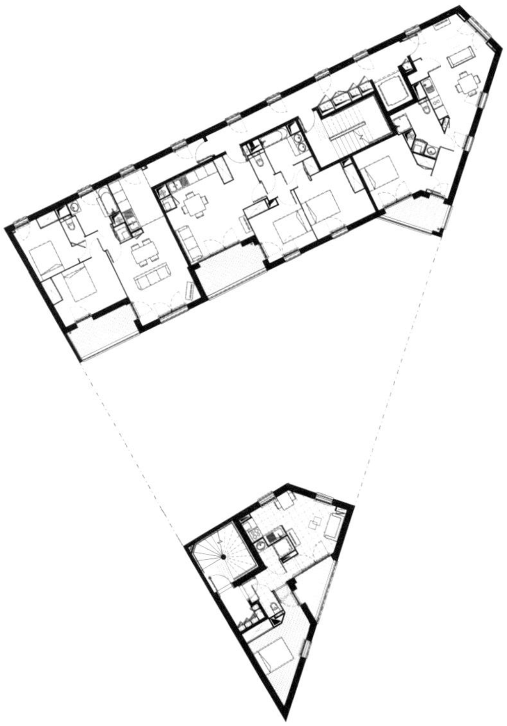

First floor plan

Second floor plan

0 2 5 10

Thomas Roszak (1966, Chicago) is an American architect, real estate developer, author, and academic. Roszak received a B.Arch from the Illinois Institute of Technology (IIT) in 1989. He founded and leads four companies: Thomas Roszak Architecture, SteelGrass Construction Management, TR Management+Consulting, and Moceri+Roszak Development. He has designed and developed projects representing more than $3 billion in the Chicago area. He was an Adjunct Professor at the IIT College of Architecture. In 2020, Roszak was elevated to a Fellow (FAIA) of the American Institute of Architects.

Thomas Roszak (1966, Chicago) ist ein amerikanischer Architekt, Immobilienentwickler, Autor und Wissenschaftler. Roszak erwarb 1989 einen B.Arch. am Illinois Institute of Technology (IIT). Er gründete und leitet vier Unternehmen: Thomas Roszak Architecture, SteelGrass Construction Management, TR Management+Consulting, und Moceri+Roszak Development. Er hat im Großraum Chicago Projekte im Wert von mehr als 3 Milliarden Dollar entworfen und entwickelt. Er war Adjunct Professor am IIT College of Architecture. Im Jahr 2020 wurde Roszak zum Fellow (FAIA) des American Institute of Architects ernannt.

Thomas Roszak (1966, Chicago) est un architecte, promoteur immobilier, auteur et universitaire américain. Roszak a obtenu un B.Arch de l'Illinois Institute of Technology (IIT) en 1989. Il a fondé et dirige quatre entreprises : Thomas Roszak Architecture, SteelGrass Construction Management, TR Management+Consulting, et Moceri+Roszak Development. Il a conçu et développé des projets représentant plus de 3 milliards de dollars dans la région de Chicago. Il a été professeur auxiliaire à l'école d'architecture de l'IIT. En 2020, Roszak a été élevé au rang de Fellow (FAIA) de l'American Institute of Architects.

Thomas Roszak (1966, Chicago) es un arquitecto, promotor inmobiliario, autor y académico estadounidense. Roszak se licenció en Arquitectura por el Instituto Tecnológico de Illinois (IIT) en 1989. Fundó y dirige cuatro empresas: Thomas Roszak Architecture, SteelGrass Construction Management, TR Management+Consulting y Moceri+Roszak Development. Ha diseñado y desarrollado proyectos que representan más de 3.000 millones de dólares en el área de Chicago. Fue profesor adjunto en la Escuela de Arquitectura del IIT. En 2020, Roszak fue elevado a miembro (FAIA) del Instituto Americano de Arquitectos.

TRA | THOMAS ROSZAK ARCHITECTURE

THOMAS ROSZAK

www.roszak.com

RECESS AND CITY HALL EVENTS

Chicago, Illinois, United States

Architect of record: **Thomas Roszak** | *Project architect:* **Paul Baulier**
Structural engineer: **Rockey Structures** | *Interior designer:* **Siren Betty**
Civil engineer: **SpaceCo** | *General contractor:* **Aberdeen Contractors**
Owner: **Marc Bushala/MAB** | *Photos:* **© Sean Henderson**

This adaptive re-use project converted two former abandoned factories built in the early 20th century and an adjacent surface parking lot into a 30,000-square-foot entertainment complex with 15,500 square feet of indoor event and restaurant space and a 14,500-square-foot open-air courtyard dining terrace.
The plan integrates two industrial buildings into a cohesive whole. New factory-style windows provide daylight as well as views of the Chicago skyline. Repurposed doors, boilers, and steel beams have been re-imagined as artwork, evoking the historic industrial aesthetic of the original buildings. On the west end of the site the architects transformed an empty parking lot into a lively outdoor terrace by surrounding it with 30 recycled shipping containers. The redevelopment improves the public realm and upholds the urban fabric by repurposing vacant facilities into a contemporary, bustling place for entertainment, enhancing the work-live-play needs.

Bei diesem Projekt wurden zwei ehemalige, im frühen 20. Jahrhundert errichtete, verlassene Fabriken und ein angrenzender oberirdischer Parkplatz in einen 3.000 m^2 großen Unterhaltungskomplex mit 1.500 m^2 Innenfläche für Veranstaltungen und Restaurants und einer 1.450 m^2 großen Terrasse für Mahlzeiten im Freien umgewandelt.
Der Plan integriert zwei Industriegebäude in ein zusammenhängendes Ganzes. Neue Fenster im Fabrikstil sorgen für Tageslicht und geben den Blick auf die Skyline von Chicago frei. Wiederverwendete Türen, Heizkessel und Stahlträger wurden als Kunstwerke neu gestaltet und erinnern an die historische Industrieästhetik der ursprünglichen Gebäude. Am westlichen Ende des Geländes verwandelten die Architekten einen leeren Parkplatz in eine lebendige Außenterrasse, indem sie ihn mit 30 recycelten Schiffscontainern umgaben. Die Sanierung verbessert den öffentlichen Raum und erhält das städtische Gefüge, indem leerstehende Gebäude in einen modernen, belebten Ort der Unterhaltung umgewandelt werden, der die Bedürfnisse von Arbeit, Leben und Freizeit erfüllt.

Ce projet de réutilisation adaptative a converti deux anciennes usines abandonnées construites au début du 20e siècle et un parking de surface adjacent en un complexe de divertissement de 30 000 pieds carrés avec 15 500 pieds carrés d'espace intérieur pour les événements et les restaurants et une terrasse de 14 500 pieds carrés pour les repas dans une cour en plein air.
Le plan intègre deux bâtiments industriels dans un ensemble cohérent. De nouvelles fenêtres de style industriel laissent passer la lumière du jour et offrent une vue sur la ligne d'horizon de Chicago. Des portes, des chaudières et des poutres d'acier réutilisées ont été réimaginées en œuvres d'art, évoquant l'esthétique industrielle historique des bâtiments d'origine. À l'extrémité ouest du site, les architectes ont transformé un parking vide en une terrasse extérieure animée en l'entourant de 30 conteneurs d'expédition recyclés. Le réaménagement améliore le domaine public et maintient le tissu urbain en réaffectant des installations vacantes en un lieu de divertissement contemporain et animé, qui répond aux besoins de travailler, vivre et jouer.

Este proyecto de reutilización adaptativa convirtió dos antiguas fábricas abandonadas construidas a principios del siglo XX y un aparcamiento de superficie adyacente en un complejo de ocio de 3.000 m^2 con 1.500 m^2 de espacio interior para eventos y restaurantes y una terraza comedor de 1.450 m^2 al aire libre.
El plan integra dos edificios industriales en un todo cohesionado. Las nuevas ventanas de estilo industrial proporcionan luz natural y vistas del horizonte de Chicago. Las puertas, las calderas y las vigas de acero reutilizadas se han reinterpretado como obras de arte, evocando la estética industrial histórica de los edificios originales. En el extremo oeste del solar, los arquitectos transformaron un aparcamiento vacío en una animada terraza al aire libre, rodeándolo con 30 contenedores de transporte reciclados. La remodelación mejora el espacio público y mantiene el tejido urbano al reutilizar las instalaciones vacías para convertirlas en un lugar de ocio contemporáneo y animado, mejorando las necesidades de trabajo-vida-juego.

CITY HALL

SS

XINES
CAPITAL
msc

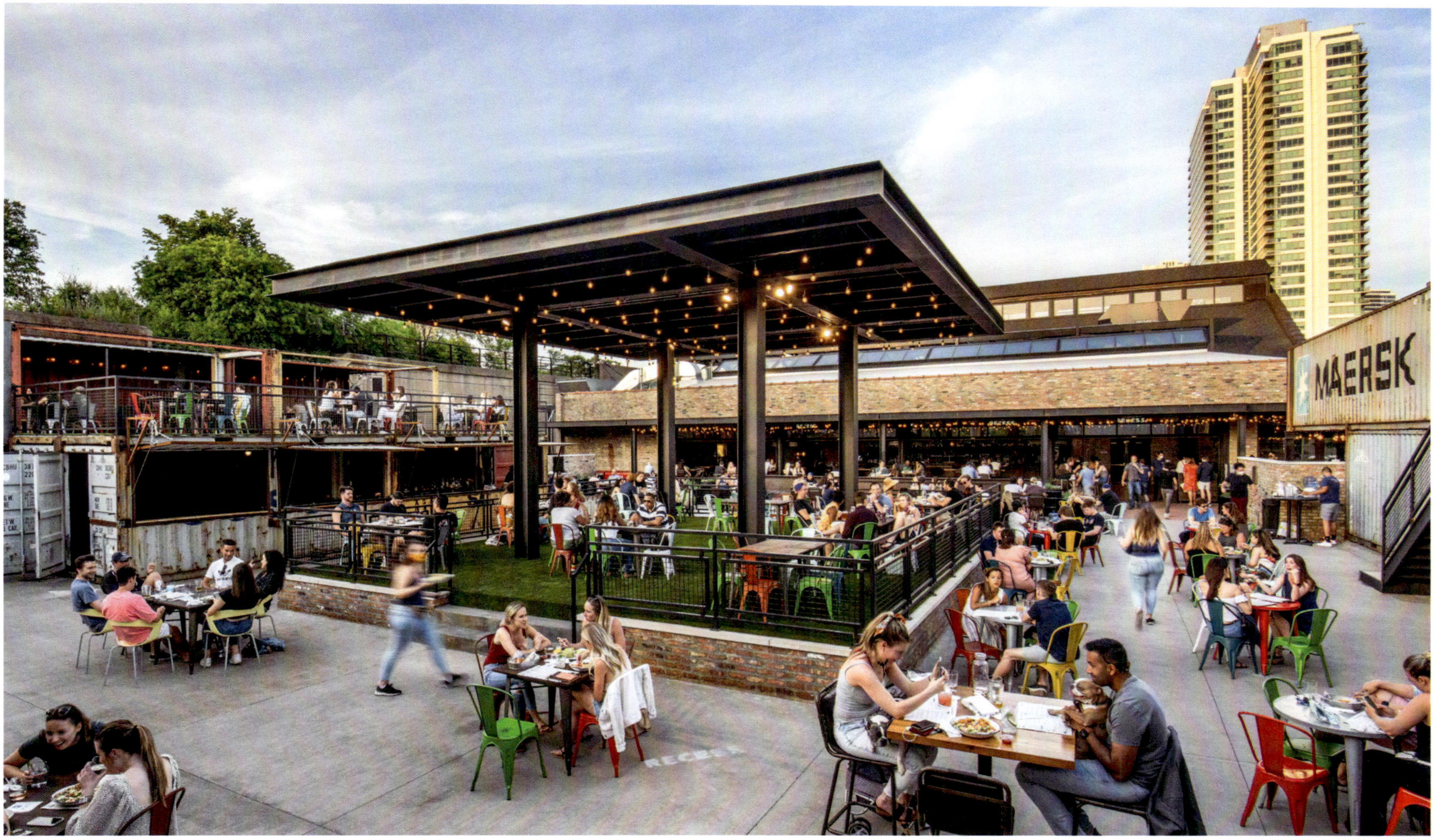
MAERSK

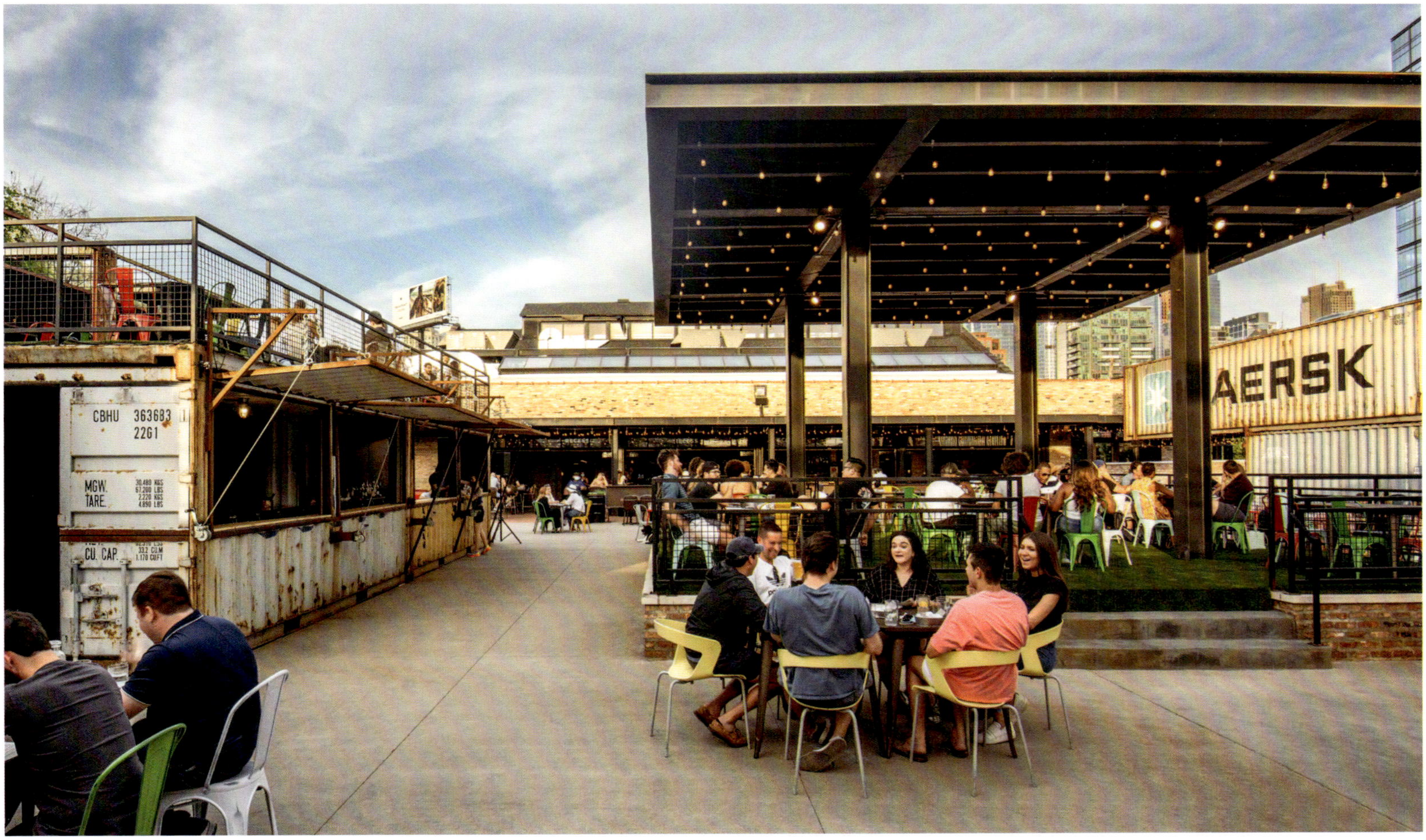
CBHU 363683
2261
MGW.
TARE.
CU. CAP.
AERSK

TOILETTES

RECES
CITY HALL

Xstudio is an architecture and interior design studio founded in 2016 by architects Leticia Romero (ETSA Madrid, 2006), and Ancor Suárez (ETSA Las Palmas de Gran Canaria, 2007), joined in 2018 by Marta Hernández (ETSA Las Palmas de Gran Canaria, 2007) and in 2019 by Tara Silva (ETSA Las Palmas de Gran Canaria, 2019).
Based in Las Palmas de Gran Canaria, Spain, they carry out works of different nature, specialising in residential space, a field in which they have received several distinctions and awards.
From the studio, each project is approached as an opportunity to explore and give shape to the work philosophy, from the general idea to the small-scale detail. This is based on the search for unique solutions in which the spatial and material definition of each project form a single whole.

Xstudio est un studio d'architecture et de décoration intérieure fondé en 2016 par les architectes Leticia Romero (ETSA Madrid, 2006) et Ancor Suárez (ETSA Las Palmas de Gran Canaria, 2007), rejoints en 2018 par Marta Hernández (ETSA Las Palmas de Gran Canaria, 2007) et en 2019 par Tara Silva (ETSA Las Palmas de Gran Canaria, 2019).
Basés à Las Palmas de Gran Canaria, ils réalisent des travaux de nature différente, se spécialisant notamment dans l'espace résidentiel, domaine dans lequel ils ont reçu plusieurs distinctions et prix.
Depuis l'atelier, chaque projet est abordé comme une occasion d'explorer et de donner forme à la philosophie de travail, de l'idée générale au détail à petite échelle. Cette démarche repose sur la recherche de solutions uniques dans lesquelles la définition spatiale et matérielle de chaque projet forme un tout unique.

Xstudio ist ein Architektur- und Innenarchitekturbüro, das 2016 von den Architekten Leticia Romero (ETSA Madrid, 2006) und Ancor Suárez (ETSA Las Palmas de Gran Canaria, 2007) gegründet wurde. 2018 kam Marta Hernández (ETSA Las Palmas de Gran Canaria, 2007) und 2019 Tara Silva (ETSA Las Palmas de Gran Canaria, 2019) hinzu.
Das in Las Palmas de Gran Canaria ansässige Unternehmen führt Arbeiten unterschiedlicher Art aus, wobei es sich insbesondere auf den Wohnbereich spezialisiert hat, ein Bereich, in dem es mehrere Auszeichnungen und Preise erhalten hat.
Im Atelier wird jedes Projekt als Gelegenheit betrachtet, die Arbeitsphilosophie zu erforschen und ihr Gestalt zu geben, von der allgemeinen Idee bis zum kleinen Detail. Dies beruht auf der Suche nach einzigartigen Lösungen, bei denen die räumliche und materielle Definition eines jeden Projekts ein einziges Ganzes bildet.

Xstudio es un estudio de arquitectura e interiorismo fundado en 2016 por los arquitectos Leticia Romero (ETSA Madrid, 2.006), y Ancor Suárez (ETSA Las Palmas de Gran Canaria,2.007), al que se incorporaron en el año 2.018 Marta Hernández (ETSA Las Palmas de Gran Canaria,2.017) y en el 2019 Tara Silva (ETSA Las Palmas de Gran Canaria,2.019).
Con sede en Las Palmas de Gran Canaria, llevan a cabo trabajos de diferente naturaleza, especializándose particularmente en el espacio residencial, campo en el que el han recibido varias distinciones y reconocimientos.
Desde el estudio cada proyecto se afronta como una oportunidad para explorar y plasmar la filosofía de trabajo, desde la idea general hasta el detalle a pequeña escala. Ésta se fundamenta la búsqueda de soluciones singulares en las que la definición espacial y material de cada proyecto formen un único conjunto.

XSTUDIO

LETICIA ROMERO, ANCOR SUÁREZ

www.x-studio.es

NAKED HOUSE

Las Palmas de Gran Canaria, Spain

Architects: Xstudio | *Constructor:* Constructora MFV | *Woodwork:* Carpintería Ángel Benítez
Toilets: Roca Gap | *Sinks:* Roca Diverta | *Taps:* Lavabo, Roca L20; Ducha, Roca Even
Mechanical: Jung LS Cube | *Client:* Great SLU | *Photos:* © David Rodríguez / Xstudio

Naked House is located in the Guanarteme neighbourhood. The urban expansion of the city has led to the coexistence of large-scale buildings with self-built dwellings. The project offers the possibility of reclaiming another way of living, by betting on the recovery and enhancement of the historical and cultural context in which the original architecture took place.
The program includes the use of a design studio throughout the house, giving shape to a new domestic space. The backbone of this project focuses on the courtyard, where its existing openings are enlarged, creating a striking relationship with the exterior.
In the material definition, elements and construction techniques of the original construction are left uncovered, allowing the incidence of light to enhance the different textures. The materials of this intervention highlight the contrast between the existing and the new.

Das Naked House befindet sich im Viertel Guanarteme. Die Ausdehnung der Stadt hat zu einer Koexistenz von Großbauten und selbstgebauten Wohnungen geführt.Das Projekt bietet die Möglichkeit, eine andere Art zu leben wiederzugewinnen, indem es auf die Wiederherstellung und Aufwertung des historischen und kulturellen Kontextes setzt, in dem die ursprüngliche Architektur entstanden ist.
Das Programm sieht die Nutzung eines Designstudios im gesamten Haus vor, wodurch ein neuer Wohnbereich entsteht. Das Rückgrat dieses Projekts ist der Innenhof, dessen bestehende Öffnungen vergrößert werden, wodurch eine auffällige Beziehung zum Außenbereich geschaffen wird.
Bei der Materialdefinition werden Elemente und Konstruktionstechniken der ursprünglichen Konstruktion offen gelassen, so dass der Lichteinfall die verschiedenen Texturen zur Geltung bringt. Die Materialien dieses Eingriffs heben den Kontrast zwischen dem Bestehenden und dem Neuen hervor.

Naked House est situé dans le quartier de Guanarteme. L'expansion urbaine de la ville a entraîné la coexistence de bâtiments de grande taille et de logements auto-construits. Le projet offre la possibilité de récupérer une autre façon de vivre, en pariant sur la récupération et la valorisation du contexte historique et culturel dans lequel l'architecture originale a pris place.
Le programme prévoit l'utilisation d'un studio de conception dans toute la maison, donnant forme à un nouvel espace domestique. L'épine dorsale de ce projet se concentre sur la cour, dont les ouvertures existantes sont agrandies, créant ainsi une relation frappante avec l'extérieur.
Dans la définition des matériaux, les éléments et les techniques de construction de la construction originale sont laissés à découvert, permettant à l'incidence de la lumière de mettre en valeur les différentes textures. Les matériaux de cette intervention soulignent le contraste entre l'existant et le nouveau.

Naked House se ubica en el barrio de Guanarteme. La expansión urbanística de la ciudad ha provocado la convivencia entre edificios de gran escala con viviendas de autoconstrucción.El proyecto ofrece la posibilidad de reivindicar otra forma de habitar, apostando por la recuperación y la puesta en valor del contexto histórico y cultural en el que la arquitectura original tuvo lugar.
El programa acoge el uso de estudio de diseño en la totalidad de la casa, dando forma a un nuevo espacio doméstico. La columna vertebral de este proyecto se enfoca en el patio, donde se amplían sus huecos existentes, propiciando una asombrosa relación con el exterior.
En la definición material se dejan al descubierto elementos y técnicas constructivas de la construcción original, logrando que la incidencia de la luz realce las distintas texturas. Los materiales de esta intervención remarcan el contraste entre lo existente y lo nuevo.

stripe

bau-
1919-25

Ground floor plan

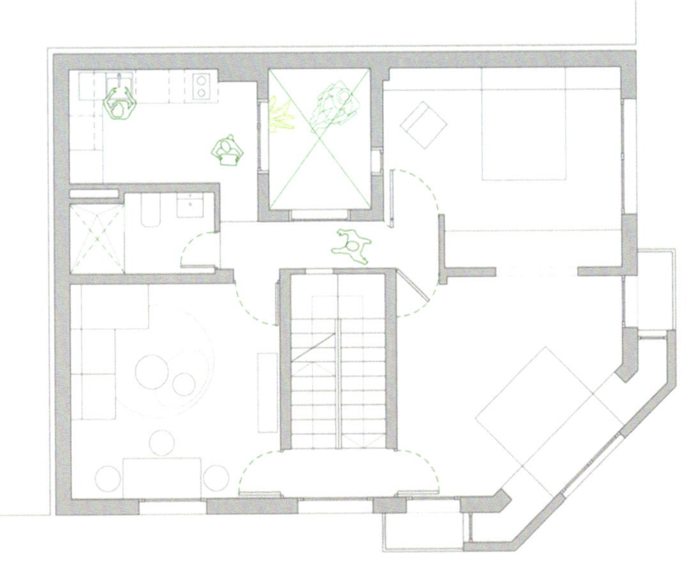
First floor plan

Construction diagram

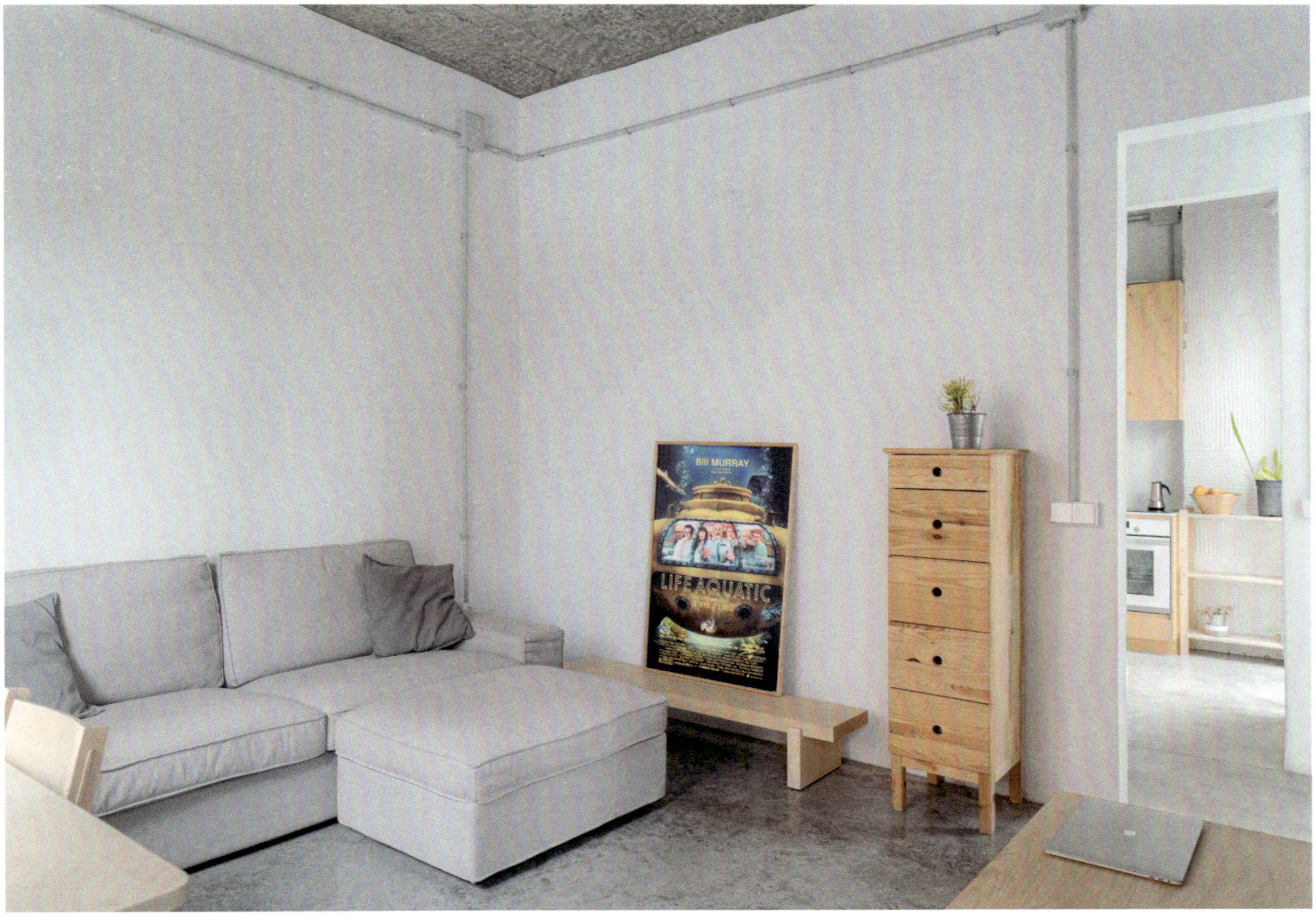
Bill MURRAY
LIFE AQUATIC

Bill MURRAY
LIFE AQUATIC
STEVE ZISSOU

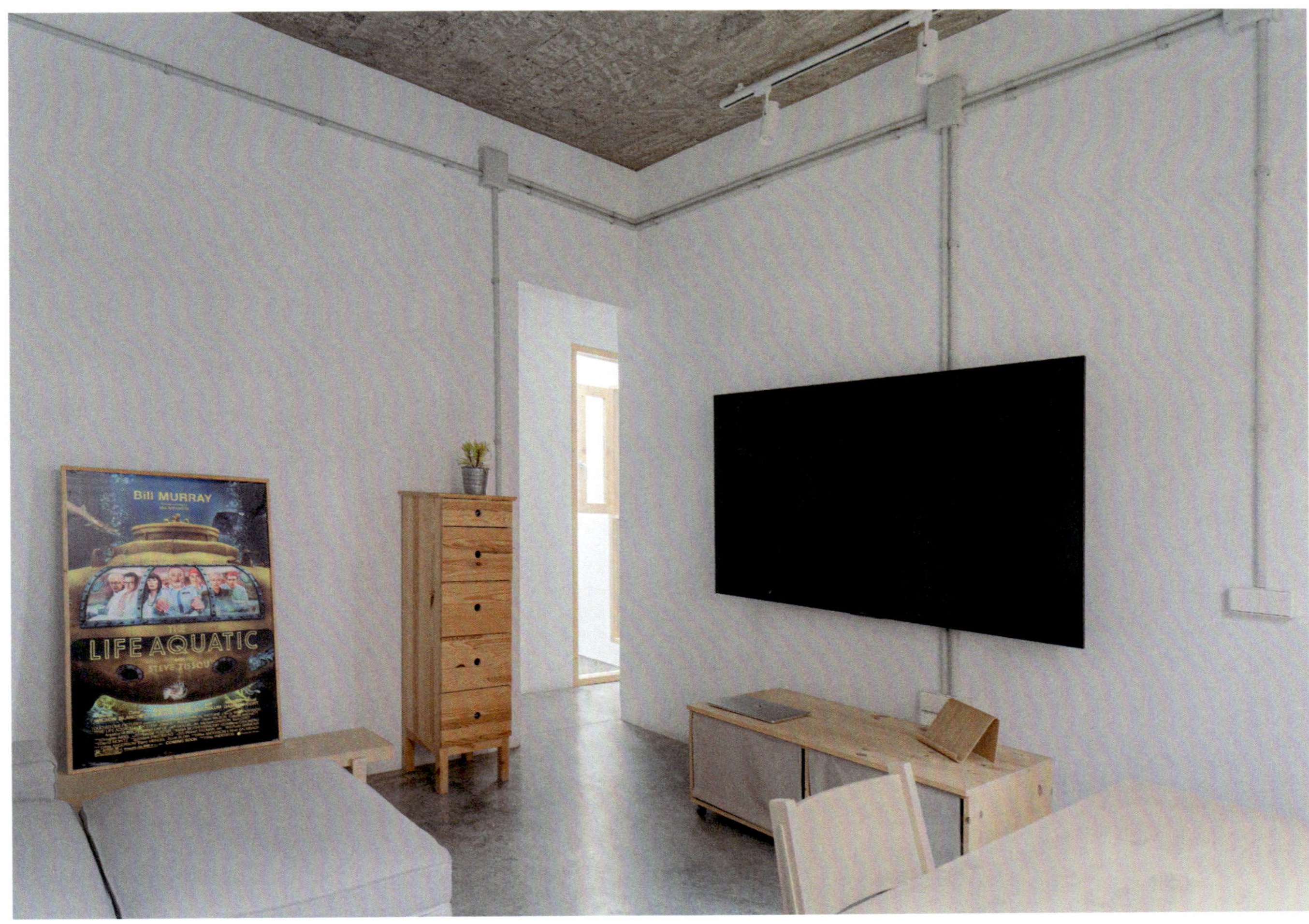

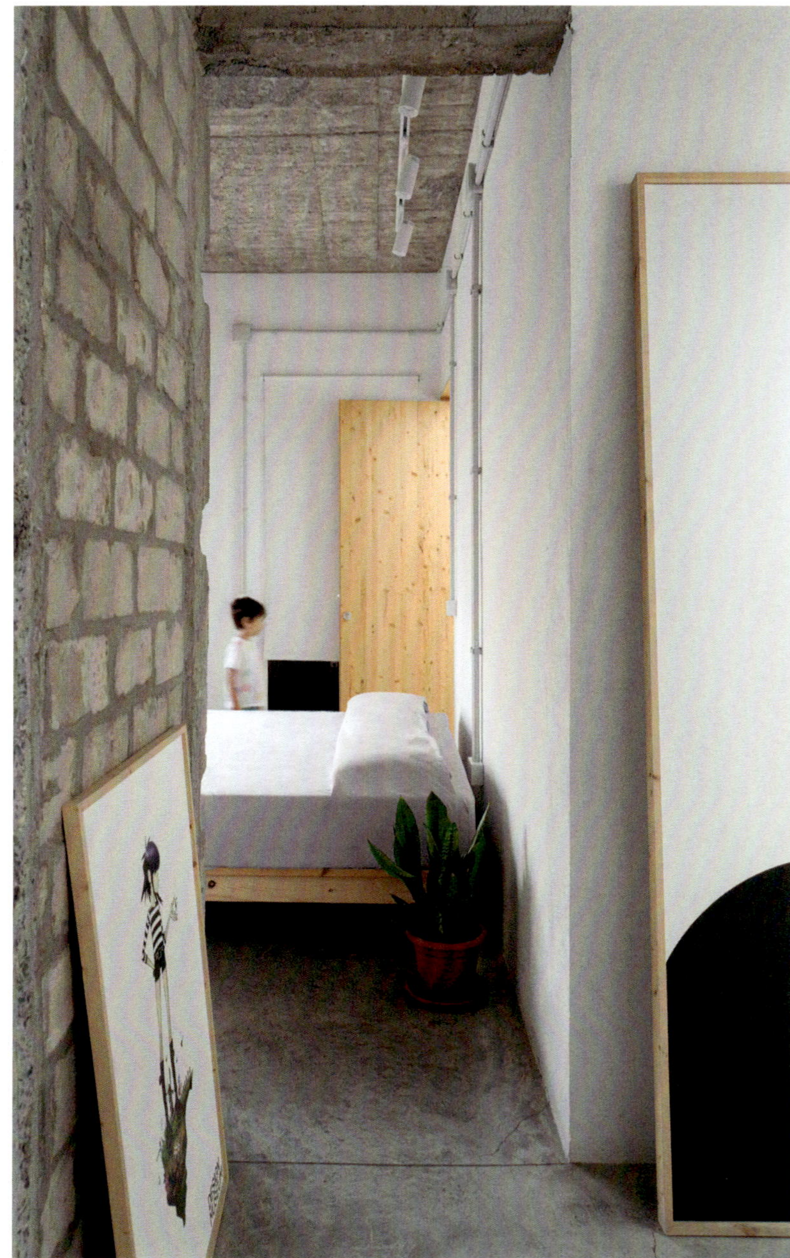